STUDIES IN ECONOMIC HISTORY AND POLICY
THE UNITED STATES IN THE TWENTIETH CENTURY

The Great Depression

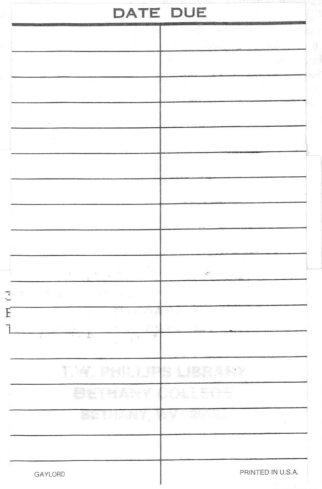

STUDIES IN ECONOMIC HISTORY AND POLICY
THE UNITED STATES IN THE TWENTIETH CENTURY

Edited by
Louis Galambos and Robert Gallman

Other books in the series:

Peter D. McClelland and Alan L. Magdovitz: *Crisis in the making: the political economy of New York State since 1945*

Hugh Rockoff: *Drastic measures: a history of wage and price controls in the United States*

William N. Parker: *Europe, America, and the wider world: essays on the economic history of Western capitalism*

Richard H. K. Vietor: *Energy policy in America since 1945: a study of business–government relations*

Christopher L. Tomlins: *The state and the unions: labor relations, law, and the organized labor movement in America, 1880–1960*

Leonard S. Reich: *The making of American industrial research: science and business at GE and Bell, 1876–1926*

Margaret B. W. Graham: *RCA and the VideoDisc: the business of research*

The Great Depression
Delayed recovery and economic change in America, 1929–1939

MICHAEL A. BERNSTEIN
Department of History, University of California, San Diego

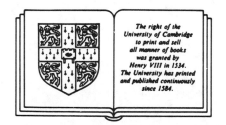

*The right of the
University of Cambridge
to print and sell
all manner of books
was granted by
Henry VIII in 1534.
The University has printed
and published continuously
since 1584.*

Cambridge University Press

Cambridge

New York   Port.Chester   Melbourne   Sydney

Published by the Press Syndicate of the University of Cambridge
The Pitt Building, Trumpington Street, Cambridge CB2 1RP
32 East 57th Street, New York, NY 10022, USA
10 Stamford Road, Oakleigh, Melbourne 3166, Australia

First published 1987
Reprinted 1989

Printed in the United States of America

Library of Congress Cataloging-in-Publication Data

Bernstein, Michael A. (Michael Alan), 1954–

The Great Depression : delayed recovery and economic
change in America, 1929–1939.
(Studies in economic history and policy)
Bibliography: p.
Includes index.
1. Depressions – 1929 – United States.   2. United
States – Economic conditions – 1918–1945.   I. Title.
II. Series
HB3717 1929.B37   1988   338.5′42   87-6403

British Library Cataloguing in Publication Data

Bernstein, Michael A.

The Great Depression : delayed recovery
and economic change in America, 1929–1939.
– (Studies in economic history and policy) :
the United States in the twentieth century.
1. Depressions   2. United States –
Economic conditions – 1918–1945
I. Title.   II. Series
338.5′42′0973   HB3743

ISBN 0 521 34048 9

For Enid Littwin Bernstein and for Those Who Loved Her

Contents

Tables

Figures

Editors' preface

In the two decades immediately following World War II, the Great Depression of the 1930s was commonly viewed as a business cycle depression, explicable in terms of standard macroeconomic theory. It had been unusually long and deep for a variety of reasons, the emphases among them differing from one analyst to the next. Monetarists stressed blunders on the part of Federal Reserve authorities; Keynesians stressed the late and inadequately passionate embrace of Keynesian fiscal policy by the federal administration. Students of the international scene looked to the concurrent depressions in the United States and Europe, to competitive devaluation and beggar-thy-neighbor tariff policies. Institutionalists spoke of the utter collapse of American financial institutions. Few doubted, however, that the Great Depression had been unique; there would be no recurrence.

This confidence stemmed from the perception that the financial reforms of the New Deal would rule out another debacle of the order of 1929–33 and from the wartime demonstration of the power of federal fiscal policy to cope with unemployment. At the close of the war, Congress had written into law federal responsibility for the maintenance of economic stability, based clearly on Keynesian macroeconomic ideas. The exact devices to be deployed (e.g., public works versus built-in flexibility) and even the relative importance of monetary and fiscal tools might be subject to debate, but there was wide agreement that the strengthened financial system and the new fiscal and monetary tools would ward off another Great Depression.

In the period since the late 1960s, however, we have learned that economic life is more complex than had appeared and that policy based on simple macroeconomic models may not achieve so easily as had been supposed the desirable state of economic stability. Michael Bernstein now proposes that we look anew at the Great Depression of the 1930s and (in his conclusion) the more recent troubled period of the 1970s. Bernstein argues that the Great Depression was not a standard business cycle depression, made deeper and longer by poor monetary and fiscal policies and widespread autarchy. Rather, he believes that the American economy was in a delicate situation when the collapse of 1929 occurred. It was in the process of negotiating a long-term structural transition, involving a change in the composition of final demand. The depth of the depression and the slowness of recovery were due to the interruption of this fundamental set of changes.

Bernstein asks us to look at the period of the 1930s – as well as the period of the 1970s, to which it bears a strong family resemblance – against the background of long-term historical change, focusing particularly on the shifting composition of the economy. His book provides a fresh perspective on these events, and we are delighted to include it in the series *Studies in Economic History and Policy: The United States in the Twentieth Century*.

Louis Galambos
Professor of History
The Johns Hopkins University

Robert Gallman
Kenan Professor of Economics and History
University of North Carolina

Preface

This book seeks to explain why the American depression of the 1930s lasted so long. It is intended for a varied audience. I have studied a system, a structure of economic life and how it came to grief in the time between the world wars. I have said little of individuals, their thoughts and feelings, their styles of life, or their perceptions of the world around them. I have examined the past with a view to answering certain questions about how modern economies behave. I have tried to avoid questions history cannot answer by focusing on what actually happened.

The economic collapse of the 1930s, inducing major changes in the role of government in American life, and preceding a war that dramatically altered the nation's role in world affairs, has been examined in a wide variety of ways. A study that explicitly offers an explanation of the depression's length should contribute to the historian's argument that in the thirties exceptional economic conditions transformed the country's political and social framework. Moreover, it should afford the economist some useful insights regarding business cycles and unemployment. Of course, the reader will ultimately have to judge to what extent these claims are true.

Economic and historical pertinence notwithstanding, I have been reluctant to engage in much normative or predictive discussion. With the exception of the last two chapters, I have avoided debates concerning policy. While I believe there is a role for social scientific theory in understanding the past, I am more comfortable with knowledge that, to paraphrase the philosopher, is gathered at dusk rather than envisaged at dawn.

I came to the study of economic history through the study of economics. Necessarily, this book is the product of the pushing and pulling of both an interdisciplinary background and two sets of colleagues. At various points, I have moved one way or the other. On some occasions, I admit I have pushed back. But at all times I have been keenly aware of the special rewards of interdisciplinary research. Such research would not have been possible in this case without the support of many people. It is a great pleasure to acknowledge them – only the conventions of publishing prevent me from listing them on the title page. Even so, some or all of them would not wish to appear thus. They do not necessarily endorse the interpretations offered here, nor should they be held responsible for errors.

Several friends and colleagues have given all or part of this project the benefit of their criticism. I thank them all: John Morton Blum, Jon Cohen, Ester Fano, Steven Fraser, Claudia Goldin, Daniel Horwitz, John Kneebone, Naomi Lamoreaux, Julie Matthaei, Donald McCloskey, John McCole, Istvan Rév, Theda Skocpol, Ross Thomson, Harold Vatter, and Michael Weinstein. I am especially grateful to Robert Gallman, Carol Heim, and James Oakes.

My colleagues at Princeton University, along with their invaluable comments, continually encouraged me. In particular I want to thank Lester Chandler, Gary Gerstle, Stephen Goldfeld, William Jordan, Stanley Katz, Arno Mayer, James McPherson, Philip Nord, Theodore Rabb, Daniel Rodgers, Stanley Stein, Robert Tignor, and Nancy Weiss.

Michael Edelstein and David Weiman were extremely important critics. Along with their helpful advice, they honored me with their friendship and sustained me with their humanity.

My mentors, David Levine and William Parker, were part of this project from its inception. They have over the years been demanding yet loyal counselors. They always insisted that I make myself clear even when they did not agree with the particular point I was trying to make. David Levine has been an inspiring tutor whose imprint on me is exemplified by the very topic of this book. My debt to William Parker will be obvious on almost every page. I find it impossible to express adequately my gratitude to him. I value him as a teacher and treasure him as a friend.

I have benefited from the outstanding research assistance of Michael Ehrlich, Nancy Goldner, Martha Hodes, Karen Itzkowitz, Linda Lierheimer, and David Stainton. The staffs of the Firestone Library, the Computer Center, and the Department of History at Princeton University were unfailingly generous in their help. Lil Hadley and Robin Huffman typed the manuscript. Morgan Phillips drafted the figures.

Financial support for this project was made available through a variety of sources. The Committee on Research in Economic History of the Economic History Association provided a stipend that allowed me to devote a summer to my research. Grants from the American Council of Learned Societies and Princeton University released me from a year of teaching responsibilities during which the manuscript was written. The Princeton University Committee on Research in the Humanities and Social Sciences and the Department of History made timely awards to defray the costs of research assistance, computer work, drafting, and typing. In this regard I would particularly like to thank Douglas Greenberg.

Charles Bowman of the United States Department of Labor and John Musgrave of the United States Department of Commerce provided important unpublished data for my research.

For permission to republish material originally presented in their forums, acknowledgment is made to the editors of *History and Technology*, the *Journal of Economic History*, and the *Rivista di Storia Economica*.

I have been very fortunate in having the exemplary assistance of Louise Calabro Gruendel, Rhona Johnson, and Frank Smith – my editors at Cambridge University Press.

Finally I must thank Teresa Odendahl. As my adviser, companion, friend, and most acute commentator, she alone knows why "Joint ventures work out better than going it alone."

Shortly before this book was completed, my mother Enid died after a long illness. She was my first and my best teacher. As I close, my thoughts are all of her.

M.A.B.
Princeton, New Jersey
and Washington, D.C.

Introduction: The puzzle of the 1930s

> The essential point to grasp is that in dealing with capitalism we are dealing with an evolutionary process. It may seem strange that anyone can fail to see so obvious a fact. . . . Yet that fragmentary analysis which yields the bulk of our propositions about the functioning of modern capitalism persistently neglects it.
>
> – Joseph A. Schumpeter

In American economic history, there is no greater puzzle than the persistent failure of investment activity during the depression of the 1930s to generate a full recovery. What investment did take place during the decade was limited by the low demand for output. But cyclical recoveries require an increase in investment expenditures large enough to make additions to productive capacity, create jobs, and expand output. In the absence of technical change, the rate of net investment will fall to zero so soon as the rate of increase in consumption levels off. For consumption expenditures to rise consistently, there must be net investment or continual injections of government spending. This is the essential paradox of the thirties. Consumption was constrained both by deficient investment and by political limits to countercyclical fiscal policy. The solution, a recovery in net investment, was not forthcoming, because of inadequate demand.

Most research concerning the Great Depression in particular, and business cycles in general, examines the behavior of economic aggregates and thereby limits its effectiveness in two ways: (1) by often ignoring structural changes within the aggregates and (2) by implicitly assuming that cycles are inherently the same irrespective of the point in the history of a given economy at which they occur.[1] Such an approach

---

1 For example, see the explanation of James Tobin in his *Essays in Economics* (London: North-Holland, 1971), vol. 1, p. vii: "Macroeconomics concerns the determinants of entire economies. . . . The theoretical concepts and statistical measures involved are generally economy-wide aggregates or averages such as national income, total employment, or a national cost-of-living index. The objective is to explain ups and downs of these magnitudes and their interrelations. The basic assumption is that this can be done without much attention to the constituents of the aggregates, that is, to the behavior and fortunes of particular households, business firms, industries, or regions."

denies the existence of long-term growth patterns that underlie, and are in turn influenced by, cyclical processes.

A systematic analysis of business cycles requires that attention be given to the fact that the performance of an economy during a fluctuation is dependent on the point in the long-run development of that economy at which the cycle occurs. As an economy grows, major structural characteristics of the system are transformed. Demand patterns, amounts of income available for discretionary expenditure, technological knowledge, raw material stocks, market size – all change, along with fundamental advances in communication, in transportation, and in the economic role of government. The basis of most of these alterations in economic structure is the continuing evolution of the nature and scope of enterprise. The stage of long-run development an economy has reached will influence responses to fluctuations and the forms that recovery will assume. It is the burden of the present argument that the absence of forces contributing toward an upturn in the American economy of the 1930s was in large part due to secular mechanisms of development rather than to the impact of short-run elements contributing to the stock market crash itself.

It is not my concern, therefore, to analyze the specific timing and causes of the downturn in 1929 that precipitated ten years of depression in the American economy. Such an investigation is very much a project of its own, and would undoubtedly involve an assessment of political and institutional issues emerging out of the ratification of the Treaty of Versailles, the structure and conduct of financial markets, and the protectionist policies pursued in international trade during the 1920s. For me, the depression is the starting point. What I wish to explain in this book is its duration.

By focusing on the experience of the American economy during the depression years, I abstract from a great many issues concerning the depression as a world-wide phenomenon. But I do not do so merely as a matter of convenience. The slump was far worse in the United States than anywhere else (with the possible exception of Germany), and the instability of economic performance was much more severe. From 1929 to 1930, the level of industrial production fell farther and faster in the United States than in Austria, Canada, France, Germany, Great Britain, Japan, or Sweden. The same is true for the so-called recession that began in 1937 and continued until the outbreak of war. Interestingly enough, the rates at which industrial production increased from the trough of 1932 were similar for the United States, Austria, Canada, and Sweden, higher for Germany and Japan, and lower for France, Great Britain, and Italy. As for unemployment, the rate for the United States was, on average, the highest among all the industrialized nations throughout the thirties.[2]

There is also every indication, and on this many authors agree, that the United States led the rest of the world into depression and that the economic contraction in America was internally based. As one authority has argued, "the depression in the United States was deeper and lasted longer than the depressions in most other industrial countries, and it was almost entirely homemade. It is true there were phases in the course of the U.S. depression when it was intensified by influences from abroad. . . . But these adverse foreign influences were largely the feedback from earlier phases of the American depression."[3]

What, then, accounts for the exceptional length of the depression of the 1930s in the United States? It is only through the application of a broad frame of reference, one that spans several decades rather than simply the few years between peak and trough, that a systematic answer to this question may be formulated. Examinations have been made of the instability of the interwar years in terms of long-term development factors, but they have been concerned with economies other than that of the United States. Ingvar Svennilson undertook such an investigation of the Western European nations. The experience of the Canadian economy during the Great Depression was studied in these terms by A. E. Safarian. Erik Dahmén did the same in his classic study of Swedish industry between the world wars. With the possible exception of Joseph Schumpeter, only one American economist, Robert A.

2 See W. Arthur Lewis, *Economic Survey, 1919–1939* (Philadelphia: Blakiston, 1950); Charles P. Kindleberger, *The World in Depression: 1929–1939* (Berkeley: University of California Press, 1973), 280; and League of Nations, *World Economic Survey: 1938–39* (Geneva), 107, as cited in Kindleberger, 280.

3 Gottfried Haberler, *The World Economy, Money, and the Great Depression: 1919–1939* (Washington, D.C.: American Enterprise Institute for Public Policy Research, 1976), 7. This point of view is also presented in W. Arthur Lewis, *Economic Survey, 1919–1939*, 52; and in H. W. Arndt, *The Economic Lessons of the Nineteen-Thirties* (New York: Augustus M. Kelley, 1965), 18–19. Erik Lundberg, in *Instability and Economic Growth* (New Haven, Conn.: Yale University Press, 1968), 73–4, also posits the American experience as unique. He quotes the following changes in industrial production during the depression era: for Sweden, output fell 12% from 1929 to 1932, and rose 1% from 1937 to 1938; for France, the relevant figures were, respectively, −26% and −7%; for Great Britain, −14% and −7%; and for the United States, −45% and −21%.

Gordon, has called for the study of economic fluctuations in the United States in a long-term historical perspective that emphasizes qualitative as well as quantitative evidence.[4]

Indeed, the older literature concerning the Great Depression in the United States may be broadly classified into three categories.[5] One group of short-run theories argued that the severity and length of the downturn were direct results of the collapse of financial markets that began in 1929. The main emphasis of such work concerned the causes of the 1929 crash and those factors that amplified its impact. Another concluded that the economic calamity of the thirties was the direct result of poorly formulated and politically distorted actions undertaken by the government. A third kind of research took a broader perspective and attempted to analyze the depression in a long-run context. It suggested that whatever the origins of the slump, the reasons for its unparalleled length and severity predated and transcended the events of the last quarter of 1929.

I   Short-run theories of the depression

All short-run arguments concerning the depression shared a common attribute. They focused on the immediate causes and impacts of the stock market collapse in 1929 and asserted that the precipitous devaluation of wealth and the disruption of the banking system occasioned by it explained the intensity of the crisis. The "business confidence" thesis was perhaps the best example of this school of thought. It held that regardless of the mechanisms that caused the collapse, the dramatic slide of the stock market created intensely pessimistic expectations in

---

4 See Ingvar Svennilson, *Growth and Stagnation in the European Economy* (Geneva: United Nations Economic Commission for Europe, 1954); A. E. Safarian, *The Canadian Economy in the Great Depression* (Toronto: University of Toronto Press, 1959); Erik Dahmén, *Entrepreneurial Activity and the Development of Swedish Industry: 1919–1939*, trans. A. Leijonhufvud (Homewood, Ill.: Richard D. Irwin, 1970); Joseph A. Schumpeter, *Business Cycles: A Theoretical, Historical, and Statistical Analysis of the Capitalist Process* (New York: McGraw-Hill, 1939); and R. A. Gordon, "Business Cycles in the Interwar Period: The 'Quantitative-Historical' Approach," *American Economic Review*, 39 (May, 1949), 47–63. Also see the intriguing article by R. R. Keller, "Factor Income Distribution in the United States During the 1920's: A Reexamination of Fact and Theory," *Journal of Economic History*, 33 (March, 1973), 252–73.

5 For an overview of the main issues that this literature attempts to confront, see G. Burck and C. Silberman, "What Caused the Great Depression?" *Fortune*, 51 (February, 1955), 94ff.

the business community. The shock to confidence was so severe and unexpected that a dramatic panic took hold, stifling investment and thereby a full recovery.[6]

A more comprehensive formulation of the short-run argument directly confronted the question of why financial markets collapsed. Looking to the political and institutional distortions created by the Treaty of Versailles, some writers, such as Irving Fisher, Jacob Viner, and Lionel Robbins, argued that the depression was the inevitable consequence of the chaotic and unstable financial structure of the twenties. The demise of the gold standard in international trade, and the demands by France and the United States that Germany make her reparations payments in gold rather than goods and services, created a net gold flow into the United States that led to an explosion of credit. Extremely unstable credit arrangements emerged thereby in the twenties, especially in mortgage markets. Because many banks in the relatively unregulated environment in which they operated at the time were committed to questionable loan contracts, when the crash came the collapse of the banking system was quick to follow. Thus, excessive credit and speculation coupled with a weak banking network caused the Great Depression.[7]

6 For an exposition of the business confidence argument, see J. J. B. Morgan, "Manic-Depressive Psychoses of Business," *Psychological Review*, 42 (January, 1935), 91–3, 98–107.

7 See Irving Fisher, *The Stock Market Crash–and After* (New York: Macmillan, 1930); and his *Booms and Depressions: Some First Principles* (New York: Adelphi, 1932), 85–110. Also see J. A. Schumpeter, "The Decade of the Twenties," *American Economic Review*, 36 (May, 1946), 1–10; Wilhelm Roepke, *Crises and Cycles* (London: William Hodge, 1936), 136–7; C. R. Noyes, "The Gold Inflation in the United States, 1921–1929," *American Economic Review*, 20 (June, 1930), 181–98; C. E. Persons, "Credit Expansion, 1920 to 1929, and Its Lessons," *Quarterly Journal of Economics*, 45 (November, 1930), 94–130; and J. Viner, "Recent Legislation and the Banking Situation," *American Economic Review*, 26 (March, 1936), 106–7. The notion of excessive speculation and "wild" stock prices was challenged in G. Sirkin, "The Stock Market of 1929 Revisited: A Note," *Business History Review*, 49 (Summer, 1975), 223–31. Lionel Robbins argued that the crash itself may have been generated by attempts by the Federal Reserve, in 1927, to reverse the net gold inflow in order to alleviate the destabilizing pressures on sterling. See his *The Great Depression* (London: Macmillan, 1934), 51–4. Also see Gustav Cassel, *The Crisis in the World's Monetary System* (Oxford: Clarendon Press, 1932), 37–9. Cassel mentioned, on p. 76, the impact of psychological factors, arguing that "American puritanism stands out as perhaps the most important . . . the stock exchange speculation of 1928–9 was regarded as particularly sinful behavior which had to get its punishment." It is certainly debatable whether or not analyses of the

Another version of the short-run approach was concerned with the immediate effects of the crash on consumer wealth and spending. The severity of the downturn, it was argued, resulted in a drastic devaluation of consumer wealth and incomes. The large stress placed on the capital markets and the lack of consumer confidence in banks ensured that effective demand could not be bolstered by increased credit. It was therefore the large decreases in purchasing power due to the crash that left the economy saddled with unused capacity and low demand.[8]

None of these short-run arguments was completely convincing or satisfying. Inasmuch as the business confidence thesis was subjective, it was virtually impossible to evaluate with historical evidence. There was also the major theoretical objection that it could mistake effect for cause; the objective circumstances of the thirties may have generated the subjective response of pessimism and panic. Such a theory could not, therefore, occupy a central place in explanations of the depression.

The excessive credit and speculation argument was frequently rejected on the grounds that it abstracted too boldly from real rather than monetary events in the interwar economy. Indeed, business cycle indicators turned down before the stock market crashed; a softness in construction activity was apparent in 1928, and indices of industrial production started to fall by the summer of 1929. Such critics as John Kenneth Galbraith held that "cause and effect run from the economy to the stock market, never the reverse. Had the economy been fundamentally sound in 1929 the effect of the great stock market crash might have been small [and] the shock to confidence and the loss of spending by those who were caught in the market might soon have worn off."[9]

consequences of the war and its settlement should be regarded as short-run arguments. The Treaty of Versailles and the protectionist era of interwar world trade could be viewed as aspects of the long run – in an institutional and political sense. I have chosen not to regard such work in this way primarily because its proponents employ institutional and political events as a means to explain one short-run incident that, for them, is crucial and decisive – the financial collapse of 1929.

8 See Peter Temin, *Did Monetary Forces Cause the Great Depression?* (New York: Norton, 1976), 169–72, for a contemporary statement of this view.

9 From John K. Galbraith, *The Great Crash, 1929* (Boston: Houghton Mifflin, 1972), 93, 192. Two separate quotations have been combined here. Also cf. W. Arthur Lewis, *Economic Survey, 1919–1939*, 52. The fact that the economy had significantly weakened before the crash was demonstrated in G. H. Moore, *Statistical Indications of Cyclical Revivals and Recessions*, N.B.E.R. Occasional Paper 31 (New York: National Bureau of Economic Research, 1950), 10–11. Also cf. E. A. Erickson, "The Great Crash of October, 1929," in H. van der

As for the wealth and spending hypothesis, the evidence did not provide a compelling proof. The dramatic decline in consumption expenditures after 1929 may have been due to the wealth effects of the stock market debacle. It may have arisen once expectations had been dampened by events after 1929. Or it may have been an outgrowth of a declining trend in construction activity and in farm incomes during the twenties. But even the most recent econometric investigations have been incapable of explaining a large portion of the decline in spending. We can speak of an autonomous drop, but we cannot say why it happened.[10]

II   Theories of the depression as a policy problem

Another approach to understanding the depression evaluated the extent to which the slump was the result of policy errors. Inadequate theory and misleading information, as well as political pressures, it was argued, distorted the policy-making process. Such writers as Melvin Brockie, Kenneth Roose, and Sumner Slichter maintained that from 1932 onward, the American economy showed a great potential for recovery, only to be set back profoundly by the 1937 recession. They found that monetary conditions were not a factor insofar as the data showed low short-term interest rates, a strong bond market, and a high incidence of excess reserves.[11] The impact of the New Deal, they asserted, was responsible for negating whatever monetary stimulus existed. The industrial codes tended to raise labor costs and material input prices.[12] The rhetoric and ideology of the Roosevelt administra-

Wee, ed., *The Great Depression Revisited: Essays on the Economics of the Thirties* (The Hague: Martinus Nijhoff, 1972), 10.

10 See Peter Temin, *Did Monetary Forces Cause the Great Depression?*

11 See C. O. Hardy, "An Appraisal of the Factors ('Natural' and 'Artificial') Which Stopped Short the Recovery Development in the United States," *American Economic Review*, 29 (March, 1939, Supplement), 170–82.

12 For a recent statement, see Michael M. Weinstein, *Recovery and Redistribution under the NIRA* (New York: North-Holland, 1980), 29–30. There was, however, substantial disagreement over the extent to which a monetary stimulus did or did not exist. Brockie argued that a doubling of Federal Reserve member-bank reserve requirements in 1936 brought on the recession of 1937. See his "Theories of the 1937–38 Crisis and Depression," *Economic Journal*, 60 (June, 1950), 292–310. In this regard, also see John P. Wernette, *The Control of Business Cycles* (New York: Farrar & Rinehart, 1940), 182; and Norman J. Silberling, *The Dynamics of Business* (New York: McGraw-Hill, 1943), 355. H. Jaeger, in his essay "Business in the Great Depression," in *The Great Depres-*

tion may also have played a role by jeopardizing the confidence of the business community.

The so-called monetarist criticism of New Deal policy, originally posed by Clark Warburton, but presented most persuasively by Milton Friedman and Anna Schwartz, focused on the impact of the external dollar drain generated by Great Britain's departure from the gold standard in 1931 and the internal drain created by the crash itself. To the extent that the Federal Reserve Board failed to understand the links between bank failures, runs on deposits, and the international pressure on the dollar, it also failed to recognize the inappropriateness of the classic policy response undertaken – the raising of discount rates.[13]

These writers did not attribute the depression's unusual severity solely to actual government policy. In some cases they criticized the government for not doing enough. They maintained that the private sector raised prices too quickly in the mid-thirties. As a result, by 1937, consumers showed an increased resistance to higher prices owing to their desire to liquidate the large debt incurred earlier in the decade and to maintain their savings in the event of another crash. The average propensity to consume subsequently fell, and a recession took hold.[14] Pro-competitive policies presumably were the solution, but government

sion Revisited, p. 137, argued that the industry codes may also have slowed recovery, because although they "seemed advisable to save weaker enterprises at the very bottom of the depression . . . in the long run [they] threatened to impede technological progress and managerial innovation."

13 See Milton Friedman and Anna J. Schwartz, A Monetary History of the United States, 1867–1960 (Princeton, N.J.: Princeton University Press, 1963), 300, 306, 315–17, 326, 358, 411–19; and Gottfried Haberler, The World Economy, Money, and the Great Depression, 31–2. Also see the following articles by Clark Warburton: "Monetary Expansion and the Inflationary Gap," American Economic Review, 34 (June, 1944), 303–27; "Monetary Theory, Full Production, and the Great Depression," Econometrica, 13 (April, 1945), 114–28; "The Volume of Money and the Price Level Between the World Wars," Journal of Political Economy, 53 (June, 1945), 150–63; and "Quantity and Frequency of the Use of Money in the United States, 1919–1945," Journal of Political Economy, 54 (October, 1946), 436–50.

14 See Kenneth D. Roose, The Economics of Recession and Revival: An Interpretation of 1937–38 (New Haven, Conn.: Yale University Press, 1954), 36–9, ch. 9; and his "The Recession of 1937–38," Journal of Political Economy, 56 (June, 1948), 239–48. Also see S. H. Slichter, "The Downturn of 1937," Review of Economics and Statistics, 20 (August, 1938), 103; and his "Corporate Price Policies as a Factor in the Recent Business Recession," Proceedings of the Academy of Political Science, 18 (January, 1939), 20–33; Alvin H. Hansen, Full Recovery or Stagnation? (New York: Norton, 1941), 269–71; and Ralph G. Hawtrey, Economic Destiny (New York: Longmans, Green, 1944), 253.

action (such as the creation of the Temporary National Economic Committee) was too little, too late, and often inspired more by political than economic concerns.

The notion that the Great Depression was essentially an outgrowth of policy failures was problematic at best. To be sure, one could, with the benefit of hindsight, engage in some forceful criticism of economic policy during the thirties. But this was a futile exercise. In many respects the Roosevelt administration did what many predecessors had done in the face of a cyclical downturn. One must ask, therefore, how government officials suddenly became so inept in the interwar period. Moreover, the question remained: Why were traditional policies, which had seemingly worked in the past and which reflected a theoretical consensus of generations of economists, suddenly so perverse in the 1930s? What had changed in the structure and operation of the national economy in the interwar period to make orthodox economic theory and policy inadequate? These are the questions that the policy approach to the Great Depression ignored. Even the monetarist school conceded this point. As Friedman and Schwartz so candidly admitted, to the extent that there was gross mismanagement of the banking system and of the crisis in capital markets after 1929, such ineptitude only made worse an economic calamity that was nonmonetary in origin.[15]

III   Long-run theories of the depression

The literature that focused on long-run factors in the depression was distinctive in holding that the crash of 1929 was less important than certain developments in the economy that had deleterious impacts throughout the interwar period. Some authors – for example, Seymour Harris and Paul Sweezy – argued that during the twenties the distribution of national income became increasingly skewed, lowering the

15 See Friedman and Schwartz, A Monetary History of the United States, 300, 306, 315–17, 326, 358, 411–19. Much controversy surrounds the claims made by Friedman and Schwartz. Considering this debate in detail is beyond the scope of this study, but it is important to note that several economists have argued that insofar as prices fell faster than the nominal money stock from 1930 to 1933, the real money supply must have risen. The argument that monetary stringency exacerbated the depression is, in their view, not tenable. See William Stoneman, A History of the Economic Analysis of the Great Depression in America (New York: Garland, 1979), preface; and Peter Temin, Did Monetary Forces Cause the Great Depression?

economy's aggregate average propensity to consume. Others, such as Charles Kindleberger, W. Arthur Lewis, and Vladimir Timoshenko, focused on a secular shift in the terms of trade between primary products and manufactured goods, due to the uneven development of the agricultural and industrial nations. This change in the terms of trade, they argued, created a credit crisis in world markets when bad crop yields occurred in 1929 and 1930. At the same time that agricultural economies were losing revenue because of poor crops and declining world demand, the developed economies were contracting credit for the developing nations and imposing massive trade restrictions such as America's Hawley-Smoot Tariff of 1930. As the agricultural nations went into a slump, the industrialized countries lost a major market for their output. Hence, the downturn of 1929 became more and more severe.[16]

Industrial organization economists, Adolf Berle and Gardiner Means most prominent among them, sought an explanation of the depression in the increasing extent of imperfect competition in the American economy of the early twentieth century.[17] Downward inflexibility of prices after the crash of 1929, caused by the concentrated structure of American industry and the impact of labor unions, intensified the effective demand problem and prevented the price system from reaching a new equilibrium at full employment. On the one side, "sticky prices" further limited the already constrained purchasing power of consumers. On the other, to the extent that noncompetitive pricing predominated in the capital goods sector, producers were less willing to buy new plant and equipment. Excessive real wages, held up by union pressure and New Deal policy, further contributed to persistent disequilibrium

16 See Seymour Harris, *Saving American Capitalism: A Liberal Economic Program* (New York: Knopf, 1948); Paul M. Sweezy, *The Theory of Capitalist Development* (New York: Monthly Review Press, 1968); John K. Galbraith, *The Great Crash, 1929*, 180–7; W. Arthur Lewis, *Economic Survey, 1919–1939*, 55–6; Vladimir P. Timoshenko, *World Agriculture and the Depression*, Michigan Business Studies, vol. 5 (Ann Arbor: University of Michigan Press, 1933), 541–3; and Charles P. Kindleberger, *The World in Depression: 1929–1939* (Berkeley: University of California Press, 1973), 292–3. Also cf. J. A. Salter, *Recovery: The Second Effort* (New York: Century, 1932), 41–4, 48.

17 See Arthur B. Adams, *Trend of Business: 1922–1932* (New York: Harper & Bros., 1932), 24–9, 30–9, 46–9, 69–70; G. C. Means, "Price Inflexibility and the Requirements of a Stabilizing Monetary Policy," *Journal of the American Statistical Association*, 30 (June, 1935), 401–13; and Gardiner C. Means and Adolf A. Berle, *The Modern Corporation and Private Property* (New York: Harcourt, Brace & World, 1968).

in labor markets. Price inflexibility thus inhibited the recovery of both final product demand and investment demand.[18]

There were several weaknesses in these theories. Those authors who focused on an increasingly unequal distribution of income or on administered pricing did not marshal unambiguous evidence to make their case, nor did they specify precisely how such factors came to life in the interwar economy.[19] The "sticky prices" thesis also relied on an assumption of perfect competition in all markets other than those where the imperfections existed, and of rising marginal costs over the entire range of output. If these assumptions were relaxed, the thesis did not hold. As Michal Kalecki pointed out, if "sticky wages" were responsible for the length of the depression, it followed that a reduction in wages would have eliminated the persistent equilibrium. If, however, there were imperfections in product markets as well, a reduction in the nominal wage would have lowered the real wage, thereby exacerbating the effective demand crisis. Only if price adjustments were general and followed *instantaneously* by increased investment would the sticky prices thesis concerning the thirties hold.[20]

The terms of trade argument similarly had a major flaw. The major weaknesses in the American economy of the interwar period were domestic, and the collapse of demand on the part of primary product exporting nations was not highly relevant. America's dependence on foreign markets was not significant in the interwar years.

The empirical and theoretical inadequacies of these long-run arguments spurred efforts to develop a more coherent and verifiable approach to the study of secular mechanisms in the Great Depression.

18 See L. G. Reynolds, "Producers' Goods Prices in Expansion and Decline," *Journal of the American Statistical Association*, 34 (March, 1939), 32–40; and W. L. Thorp and W. F. Crowder, "Concentration and Product Characteristics as Factors in Price-Quantity Behavior," *American Economic Review*, 30 (February, 1941), 390–408. J. Backman, in "Price Inflexibility and Changes in Production," *American Economic Review*, 29 (September, 1939), 480–6, challenged the empirical relevance of the administered prices theory and argued (on p. 486) that in order to understand the low levels of output that prevailed during the thirties, one had to examine the "character of the market; durability of the product; capital goods versus consumers' goods; joint demand; stage of development of an industry; [and] necessaries versus luxury products."

19 Moreover, there was an obvious criticism to be made of the administered prices thesis: Insofar as prices fell by one-third in the early thirties, how inflexible could the general price system have been?

20 See Michal Kalecki, *Studies in the Theory of Business Cycles, 1933–39* (New York: Augustus M. Kelley, 1969), 40–59.

These efforts had as their intellectual precursor the work of Joseph Schumpeter on cyclical processes in modern economies. Schumpeter held that the interwar period was an era in which three major cycles of economic activity in the United States (and Europe) coincidentally reached their nadir.[21] These cycles were (1) the Kondratieff, a wave of fifty or more years associated with the introduction and dispersion of major inventions, (2) the Juglar, a wave of approximately ten years' duration that appeared to be linked with population movements, and (3) the Kitchin, a wave of about forty months' length that had the appearance of a typical inventory cycle.

Schumpeter's efforts were paralleled by those of Simon Kuznets and, more recently, Moses Abramovitz and Richard Easterlin. Kuznets was successful in documenting the existence of waves of some fifteen to twenty years in length. These periodic swings, according to Abramovitz, demonstrated that in the United States and other industrialized countries "development during the nineteenth and early twentieth centuries took the form of a series of surges in the growth of output and in capital and labor resources followed by periods of retarded growth." Significantly, "each period of retardation in the rate of growth of output . . . culminated in a protracted depression or in a period of stagnation in which business cycle recoveries were disappointing, failing to lift the economy to a condition of full employment or doing so only transiently."[22]

Most, if not all, of the "Kuznets cycle" literature was concerned with the explicit dating of the long swings that appeared in the data. It seemed clear that these swings involved changes in resource endowments (including the size of population) and alterations in the intensity of resource utilization.[23] The specific behavioral mechanisms that could account for the Kuznets phenomenon (and its precise manifestation in

---

21 See Joseph A. Schumpeter, *Business Cycles*, vol. 2, 905–1050.

22 See S. Kuznets, "Long Swings in the Growth of Population and in Related Economic Variables," *Proceedings of the American Philosophical Society*, 102 (February, 1958), 25–52; and M. Abramovitz, "The Nature and Significance of Kuznets Cycles," *Economic Development and Cultural Change*, 9 (April, 1961), 229, 234. Eventually Abramovitz argued that the "Kuznets cycle" applied only to the years 1840–1914. See his "The Passing of the Kuznets Cycle," *Economica*, N.S., 35 (November, 1968). Also see Richard A. Easterlin, *Population, Labor Force, and Long Swings in Economic Growth: The American Experience* (New York: National Bureau of Economic Research, 1968); and his "American Population Since 1940," in Martin Feldstein, ed., *The American Economy in Transition* (Chicago: University of Chicago Press, 1980), 275–321.

23 Abramovitz, "The Nature and Significance of Kuznets Cycles," 241.

the United States in the 1930s) were necessarily the focus of continued debate. It is in this context that one can understand the large literature on "secular stagnation."

Broadly speaking, the stagnation theorists were divided between those who evinced a "Schumpeterian pessimism" about the emergence of innovations and new technologies, and those who shared a "Keynes-Hansen pessimism" concerning the shrinkage of investment outlets owing to a decline in the rate of population growth.[24] Both groups agreed that stagnation or, as it was sometimes called, economic maturity involved a "decrease of the rate of growth of heavy industries and of building activity [and] the slowing down of the rate of growth of the total quantity of production, of employment, and usually of population. It [also involved] the rising relative importance of consumer goods." They also believed that "the appearance of industrial maturity raise[d] profound questions concerning the ability of an enterprise system to produce a progressive evolution of the economy."[25]

The Keynes-Hansen pessimism, as presented by John Maynard Keynes and Alvin Hansen in the late thirties, held that as population growth fell off, and major markets consequently contracted, outlets for new investment were limited to those created by the introduction of new technology or new products. To the extent that recovery from a depression required investment outlays above and beyond the level of depreciation allowances, an upturn became dependent on the availability, in an adequate volume, of opportunities in new industries and processes. If these were not forthcoming (as stagnation theorists believed was true of the 1930s), the only solution was deficit spending to augment consumer purchasing power. But political barriers to such government action in the thirties left the economy in a slump.[26]

24 As suggested by William Fellner in his "Full Use or Underutilization: Appraisal of Long-Run Factors Other than Defense," *American Economic Review*, 44 (May, 1954), 423–33. It should be pointed out that Fellner had earlier rejected all arguments concerning stagnation. See his "The Technological Argument of the Stagnation Thesis," *Quarterly Journal of Economics*, 55 (August, 1941), 638–51.

25 The quotations are taken from G. E. McLaughlin and R. J. Watkins, "The Problem of Industrial Growth in a Mature Economy," *American Economic Review*, 29 (March, 1939, Supplement), 1–14.

26 See A. H. Hansen, "Economic Progress and Declining Population Growth," *American Economic Review*, 29 (March, 1939), 1–15; and J. M. Keynes, "Some Economic Consequences of a Declining Population," *Eugenics Review*, 29 (April, 1937), 13–17. A complete, if rather polemical, exposition of the stagnation thesis may be found in George Terborgh, *The Bogey of Economic Maturity* (Chicago: Machinery and Allied Products Institute, 1945).

The inadequacies of this argument were discussed by several writers. One critic, Michal Kalecki, pointed out:

> It is sometimes maintained that the increase in population encourages investment because the entrepreneurs anticipate a broadening market. What is important, however, in this context is not the increase in population but in purchasing power. The increase in the number of paupers does not broaden the market. For instance, increased population does not mean necessarily a higher demand for houses: without an increase in the purchasing power the result may well be crowding of more people into the existing dwelling space.[27]

A more systematic theory had to argue that, for secular reasons, the purchasing power of the population, rather than the size of the population itself, fell in the interwar period.[28]

There was a further wrinkle to the Keynes-Hansen pessimism concerning investment behavior in advanced economies. It was argued that as a society became more affluent, an ever-increasing volume of savings

27 From Michal Kalecki, *Studies in Economic Dynamics* (London: George Allen & Unwin, 1943), 88. Also cf. A. R. Sweezy, "Population Growth and Investment Opportunity," *Quarterly Journal of Economics*, 55 (November, 1940), 64–79. As Terborgh argued in *The Bogey of Economic Maturity*, p. 181: "There is no rigid physical relation . . . between the number of families in the country and the amount and value of the housing they will pay to occupy. Demand depends not only on their number but on their incomes." It should be added that there was disagreement in later years over the empirical validity of the argument concerning excessive expansion in the housing and automobile industries. The notion of overbuilding in residential construction in the interwar period was challenged in R. F. Muth, "The Demand for Non-Farm Housing," in A. C. Harberger, ed., *The Demand for Durable Goods* (Chicago: University of Chicago Press, 1960), 29–96. And a critique of the general idea of excess capacity in the American economy of the 1920s was offered in L. J. Mercer and W. D. Morgan, "The American Automobile Industry: Investment Demand, Capacity, and Capacity Utilization, 1921–1940," *Journal of Political Economy*, 80 (December, 1972), 1214–31.

28 It was also true that most of the secular stagnation literature did not address the impact of demographic changes on the population's age structure and thereby on the composition of final demand. For instance, one could argue that as the rate of population growth (and immigration) fell in the 1920s, the resulting increase in the age structure raised the economy's marginal propensity to save, thereby slowing the growth rate of consumption. Moreover, an increasingly older population would most likely have jeopardized the growth of such important industries as automobiles and residential construction. Some evidence on these matters is presented in Robert M. Coen and Bert G. Hickman, *An Annual Growth Model of the U.S. Economy* (New York: North-Holland, 1976). Also cf. R. B. Zevin, "The Economics of Normalcy," *Journal of Economic History*, 42 (March, 1982), 43–52, where the role of a changing age structure in the downturn of the early thirties is explicitly examined.

was generated. Such savings could find no outlets except at unrealistically low rates of interest – rates at which investors preferred to hold their wealth in cash rather than securities, bonds, or other titles to real capital.[29] In a certain sense this argument was analogous to the Schumpeterian notion of vanishing investment and technological opportunities. It presumed that at very low rates of interest the demand for money became so high as to create a "liquidity trap." This notion was never unequivocally accepted.[30]

Much like the population theory, the variant of the stagnation theory that focused on the decline of innovation and technical change embodied certain inconsistencies and questionable assertions. The lower rate of technical change and the decline in the number of major innovations were deemed to be exogenous factors derived from the state of technical knowledge at the time.[31] Little justification of this position was offered by such leading proponents as Hansen, Kalecki, and David Weintraub. Furthermore, meager attention was given to a seeming contradiction in the argument. If during the thirties little technical change took place, why did the eventual reduction in the amount of capital equipment available (owing to firm exits and the periodic obsolescence of plant) not result in a revival in capital goods output?[32]

29 See John Maynard Keynes, *The General Theory of Employment, Interest, and Money* (London: Macmillan, 1936), 31. Also see C. E. Ayres, "The Impact of the Great Depression on Economic Thinking," *American Economic Review*, 35 (May, 1946), 112–25.

30 There is an enormous literature on this debate. For well-known examples of it, see J. R. Hicks, "Mr. Keynes and the 'Classics': A Suggested Interpretation," *Econometrica*, 5 (April, 1937), 147–59; Don Patinkin, *Money, Interest, and Prices* (New York: Harper & Row, 1965); J. Tobin, "Liquidity Preference and Monetary Policy," *Review of Economics and Statistics*, 29 (February, 1947), 124–31; and M. Friedman and A. J. Schwartz, "The Quantity Theory of Money – A Restatement," in M. Friedman, ed., *Studies in the Quantity Theory of Money* (Chicago: University of Chicago Press, 1956), 3–21.

31 See Alvin H. Hansen, *Full Recovery or Stagnation?* (New York: Norton, 1941), 279ff.; and M. Kalecki, "Observations on the Theory of Growth," *Economic Journal*, 72 (March, 1962), 134–53. Kalecki did concede, on pp. 134 and 147, that innovations were not wholly exogenous and could, in fact, be influenced (with appreciable lags) by changes in profit rates, output, and the size of the capital stock. Even so, he argued elsewhere that the exogeneity of technical change indicated that "long-run development [was] not inherent in the capitalist economy." See his *Theory of Economic Dynamics: An Essay on Cyclical and Long-Run Changes in Capitalist Economy* (New York: Monthly Review Press, 1968), 161.

32 As admitted by Michal Kalecki, *Selected Essays on the Dynamics of the Capitalist Economy, 1933–1970* (Cambridge University Press, 1971), 30.

There was one further objection to the technology argument that was apparent to some of the stagnation theorists themselves. There was an implicit assumption made that new innovations were capital-using; thus, had innovations occurred in the thirties, net investment demand would have absorbed large capital outlays and generated an upturn. But if innovations were capital-saving, this argument was contradicted. In fact, investment during the earlier growth of the American economy in, for example, railroads, motor cars, and housing had given way in later periods to newer forms of investment in materials handling, managerial technique, and information processing. These latter innovations did not absorb large amounts of investment expenditure, but did improve the organization and efficiency of production.[33]

The implications of the stagnation thesis for the role of government and external market penetration were quite profound, because it linked outlets for net investment expenditure with (1) deficit spending to bolster effective demand, (2) direct government purchases of goods and services, (3) increasing outlays on sales efforts and distribution mechanisms by firms, and (4) the penetration of foreign markets that were unsaturated.[34] Unlike those who conceived of fiscal and monetary mechanisms as instruments of countercyclical policy, the stagnation theorists (Paul Baran and Paul Sweezy being the best examples) saw government involvement in mature economies as permanent and increasing over time.

A more sophisticated version of the economic maturity idea was

33 See Michal Kalecki, *Theory of Economic Dynamics*, 159; and Alvin H. Hansen, *Full Recovery or Stagnation?* 310, 315. Reflecting on the differences in innovation that obtain in an economy over time, Hansen noted on p. 314: "The transformation of a rural economy into a capitalistic one is something distinctly different from the further evolution of a society which has already reached the status of a fully-developed machine technique."

34 See D. Weintraub, "Effects of Current and Prospective Technological Developments upon Capital Formation," *American Economic Review*, 29 (March, 1939, Supplement), 32; M. Kalecki, "The Problem of Effective Demand with Tugan-Baranovski and Rosa Luxemburg," in his *Selected Essays on the Dynamics of the Capitalist Economy*, 146–55; Paul A. Baran and Paul M. Sweezy, *Monopoly Capital: An Essay on the American Economic and Social Order* (New York: Monthly Review Press, 1966), chs. 5–7; and P. Patnaik, "A Note on External Markets and Capitalist Development," *Economic Journal*, 82 (December, 1972), 1316–23. Josef Steindl pointed out that expanded systems of consumer credit were yet another means by which investment opportunities could be maintained in mature economies. See his note "On Maturity in Capitalist Economies," in *Problems of Economic Dynamics and Planning: Essays in Honour of Michal Kalecki*, no ed. (New York: Pergamon, 1966), 423–32.

developed by Josef Steindl in 1951. His work linked economic stagnation directly with the behavior of firms, thereby avoiding the mechanistic qualities of the earlier stagnation arguments and their frequent and often unexplained appeals to exogenous factors. Steindl argued that long-run tendencies toward capital concentration, which he took to be inherent in capitalist development, led to a lethargic attitude toward competition and investment.[35] Specifically, the emergence of concentrated markets made difficult, and in some cases impossible, that expulsion of excess capacity required for revival after the 1932 trough.

Steindl argued that price inflexibility in concentrated industries was intensified during depressions, and this had an important impact on the responses of firms to economic fluctuations. The net revenue of firms tended to be so attenuated in a slump that strategies of price reduction were viewed as unfeasible. There may even have been incentives to raise prices in order to compensate for the reduction in the volume of sales.[36] For a given industry, therefore, the impact of a decline in the rate of growth depended on the extent to which the industry was concentrated. In sectors where the squeezing out of competitors was relatively easy, declines in demand resulted in a reduction of profit margins for each firm as prices were cut. By contrast, in more concentrated markets, profit margins tended to be stable in the face of reductions in demand.[37]

35 The idea that large concentrated firms avoided major investment opportunities, owing to a desire to maintain their dominant market position, also played a role in the conception of economic stagnation developed by Michal Kalecki. See his *Studies in Economic Dynamics*, 92; and his *Theory of Economic Dynamics*, 159. This exposition is derived from Josef Steindl, *Maturity and Stagnation in American Capitalism* (New York: Monthly Review Press, 1979), chs. 2–5, 9, 13; and his *Small and Big Business: Economic Problems of the Size of Firms* (Oxford: Basil Blackwell, 1945), 48–54, 63–6.

36 This argument was analogous to what James Tobin has often called the "Blough effect." Simply put, for the nonagricultural sector, let $P = (W/Q^*) [1 + Z(u)]$, where P is price, W the wage rate, Q^* a productivity parameter, Z the firm's percentage markup, and u the level of unemployment. The Blough effect obtains when $Z'(u) > 0$. See J. Tobin, "The Wage-Price Mechanism," in his *Consumption and Econometrics*, vol. 2 of *Essays in Economics* (New York: North-Holland, 1975), 17–32.

37 It may make the argument clearer (at the risk of doing some violence to Steindl's assumptions) to employ the calculus of profit maximization. For a firm in an oligopolistic industry, marginal revenue may be expressed as

$$MR = \delta(Pq)/\delta q = (\delta P/\delta q)(q) + P$$
$$= (\delta P/\delta Q)(\delta Q/\delta q)(q) + P$$

where P is the price charged for the firm's output q, and Q is the output of the industry as a whole. Rearranging terms,

At the macroeconomic level, the implications of rigid profit margins for cyclical performance were profound. If price reductions did not occur when the rate of growth declined, the necessary adjustment of sectoral rates of expansion to the aggregate rate required reductions in the rate of capacity utilization. If industrial structure was more competitive, however, excess capacity did not result from a decline in the rate of accumulation; rather, prices fell.

Reductions in capacity utilization implied not only lower national income but also higher unemployment. In the presence of underutilized capacity, firms were disinclined to undertake net investment. A cumulative process was thereby established wherein a decline in the rate of growth, by generating reductions in the rate of capacity utilization, led to a further decline in the rate of expansion as net investment was reduced. Individual firms, believing that decreases in investment would alleviate their own burden of excess capacity, merely intensified the problem economy-wide. The greater the proportion of a nation's industry that was highly concentrated, the greater the tendency for a cyclical downturn to develop into a progressive decline.

Central to Steindl's thesis was a conception of long-term alterations in industrial structure that made the economy less able to recover from

$$MR = (\delta P/\delta Q)(Q/P)(q/Q)(\delta Q/\delta q) + 1$$
$$= P\{(s/\epsilon)(\delta Q/\delta q) + 1\}$$

where s is the firm's market share as denoted by q/Q, and ϵ is the elasticity of demand. Assuming that the firm maximizes profits, marginal revenue will equal marginal and average cost. Thus,

$$P/AC = 1/\{(s/\epsilon)(\delta Q/\delta q) + 1\}$$

The ratio of profits, π to revenue, R, may be denoted as

$$\pi/R = \{(P - AC)Q - FC\}/PQ$$

where FC equals the fixed costs of production. Therefore,

$$(P - AC)/P = \pi/R + FC/Q$$
$$= 1 - \{1 + (s/\epsilon)(\delta Q/\delta q)\}/1$$
$$= (s/-\epsilon)(\delta Q/\delta q)$$

The ratio π/R may then be expressed as

$$\pi/R = (-s/\epsilon)(\delta Q/\delta q) - FC/q$$

To the extent that the firm has lower costs, s is higher according to Steindl's argument. If s rises, π/R rises because $\epsilon < 0$ and FC/q falls. And it is also clear that as s rises, MR becomes steeper, and the less are prices reduced in response to declines in demand.

cyclical instability and to generate continued growth. The emergence of oligopolistic market structures was taken to be inherent in the development of large-scale manufacturing techniques. Economic maturity and the threat of stagnation resulted because the growing incidence of "[o]ligopoly [brought] about a maldistribution of funds by shifting profits to those industries which [were] reluctant to use them."[38] To escape stagnation, capital had to be redistributed either to more competitive sectors or to new industries, although such shifts could proceed, given the difficulties of obtaining the technical knowledge, labor skills, and "goodwill" in new product lines, only with considerable time lags.

By the terms of Steindl's thesis, one should expect an inverse relation between net investment and the degree of concentration in American manufacturing during the Great Depression. But statistically this relation cannot be confirmed. Data on concentration and investment provide no information concerning interfirm differentials in costs, which are the basis of firms' pricing strategies.[39] Large disparities in techniques and costs among even a small number of firms may, over time, permit and encourage severe competition. Conversely, a large number of identical firms may prove to be quite lethargic, lacking significant cost differentials that can be competitively exploited. In short, whatever the "Steindl effect" may be, it is masked in the record. Some highly concentrated industries were relatively vibrant during the 1930s, whereas others that were less concentrated were virtually moribund.[40]

Many theorists and historians thus looked on the interwar period of American economic development as the final stage of internally

38 From Steindl, *Maturity and Stagnation in American Capitalism*, preface.

39 For a survey and criticism of static analyses of industrial structure that focus on the number of sellers and demand elasticities of a given market, see R. W. Pfouts and C. E. Ferguson, "Market Classification Systems in Theory and Policy," *Southern Economic Journal*, 26 (October, 1959), 111–18; and also see J. P. Miller, "Measures of Monopoly Power and Concentration: Their Economic Significance," in *Business Concentration and Price Policy*, no ed. (Princeton, N.J.: Princeton University Press, 1955), 119–39.

40 In addition, the data on sectoral shares of wages in the value added, which Steindl cited as indices of competitiveness, are similarly misleading. A rising (falling) trend in the wage share may not necessarily indicate a competitive decline (noncompetitive rise) in the industry's gross margin, but may rather demonstrate changes in the labor intensity of that sector's technology over time. See Steindl, *Maturity and Stagnation in American Capitalism*, ch. 8. Also see Michael A. Bernstein, *Long-Term Economic Growth and the Problem of Recovery in American Manufacturing: A Study of the Great Depression in the United States, 1929–1939* (Ph.D. dissertation, Yale University, 1982), 183–4, 235, 240, 296.

generated accumulation. They argued that the American economy stagnated by the 1930s and was revived only by the impact of wars, state expenditures, and the penetration of foreign markets.

What the stagnation theorists focused on were those characteristics of the early twentieth-century economy that seemed to presage an end to the endogenous growth of the system. By the interwar period the geographic expansion of the United States had ceased, and with it so had the dramatic rates of increase in infrastructural and heavy investment. Population growth had also slowed, along with the rate of immigration. The opportunities offered by foreign markets were reduced by increasingly protectionist policies, and an unequal distribution of income in the nation may have generated tendencies toward underconsumption.

Yet even if all of the foregoing descriptions of the interwar economy are accepted (despite empirical studies noted earlier that challenge their accuracy), there is an implicit assumption embedded within them that is problematic – that is, that such systemic changes in the economy created fundamental barriers to continued growth, rather than a new structure of demand that required a change in the composition of investment and output. This is to say that the stagnation argument mistook qualitative changes in demand during the interwar period for the permanent exhaustion of a fixed set of investment opportunities. It neglected the powerful ability of modern enterprise to respond to and influence secular change.

I want to suggest in this study that the difficulty experienced by the American economy in the 1930s was an outgrowth of secular trends in development. By the 1920s, the economy had entered an era characterized by the emergence of dramatically new demand patterns and investment opportunities. These patterns and opportunities foreshadowed and indeed encouraged a shift in the composition of national output. But such a qualitative transformation created impediments to the recovery process in the thirties. These impediments derived from the difficulty of altering technology and labor skills to meet demands for new investment and consumer goods at a time of severe financial instability. In this sense, long-term growth mechanisms played a major role in the cyclical problems of the interwar period.

1. Long-term economic growth and the problem of recovery in the United States: 1929–39[1]

> It has generally been the fate of economic theory to run a losing race against the course of history, and never to have completed the analysis of one phase of economic development before another takes its place.
>
> – Joan Robinson

Although the American economy has suffered several financial panics in its history, none had the legacy of the panic of 1929. My concern is to examine the economy's failure to recover in the thirties – a failure epitomized by the fact that it was not until the outbreak of war in Europe that industrial production reached its pre-crash levels and the unemployment rate fell below a decennial average of 18 percent.[1]

I   A theory of long-term growth

Secular economic growth is not well understood. Most analytical traditions view the trend in strictly quantitative terms, by means of the concept of the "natural rate of growth," with qualitative change most often relegated to the status of an exogenous factor.[2] In the one major analytical tradition that seeks to integrate the secular development of an economy with its short-run behavior, namely the Marxian, the theory of long-term growth is subsumed within a theory of the firm that focuses on the concentration of capital into larger enterprises and a decline in the number of independent firms.[3]

In order to move beyond the limitations of such views, it is necessary

1 See Stanley Lebergott, *Manpower in Economic Growth: The American Record Since 1800* (New York: McGraw-Hill, 1964). But also cf. M. R. Darby, "Three-and-a-Half Million Employees Have Been Mislaid: Or, an Explanation of Unemployment, 1934–1941," *Journal of Political Economy*, 84 (February, 1976), 1–16. Also see "The Immediate Impact of War on the American Economy," by the editors, *Plan Age*, 5 (December, 1939), 313–26.

2 Cf. F. H. Hahn and R. C. O. Matthews, "The Theory of Economic Growth: A Survey," *Economic Journal*, 74 (December, 1964), 779–902.

3 See Karl Marx, *Capital*, trans. S. Moore and E. Aveling (New York: International Publishers, 1967), vol. I, ch. 25.

21

to develop theoretical propositions that are rooted in historical experience. Modern economy may on one level be characterized as a system of production that fashions useful objects by whose sale it accumulates wealth. Thus, the cost conditions affecting supply as well as the determinants of needs and desires affecting demand play a central role in delimiting growth performance. It is the secular changes in these factors of which a theory of long-term economic development is made.

The classification of expansion by periods or phases is undertaken by logically distinguishing between and showing the interconnections of the forms that growth assumes.[4] Each phase eventually confronts impediments to its continuation that arise out of the economic structure posited by history up to that time. Specific phases of the growth process may be defined by these impediments. The barriers are themselves overcome and transformed by the accumulation of capital over time.

At its inception, economic growth proceeds on the basis of a strictly limited set of commodities. Immaturity in technological knowledge, raw material constraints due to technical bottlenecks and difficulties in transportation, and a scarcity of sufficiently disciplined and skilled workers severely limit the set of goods that can be produced. At the same time, the market for commodities is small, for two reasons. First, the modest extent of production as a whole, coupled with the fairly primitive techniques in use, dictates a low level of demand for producers' goods. Second, the generally low level of income of the population, along with the existence of much productive activity that is either traditional or domestic, generates a very small demand for marketed consumer goods.

Expansion, then, is dependent on the rate of growth of the industrial labor force.[5] On the one hand, levels of output and of profits are

---

4 See D. P. Levine, "The Theory of the Growth of the Capitalist Economy," *Economic Development and Cultural Change*, 24 (October, 1975), 47–74. As Levine puts it on p. 47: "The theory of economic growth needs to go beyond the specification of the movement of economic magnitudes in order to establish the organic connections between economic growth and the development of the economic structure as a whole." Readers familiar with recent contributions to the literature in Europe will recognize some links between the French tradition of "regulation theory" and both the work of Levine and my own approach. See, for example, M. DeVroey, "A Regulation Approach Interpretation of Contemporary Crisis," *Capital and Class*, 23 (Summer, 1984), 45–66.

5 See W. A. Lewis, "Economic Development with Unlimited Supplies of Labour," *Manchester School of Economic and Social Studies*, 22 (May, 1954), 139–91; and John C. H. Fei and Gustav Ranis, *Development of the Labor Surplus Economy: Theory and Policy* (Homewood, Ill.: Irwin, 1964), ch. 2.

directly proportional to levels of employment. On the other, the greater the size of the wage-earning population, the more extensive the market. An increase in the labor force, however, depends on certain mechanisms. First, domestic labor must be displaced by the purchase of commodities. Second, artisans and petty-commodity producers must be competed out of the market. The former will depend on the extent to which the prices of products also made in the home can be lowered. The latter will involve the achievement of greater productive efficiency by the merging in space of processes once carried out in isolation, and by the increasing division of tasks.

Yet the inherent limit to accumulation in this period remains the low level of wages. Given the labor-intensive character of production, the preservation of the profitability of enterprise depends on keeping labor costs down. This contradiction in the character of accumulation may be temporarily relieved by increasing the rate of capacity utilization, thereby increasing the amount of labor expended at a given wage, and by lowering per-unit labor costs by means of the elimination of skill requirements and by the introduction of secondary laborers into the work force. These strategies, however, tend to interfere with the reproduction of labor to the extent that they jeopardize the cohesiveness of families and the health and education of children. They also may poison, by virtue of the labor-management hostility they engender, the political environment in which the wage bargain is made. As a result, the drive to increase labor productivity is frustrated. But this need not be a permanent state of affairs. The potential for growth eventually becomes linked with process innovation and the impact of labor-saving technical change.[6]

Early economic growth is therefore based on goods that are rudimentary and labor-intensive in their production and enjoy flexible responses to price changes by both supply and demand.[7] Historically, such commodities have been simple consumer items – nonluxury clothing, foods, and household implements. The early production of textiles in

6 Some writers have argued that in the early stages of development, the theory of accumulation posited by Karl Marx is most appropriate. See N. Kaldor, "Capitalist Evolution in the Light of Keynesian Economics," in his *Essays on Economic Stability and Growth* (Glencoe, Ill.: Free Press, 1960), 243–58; and P. M. Sweezy, "Karl Marx and the Industrial Revolution," in R. Eagly, ed., *Events, Ideology, and Economic Theory* (Detroit: Wayne State University Press, 1968), 107–26.

7 Certain luxury goods may also be produced (as the historical evidence shows) to meet the demands emanating from the landowning class.

the United States, for example, took advantage of certain key characteristics of the product: (1) a natural resource base easily cultivated, prepared for use, and cheaply transported, (2) a relative simplicity of technique in production, (3) a high price elasticity of demand, and therefore (4) an ability to encourage the substitution of manufactured clothing for household production, releasing labor inputs to a growing market for wage labor.

Over time, the initial focus on consumer goods generates linkages with other sectors and broadens to include an ever-increasing range of consumption items. Linkages arise for two reasons: (1) Market development calls forth transportation improvements that in turn stimulate development in the heavy sectors. (2) The opportunities for growth center on reduction of costs in the production process, which in turn requires the development of new, nonhuman inputs. But given some lower bound to the wage, for both institutional and biological reasons, the lowering of costs becomes linked with process innovation – that is, labor saving technical progress. (If the costs of raw material inputs are fundamentally dependent on improvements in transportation and the technique of extraction, process innovation will lower these costs as well.) The increasing mechanization of production creates new sectors whose outputs are the machinery and tools to be used by the consumer industries.

The potential for growth thus ultimately shifts from the extensive increase in markets owing to the growth of the labor force to the intensive development of profitability by means of lowering the costs of production. For the individual firm, accumulation, at one time primarily dependent on the extent to which output could displace petty and domestic producers, is now constrained by the market share of other enterprises. Growth thus becomes linked with the elimination of competitors by price cutting. Hence, process innovation becomes even more important as a mechanism of expansion.[8]

As process innovation proceeds, the growth of heavy industrial sectors is stimulated. A related factor in the rise of heavy industry is the increasing extent and improving quality of transportation, communication, and other elements of the infrastructure. The incentives to reduce costs, originally arising in the leading consumer sectors, also emerge in the producer goods industries themselves. Production of machinery itself becomes more and more mechanized, and the creation of ma-

---

8 Cf. Paolo Sylos-Labini, *Oligopoly and Technical Progress*, trans. E. Henderson (Cambridge, Mass.: Harvard University Press, 1969), 33–77, 161–73.

chinery by machinery becomes widespread. As a result, this epoch of development is characterized by high rates of investment in producer durables and other heavy industries.

The development of heavy industries has fundamental implications for subsequent patterns of growth. Techniques in use in these industries require large investments of capital in plant and equipment. In addition, production and management tasks require higher degrees of skill and expertise. Because of larger capital requirements, economies of scale, and the need for a well-trained, highly motivated, and disciplined work force, the rise of heavy industry coincides with the concentration of capital in a smaller number of firms over time. This structural trend also takes hold in the consumer goods sectors for similar reasons.

Increasing capital concentration alters the growth performance and cyclical stability of the economy. Consider that a firm's potential market, in a given year, is a function of the number of potential consumers that year and the frequency with which the given product is consumed per individual per year. The number of potential consumers is linked with the rate of growth of population and with the level of the real wage. Frequency of purchase is linked with the durability and characteristics of the commodity itself. A durable good may be purchased once every several years; a nondurable, like food, is purchased virtually every day. To the extent that the expansion of markets by price reductions is limited, durable goods firms will face severely limited opportunities. Their sales prospects become linked ever more closely with general income standards, the rate of increase of the population, and the overall rate of economic growth. In addition, as the proportion of the nation's industry that is conducted in oligopolistic markets increases, the destabilizing impact of cyclical fluctuations becomes increased. A large decline in the aggregate rate of accumulation, in an economy now predominantly concentrated, has the potential to initiate a continuous decline in utilization, output, and employment. The prospects for a reversal of this process, as a consequence of the long-term alteration of the economy's structure, become increasingly dim. Unless the macroeconomy grows in steady-state fashion, a business cycle can precipitate a long period of cumulative decline. Given the many factors militating against the achievement of balanced expansion, such as population changes, alterations in the geographic size of markets, natural events, and the uncoordinated actions of firms themselves, the likelihood of the system's avoidance of fluctuations in growth rates is small.

In a major sense, the foregoing is the foundation of an argument concerning economic stagnation. Typically the continuation of such an argument would view further growth as dependent on intervention by the state. But revivals of activity in a mature economy are linked with the creation of new markets through product innovation and with the increasing intensity of sales efforts and advertising. Insofar as the loci of new net investment shifts to new product lines, this era of development formally recapitulates the earliest phases of growth. The ongoing accumulation of capital is once again dependent on the establishment of new demand patterns, not on the more profitable exploitation of already existing patterns by means of cost reduction and pricing strategies. Investment decision making becomes oriented toward the development of new products, active efforts to create the market for new commodities, and the establishment of distribution and service channels.[9] Except in cases where the created item or its development has close linkages with heavy sectors (e.g., automobiles and refrigerators), this trend in investment activity provides little stimulus to the previously dynamic sectors of the economy. The creation of new products and the establishment of new uses for existing products are activities centered by their nature in the industries producing consumer goods. For it is in the markets for consumer goods where changes in styles, fashions, and characteristics have the most sales potential.

Consumer product innovation, therefore, provides an avenue for further expansion and may act by virtue of the competitive pressures it unleashes to slow or reverse the trend of increasing concentration and relatively stagnant investment activity set in motion in the past. The precise venue of the innovative activity undertaken is difficult to specify, but historical factors having to do with technology and income levels will be decisive.[10] Technical factors may favor development in nondurable products insofar as innovations in durables tend to require long

9 See Edith T. Penrose, *The Theory of the Growth of the Firm* (New York: Wiley, 1959), 104–52; and Robin Marris, *The Economic Theory of 'Managerial' Capitalism* (London: Macmillan, 1967), 133–203. Both of these works focus on the activities of the individual firm rather than on those of the economy as a whole.

10 There will also be influences on the location of innovative activity that are tied to conditions in international trade having to do with cost differentials prevailing in foreign economies. In other words, historical factors will affect not only the sectoral location but also the geographic location of innovative activity. Cf. R. Vernon, "International Investment and International Trade in the Product Cycle," *Quarterly Journal of Economics*, 80 (May, 1966), 190–207. I cannot pursue this issue here.

gestation periods of design and development. Moreover, the production of durable commodities takes place by means of equipment that is difficult to retool for other purposes or to liquidate. It is in the non-durable product lines where technology tends to be more flexible. Indeed, the production of a given product may create by-products that themselves are marketable. This is obviously the case with industries like chemicals and foodstuffs.

Nondurable products will also have a high potential for growth, because their prices tend to be lower than those for most other goods, and as a result the financing of consumer purchases is less difficult. In addition, the frequency of nondurable sales in a market of given dimensions (with respect to both numbers of individuals and levels of income) will act as yet a further incentive for new ventures to cluster in consumer nondurable product sectors.[11]

II Long-term growth and the problem of recovery

It is now possible to integrate the analysis of long-term growth with an investigation of the Great Depression in the United States.[12] Recovery was lacking in the thirties because at the same time that long-run potentials for growth were shifting under the influence of a secular transformation to sectors whose presence in the aggregate economy was still relatively insignificant, short-run obstacles to a smooth transition emerged. An unprecedented derangement of financial markets, and the resultant fall in consumer purchasing power, interrupted the long-term development process. What in principle might have been a relatively brief panic became, by virtue of the delicate condition of the economy at the time it occurred, a prolonged slump.

The process of secular change that interfered with recovery had four major components. Patterns of consumer demand were modified because of a rising standard of living and changes in the distribution of income. As a consequence, investment activity was altered both qualitatively and quantitatively so as to meet this new demand. In turn, as investment changed, the need for labor was transformed at the same time as alterations in the capital-output ratio interfered with the econo-

---

11 The high turnover of nondurable output will also often allow the firm to secure better terms in the credit markets because the time horizon of loans will be relatively short.

12 A formal representation of the argument is presented in this chapter's appendix.

my's capacity to recover from a financial shock. On the one side, the demand for new kinds of capital goods changed the industrial distribution of employment needs. As a result there emerged an effective demand crisis as large amounts of structural unemployment were generated. On the other, changes in the capital requirements of production for new consumer demands made it more difficult for the economy to rebound from a financial shock and decline in its rate of growth. Let us look more closely at the impact of these different elements of the crisis – elements that will be analyzed in more detail in the following chapters of this study.

Consumption trends

During the interwar period the composition of consumer demand changed as a direct result of the secular rise in national income during the "New Era." The new, more affluent consumer markets that emerged as a consequence showed greater potential and faster rates of growth than others that had in the past figured prominently in total consumption expenditures. In a certain sense this phenomenon was a direct result of the kind of behavior described by Ernst Engel in his classic studies of demand. Engel found that as people grew richer, they spent proportionately less on basic foods, clothing, and housing and more on manufactures and, as they grew still more affluent, on services.[13] These shifts in consumer demand during the New Era had important macroeconomic consequences. The new pattern of consumer demand differentially affected manufacturing industries – benefiting some, harming others. As I shall show, this uneven growth of American industries forestalled recovery after the financial collapse of 1929. Certain major industries such as textiles, iron and steel, and lumber saw their markets weaken; others, notably appliances, chemicals, and processed foods, faced a new set of opportunities, but were not yet sufficiently strong to ensure recovery.

The general tendency during the interwar period was for the share of consumer spending devoted to traditional durable goods such as

---

13 See G. J. Stigler, "The Early History of Empirical Studies of Consumer Behavior," *Journal of Political Economy*, 62 (April, 1954), 95–113. Engel first published his findings in 1857 in his "Die Productions und Consumtionsverhältnisse des Königreichs Sachsen," reprinted in *International Statistical Institute Bulletin*, vol. 9, no. 1, supplement 1.

housing and standard clothing to fall. The share expended on equipment and services was roughly stable. Yet at the same time, increasing percentages of demand expenditures were made on processed food products, tobacco, household appliances and operations, medical care and insurance, recreation, and education. It was the fact that the shift to this new pattern of spending was taking place when the crash intervened, and that the economy was therefore blocked from sustaining the transition, that is essential to an understanding of why the slump continued for as long as it did.

Investment trends

The divergent growth potentials of American industries during the interwar period can be discerned from the changing pattern of demand for capital goods in major manufacturing sectors. Movements in the demand for capital goods indicate which industries were expanding and which were contracting during the interwar years. As the composition of final consumer demand changed during the New Era, so the derived demand for investment inputs was altered. The consumption patterns of the twenties favored the emergence and expansion of certain industries and generated a slower rate of growth, if not actual contraction, for others.[14]

For example, an average of 2.1% of the total real expenditures on productive facilities in the American economy during the twenties was spent in the processed foods sector. That average rose to 2.5% during the decade of depression, paralleling the change in the share of consumer spending going to processed foods. By contrast, in the textile industry the mean was 1.54% during the twenties and 1.2% during the thirties. The same shrinkage occurred in the lumber industry, where the relevant figures are 0.8% in the 1920s and 0.4% in the 1930s. In the petroleum sector there was expansion as the average share rose from 0.6% in the twenties to 1% during the thirties. Expansion in petroleum was linked to consumers spending more of their income on transportation and home heating.

Certain relatively new industries expanded quickly during the inter-

14 The evidence for this section is compiled and reported in J. Frederic Dewhurst and Associates, *America's Needs and Resources* (New York: Twentieth Century Fund, 1947), Appendix 21. See the statistical appendix to this chapter, where the evidence is presented in tabular form.

war years. Aircraft production and chemicals manufacturing were two sectors where the rate of investment in new productive facilities was high. There was also a rise in investment in the manufacture of office machinery and related equipment, absorbing an average of 3.3% of real total domestic investment during the twenties and 3.9% in the thirties. In iron and steel production there was also a moderate increase in the investment share, but this expansion was limited to firms producing for appliance, food container, and other new markets. The automobile sector experienced a slight rise in its investment share, but again such expansion was limited to firms producing newer styles of cars endowed with what had previously been regarded as luxury items.

I undertake a more detailed consideration in the next chapter of the precise markets in which the expanding sectors flourished during the interwar period. In the most general terms, such sectors were those producing consumer nondurable goods, services, and newer durable products such as appliances, automobiles with luxury amenities, and communications equipment. Durable goods industries typically suffer proportionately more than other industries during cyclical downswings. But the evidence from the interwar period suggests that a secular dynamic was at work as well – one that favored the emergence of industries producing for a more affluent population subsisting within a relatively sophisticated and developed infrastructure.

The financial collapse of 1929 interfered with a smooth transition in the focus of American manufacturing activity along the lines of the secular transformation described earlier. It thus precipitated a decade of poor macroeconomic performance. The crash created a massive disruption in the financial markets of the country, drastically devalued capital stocks, greatly depressed levels of disposable income, and, by virtue of the high unemployment and rapid deflation it generated, so biased the already unequal distribution of purchasing power as to virtually eliminate consumer and investor confidence. Idle plant and unemployed workers dampened entrepreneurial spirits and depressed the rate of net investment. At the same time, reduced investment lowered effective demand by lessening employment and thereby idled plant and employees. In the absence of bold government intervention to stimulate investment or direct government investment itself, the only road to recovery lay in an increase in private net investment expenditures.

Yet those firms generating enough revenues to make possible net investment and enjoying the kind of prospects to justify net investment were unfortunately not present in sufficient numbers to lead a general advance. For hard-hit firms, liquidation was undesirable in a period of severe depression and deflation. Moreover, the capital markets, because of massive bank failures and public suspicion, were in no position to float large equity issues and loans.[15] Firms were loath to incur more debt as the real costs of borrowing rose in the wake of deflation. All this merely intensified the need for comparatively prosperous enterprises to spearhead an upswing. It was only by means of their net revenues that investment activity could be funded.

Had there been no financial disruption in 1929, the secular transformation I have outlined here would have proceeded relatively smoothly. What might have happened if the crash had occurred at a different point in the long-term trend of development – specifically at a time when the newer industries were more fully established? The length of the disruption would have been significantly shortened. Profitable new enterprises would have been more resilient to cyclical setbacks. Their surplus funds would have been ample, and eventually they would have been able to finance their own recovery. Most important perhaps, business expectations would have been less depressed, and net investment commitments would have increased at an earlier date. This is all by way of saying that it was the interaction of cycle and trend that accounted for the length of the Great Depression, not the cycle or the trend alone.

Employment trends

The changing composition of consumer and investment demand, combined with the cyclical problems of the early thirties, generated a severe structural employment problem. The limited size of the dynamic sectors made the absorption of the unemployed exceedingly difficult. The net result was a continuation of the unpropitious demand conditions facing the economy as a whole. Any large increase in employment had to come from a general revival of all sectors.[16]

---

15 See Lewis Kimmel, *The Availability of Bank Credit: 1933–1938* (New York: National Industrial Conference Board, 1939); and B. S. Bernanke, "Nonmonetary Effects of the Financial Crisis in the Propagation of the Great Depression," *American Economic Review*, 73 (June, 1983), 257–76.

16 There is an interesting implication of this argument for contemporary macroeconomic theory. The discussion in the text suggests that during the thirties there was an increase in the so-called natural rate of unemployment. Of course,

A comparison of net investment data for the 1930s with the interwar ranking of industries with respect to their share of national employment and value of output demonstrates the uneven development of manufacturing that interfered with recovery.[17] The evidence in Table 1-1 shows that sectors where net investment recovered relatively quickly after the trough of 1932 had low shares of national employment and national value-product. Conversely, those industries that in the interwar period accounted for large shares of employment and output engaged in little if any expansion in the immediate wake of the crash. Notable examples of the former are food products, tobacco products, chemicals, and petroleum products – precisely those sectors most stimulated by the new patterns of consumer spending in the New Era. Of the latter, the best demonstrations are afforded by textile mill products, lumber products, primary metal industries, and transportation equipment.

Thus, a massive structural unemployment problem emerged during the thirties that in the absence of an exogenous shock like war would have taken some time to solve. But this problem, which began to emerge prior to 1929, was not derived from interferences with the price mechanism of labor markets. Rather, it was one of mobilizing the necessary capital, information, and confidence to retrain and reallocate the labor force in conformity with prevailing employment trends and opportunities. Indeed, there had been a steady decline since the early twenties in the percentage of national employment accounted for by the manufacturing and construction sectors. The same decline took place in agriculture and mining. In the service industries, such as transportation, trade, finance, selected services, and government operations, there was a rise (Table 1-2). Even if there had been no financial crash in 1929, these trends show that structural unemployment would have been a recurrent problem in the interwar period.

The capital-output relation

Superimposed on an already weak recovery mechanism was yet another secular development that made matters worse. Since 1919 the aggregate

insofar as the interwar period witnessed a decline in the proportionate share of the agricultural sector in national economic activity, the observed natural unemployment rate would necessarily be higher. See L. Spaventa, "Dualism in Economic Growth," *Banca Nazionale del Lavoro Quarterly Review*, 12 (December, 1959), 386–434.

17 I focus on net investment data because gross expenditures would include disbursements for amortization and replacement of existing capacity. A full economic recovery requires investment in new plant and equipment.

Table 1-1. *Data on industrial recovery in the 1930s*

Industry	Net investment in equipment as percentage of 1929 level			Share of national employment by rank			Share of national value-product by rank		
	1937	1938	1939	1931	1933	1935	1931	1933	1935
Chemicals and allied products	369.9	256.6	401	32	27	25	20	18	14
Stone, clay, and glass products	850.3	422.9	306.3	29[a]	30[a]	24[a]	46[a]	40[a]	41[a]
Petroleum and coal products	131.9	50.1	21.2	23	22	21	8	2	4
Tobacco products	130.2	85.6	159.6	19	54[b]	67[b]	10	11	10
Food and kindred products	178.2	61.2	115.7	18[c]	13[c]	14[c]	1[c]	1[c]	2[c]
Nonelectrical machinery	96.9	58.5	148.9	NA[d]	NA	NA	NA	NA	NA
Apparel and other textile products	32.6	Neg.[e]	114.4	15[f]	12[f]	18[f]	19[f]	20[f]	19[f]
Rubber and plastic products	22.2	14.8	74	30	28	32	27	27	22
Transportation equipment	34.7	8	53.2	12	18	8	2	4	1
Paper and allied products	27.4	8.6	29.5	20	19	17	14	13	12
Primary metal industries	38.6	Neg.	Neg.	4	2	1	5	3	3
Fabricated metal products	18.7	25.3	100.2	NA	NA	NA	NA	NA	NA
Printing and publishing	Neg.	Neg.	Neg.	16	15	13	4	5	7
Leather and leather products	19	Neg.	3.6	36	35	38	36	34	35
Lumber and wood products	Neg.	Neg.	Neg.	5	7	3	25	23	18
Textile mill products	Neg.	Neg.	Neg.	3	3	3	3	3	3

[a]Glass products only.
[b]Cigarettes only.
[c]Meat packing only.
[d]Data not available.
[e]Neg. indicates net disinvestment in relevant year.
[f]Men's clothing only.

Sources: U.S. Bureau of the Census, *Census of Manufactures*, relevant years; U.S. Bureau of Labor Statistics, *Capital Stock Estimates for Input-Output Industries: Methods and Data*, Bulletin 2034, 1979; U.S. Internal Revenue Service, *Statistics of Income*, relevant years; L. Chawner, "Capital Expenditures for Manufacturing Plant and Equipment – 1915 to 1940," *Survey of Current Business* (March, 1941); L. Chawner, "Capital Expenditures in Selected Manufacturing Industries," *Survey of Current Business* (May, 1941); L. Chawner, "Capital Expenditures in Selected Manufacturing Industries – Part II," *Survey of Current Business* (December, 1941). I am indebted to Charles Bowman of the U.S. Department of Labor and John Musgrave of the U.S. Department of Commerce for providing me with some unpublished data used in this table.

Table 1-2. *Percentage distribution of employment by major groups, 1919–39*

Year	Primary industries[a]	Secondary industries[b]	Service industries[c]
1919	28.5	29.4	42.1
1920	28.9	28.6	42.5
1921	30.2	25.1	44.7
1922	28.9	26.8	44.3
1923	27.6	28.2	44.2
1924	27.3	27.3	45.4
1925	26.8	27.7	45.5
1926	26.3	27.8	45.9
1927	25.5	27.7	46.8
1928	25.4	27.5	47.1
1929	25.1	28.1	46.8
1930	25.8	26.6	47.6
1931	27.1	24.5	48.4
1932	28.7	22.5	48.8
1933	30.1	22.7	47.2
1934	27.0	24.8	48.2
1935	26.6	25.5	47.9
1936	25.3	26.6	48.1
1937	24.0	27.6	48.4
1938	24.5	25.5	50.0
1939	23.6	26.8	49.6

[a]Agriculture and mining.
[b]Contract construction and manufacturing.
[c]Transportation, trade, finance, selected services, and government.

Sources: U.S. Department of Labor, Bureau of Labor Statistics, *Employment and Earnings* (June, 1968), vol. 7, no. 1, p. 11, as cited in John P. Henderson, *Changes in the Industrial Distribution of Employment: 1919–59*, University of Illinois, Bureau of Economic and Business Research, Bulletin 87, 1959, p. 10.

ratio of capital to output had been falling. The capital deepening of the late nineteenth and early twentieth centuries had given way by the end of World War I to an era of adjustment in production technique and product development. Capital-saving innovations became more common.[18] As a consequence, for any given increase in output, the response of investment spending was smaller because the capital requirements per unit of output had decreased. During the interwar period, there-

18 See Levine, "The Theory of the Growth of the Capitalist Economy," 58–67.

Table 1-3. *Ratio of total capital to output:*
manufacturing sector, 1900–53

Year	Ratio
1900	0.79
1909	0.97
1919	1.02
1929	0.88
1937	0.74
1948	0.61
1953	0.59

Source: Simon Kuznets, *Capital in the American Economy:*
Its Formation and Financing (Princeton, N.J.: Princeton
University Press, 1961), p. 209.

fore, emergent industries that tended to rebound quickly from the crash
of 1929 were not successful in stimulating net investment activity
economy-wide. This is but another demonstration of the fact that the
particular input requirements of these sectors were not those that could
be met by a large portion of the extant capital stock at the time.

John Kendrick reports a falling capital-output ratio for the manufacturing sector as a whole for the period 1899 to 1953. The fastest
decline during these years took place from 1919 to 1929. Simon
Kuznets has published similar findings, as Table 1-3 shows. Clearly, the
cyclical performance of the economy during the interwar period was
qualitatively different from that of earlier decades.[19] A rising aggregate

19 See John W. Kendrick, *Productivity Trends in the United States* (Princeton,
N.J.: Princeton University Press, 1961), 164–70. Findings similar to Kendrick's
are given in S. Kuznets, "Quantitative Aspects of the Economic Growth of
Nations, VI: Long Term Trends in Capital Formation Proportions," *Economic
Development and Cultural Change*, 9 (July, 1961), part 2, 34–5. Also see
Daniel Creamer, *Capital and Output Trends in Manufacturing Industries: 1880–
1948*, N.B.E.R. occasional paper 41 (New York: National Bureau of Economic
Research, 1954); Lance E. Davis et al., *American Economic Growth: An Economist's History of the United States* (New York: Harper & Row, 1972), 290–4;
and H. G. Vatter, "The Atrophy of Net Investment and Some Consequences for
the U.S. Mixed Economy," *Journal of Economic Issues*, 16 (March, 1982),
237–53. Further confirmation of this point may be found in J. E. La Tourette,
"Potential Output and the Capital-Output Ratio in the United States Private
Business Sector: 1909–1959," *Kyklos*, 18 (1965), 316–32. La Tourette also
notes in his "Sources of Variation in the Capital-Output Ratio in the United
States Private Business Sector: 1909–1959," *Kyklos*, 18 (1965), 647: "In view
of the tendency for American and English economists to emphasize market
factors as the cause for dynamic disequilibrium, it is interesting that our results

capital-output ratio in the late nineteenth century was linked with the emergence of heavy industry and infrastructural development. Investment at that time took the form of large capital commitments in, for example, railroad rights-of-way and construction. Subsequent investment had lower capital-output ratios insofar as it could utilize the fixed capital already in place. These long-term developments interfered with the workings of what economists call the accelerator mechanism. Hence the depression was prolonged despite the growth of the newer industries.

What made the interwar American economy so vulnerable to the business cycle was the fact that by 1929, dramatic changes were occurring in the composition of consumer demand, investment demand, technology, and employment requirements. These secular developments made previous investment patterns less capable of withstanding a cyclical downturn.[20] As national income rose during the twenties, new patterns of consumer demand emerged. These patterns created weaknesses in some markets and strong sales in others. Concomitantly, demands were created for new kinds of human and physical capital. And the technological developments of the period generated a lower capital-output ratio, leaving the economy with a less effective accelerator mechanism.

As the experience of the more successful industries of the interwar period shows, the creation of new products, techniques, and labor force skills was not, as the stagnation theorists have suggested, an impossible or wholly exogenous process. It was a lengthy one. The difficulty lay in the fact that the dynamic industries were predominantly dependent on

point to the nature of technological progress as a possible cause." Bert G. Hickman, in his *Investment Demand and U.S. Economic Growth* (Washington, D.C.: Brookings Institution, 1965), shows a downward trend in the aggregate capital-output ratio during the war years as well. Despite an upturn in the late forties, the ratio remained well below its predepression value throughout the postwar era. Also see M. Abramovitz and P. A. David, "Reinterpreting Economic Growth: Parables and Realities," *American Economic Review*, 63 (May, 1973), 428-39.

20 Indeed, in the wake of the Great Depression, cyclical movements in economic activity came to be regarded no longer as the result of inherent, periodic, self-rectifying fluctuations in certain economic variables, but rather as aberrations in the economy that could be removed by appropriate fiscal and monetary policies. It would be interesting to consider that such a change in the conception of business cycles was closely linked in time with a change in the kind of business cycle the economy experienced – namely, a cycle that was not self-correcting or short-lived. See M. N. Baily, "Stabilization Policy and Private Economic Behavior," *Brookings Papers on Economic Activity*, 1 (1978), 11-59.

consumer markets for their growth.[21] These markets grew slowly because of a relatively skewed distribution of income and a structural
unemployment problem and because of the effective demand failure
that took hold after 1929. It took the shock of the world war and the
impact of pent-up demand in the aftermath of war to overcome these
obstacles to renewed expansion.

A long-term perspective concerning the Great Depression poses several questions about the need for and desirability of state intervention in
the recovery process. The Keynesian solution of deficit spending and
public sector employment schemes certainly provides a short-run solution to dynamic instability. Priming the pump increases the sales of
both new and old industries. It expands consumer spending and may
even stimulate investment.[22] But can such fiscal intervention have long-
term effects? An answer to this question requires determining to what
extent the state can influence the secular process by which old and new
industries decline and expand. The difficulty may be that the state
apparatus can be "captured" by industrial and/or labor interest groups,
thereby forestalling or distorting the process of long-term development.
Clearly the analysis of the Great Depression as a secular phenomenon
poses an entirely new agenda for the study and formulation of policy
responses to economic instability – a subject pursued in the final two
chapters of this study.

After World War II, the process of secular adjustment continued. Industries such as food products, chemicals, and fabricated metals gained
larger shares of total manufacturing employment. But as Table 1-4
shows, these increasing shares were acquired from 1947 to 1972 –
obviously too late to spur recovery in the 1930s. The tobacco and
petroleum industries, no doubt because of their increasing capital intensity, played less and less of a role in national employment during
this period. Overall, however, the largest increases in shares of national
employment from 1929 to 1970 occurred in the service, finance, and
government sectors (Table 1-5). And from 1929 to 1972, the service,
government, and communications sectors secured the largest increase of
all sectors in their share of national income (Table 1-6). Along with the

21 A theoretical investigation of this issue may be found in D. P. Levine, "Determinants of Capitalist Expansion," *Economic Development and Cultural Change*,
   30 (January, 1982), 314–20.
22 Even so, as Alvin Hansen pointed out, New Deal relief policies were insufficient
   for the task of stimulating recovery while at the same time investment net of
   replacements was virtually zero. See his *Full Recovery or Stagnation?* 274–82.

Table 1-4. *Percentage share of total manufacturing employment, by sector, 1947–72*

Sector	1947[a]	1954[a]	1958	1963	1967	1972
Food	NA[b]	9.2	11.1	10.1	8.9	8.7
Tobacco	0.87	0.7	0.55	0.48	0.41	0.37
Textiles	9.6	7.7	5.9	5.3	5	5.3
Apparel	8.2	8.6	7.7	7.9	7.3	7.6
Lumber	NA	4.7	3.8	3.5	3	3.8
Furniture	2.3	2.3	2.3	2.3	2.3	2.6
Paper	3.3	3.5	3.6	3.6	3.5	3.5
Printing	3.7	4	5.6	5.6	5.6	5.9
Chemicals	3.9	4.1	4.5	4.5	4.6	4.6
Petroleum	1.4	1.3	1.2	0.95	0.77	0.77
Rubber[c]	1.8	1.6	2.3	2.6	2.8	3.4
Leather	2.9	2.6	2.3	2	1.8	1.5
Stone, clay, and glass	3.4	3.3	3.6	3.5	3.2	3.5
Primary metals	8.5	7.6	7.1	6.9	6.9	6.3
Fabricated metals	6.9	6.6	6.9	6.7	7.3	8.3
Nonelectrical machinery	10.5	9.5	8.8	9	10.1	10.1
Electrical machinery	5.3	5.8	7.4	9.3	10.1	9.2
Transportation equipment	8.2	10.7	10.1	9.9	9.9	9.5
Instruments	1.6	1.6	1.9	1.9	2.1	2.5

[a]For production workers only; all other years for total
employees.
[b]Data not available.
[c]Includes plastics products.
Source: *Census of Manufactures*, 1947, 1954, 1958, 1963,
1967, 1972.

manufacturing industries already noted, these sectors are the leaders in
contemporary American economic growth. The origins of their emergence can in most cases be traced to the interwar period. But the mass
of their activity during the 1930s was insufficient to stimulate recovery.
It took several more years before their share of national product and
employment was large enough to secure full employment without dramatic government intervention or exogenous stimuli such as wartime
production.

Table 1-5. *Percentage share of total national employment, 1929-70*

Year	Sector[a]							
	1	2	3	4	5	6	7	8
1929	34.1	NA[b]	NA	19.5	4.8	11	1.7	8.1
1939	33.6	15.4	18.2	21	4.8	11.5	3	10.1
1949	33	17.1	15.9	21.2	4.2	12	4.4	9
1959	31.3	17.6	13.7	20.9	4.9	13.4	4.2	11
1970	27.4	15.9	11.6	21.1	5.2	16.5	3.8	14

[a]Sectors: 1, total manufacturing; 2, durables; 3, nondurables; 4, wholesale and retail trade; 5, finance, insurance, real estate; 6, services; 7, federal government; 8, state and local government.
[b]Data not available.
Source: U.S. Council of Economic Advisers, *Economic Report of the President: 1972*, p. 226; computations by the author.

The notion of "development blocs" (associated with the work of Erik Dahmén) is analogous to the argument presented here. In the interwar American economy, the greatest potential for expansion lay with a set of industries (i.e., blocs) that were interdependent with respect to the final demand for their products (for example, processed food products and household appliances) and/or the inputs they required (for example, the petroleum and chemicals industries). The successful establishment of development blocs can be obstructed because of the absence of certain preconditions such as entrepreneurial skill and breadth of vision, the availability of large amounts of capital to underwrite whole blocs, and a sustained level of effective demand. To whatever extent such preconditions were present in the twenties, after 1929 the barriers to the full development of industry blocs were quite severe owing primarily to the dramatic disruption of the financial mechanisms of the American economy. Consequently, a financial crisis combined with a secular trend to create America's longest depression on record.[23]

The Great Depression in America thus appears to have been the result of two mechanisms, one cyclical, the other secular. The problem is to make explicit the significance of long-term trends in the industrial

23 See Dahmén, *Entrepreneurial Activity and the Development of Swedish Industry*, 73-5, 424, 427.

Table 1-6. *Percentage change in industry share of national income, 1929–72*

Industry division	Change (%)
Government and government enterprise	174
Communication	75
Services	26.7
Contract construction	25
Durable goods manufacturing	24.6
Total manufacturing	6.3
Electric, gas, and sanitary services	5.6
Nondurable goods manufacturing	−13.1
Wholesale and retail trade	−4.5
Finance, insurance, and real estate	−21.8
Transportation	−50
Agriculture, forestry, and fisheries	−67
Mining	−62.5
Rest of the world	−11.2

Source: U.S. Department of Commerce, *Survey of Current Business*, August, 1965, pp. 42–5; July, 1966, p. 15; July, 1970, p. 21; July, 1973, p. 22.

fluctuations of the 1930s. A collapse in the nation's financial markets in 1929 precipitated ten years of economic distress because full recovery was delayed. An analysis of long-term trends in American economic development shows the significance of this delay without reference to unexplained shifts in investor confidence, political events, or world market conditions. The Great Depression must be viewed as an event triggered by random historical and institutional circumstances, but prolonged by the timing of the process of long-term industrial development in the United States – in particular, by a transition in the structure of consumer and investment demand at the higher levels of income reached by the 1920s. The financial machinery of the American economy, caught in heavy deflation, was not equal to the task of pushing open the doors to the patterns of growth characteristic of the postwar era.

Statistical appendix to Chapter 1

Evidence on percentage distribution of real capital goods expenditures 1920–39

In the following table, the percentage distributions of capital expenditures from 1920 to 1939 are presented. Current dollar data were

Percentage distribution of investment spending, 1920–39

	1920	1921	1922	1923	1924	1925	1926	1927	1928	1929	1930	1931	1932	1933	1934	1935	1936	1937	1938	1939
Food	2.8	2.3	2.3	1.7	1.6	1.7	2.1	2.0	2.5	2.1	1.9	1.7	2.2	4.5	3.2	2.5	2.6	2.6	2.1	1.8
Textiles & apparel	2.4	1.9	1.9	1.8	1.2	1.2	1.1	1.3	1.2	1.3	0.9	0.9	1.0	1.7	1.7	1.2	1.1	1.3	0.9	1.1
Lumber	1.3	0.7	1.1	0.8	0.7	0.7	0.8	0.6	0.5	0.6	0.3	0.3	0.3	0.4	0.4	0.4	0.5	0.5	0.4	0.5
Stone, clay, glass	1.3	1.2	1.8	1.4	1.1	1.1	1.3	1.2	1.7	1.3	0.8	0.7	0.7	0.6	0.7	0.9	1.0	0.8	0.7	0.6
Iron & steel products	1.5	0.6	0.9	0.8	1.2	1.2	1.3	0.9	1.2	0.8	2.1	1.2	0.7	1.1	0.6	1.6	1.9	2.6	1.3	1.6
Automobiles	1.4	0.7	0.5	0.7	0.8	0.7	0.8	0.9	0.9	1.0	0.8	0.8	1.2	1.0	1.3	1.7	1.5	1.3	1.5	1.1
Airplanes	—	—	—	—	—	—	—	—	—	—	—	—	—	—	—	0.1	0.1	0.1	0.1	0.3
Petroleum	0.8	0.6	0.6	0.5	0.4	0.4	0.5	0.5	0.7	0.7	0.6	0.6	0.9	1.4	1.2	0.7	0.9	1.2	1.3	1.1
Chemicals	—	—	—	—	—	—	—	—	—	—	—	—	—	—	—	—	—	—	—	1.4
Machinery	—	—	—	—	—	—	—	—	—	—	—	—	—	—	—	—	—	—	—	0.4
Miscellaneous	—	—	—	—	—	—	—	—	—	—	—	—	—	—	—	—	—	—	—	0.7
Office machinery	2.8	3.0	3.0	3.3	3.7	3.3	3.3	3.5	3.5	3.7	3.7	3.8	4.1	4.5	4.2	4.1	3.5	3.7	3.8	3.7
Aircraft	0.1	0.1	0.1	0.1	0.1	0.1	0.1	0.1	0.3	0.3	0.4	0.5	0.5	0.6	0.5	0.5	0.6	0.7	0.8	1.2
Telephone	1.0	1.5	1.3	1.4	1.7	1.5	1.5	1.5	1.7	2.1	2.7	2.5	2.7	2.4	1.9	1.7	1.7	2.1	2.3	2.1
Electric light and power	3.5	2.9	3.6	5.0	5.6	4.7	4.0	4.3	4.0	4.2	4.2	5.3	4.4	2.5	2.1	2.5	2.9	3.8	3.9	3.0

gathered from J. Frederic Dewhurst and Associates, *America's Needs and Resources*, pp. 756–7. The data were deflated to 1967 constant dollars by use of the annual wholesale price indices (for all commodities) reported in *Historical Statistics of the United States*, series E23-29, vol. I, p. 199. The percentage shares of total real capital expenditures were then computed.

Appendix to Chapter 1

A schematic representation of the argument

A formal analysis of the transitional difficulties faced by the American economy in the interwar period is posed here. Those readers with more empirical concerns may proceed, without loss of continuity, directly to the next chapter.

At any given time, the macroeconomy is composed of (1) dynamic industries, (2) maturing industries, and (3) declining industries. The dynamic industries are composed of those firms just beginning their development and that therefore enjoy a large potential for market development and growth. Those firms that have established their markets compose the maturing industries. Declining industries contain firms whose rates of growth are constant or falling.

The performance of the whole economy at any given moment is the result of the behavior of the industries within it. With respect to shares of aggregate output, the relative importance of the dynamic, maturing, and declining industries will statistically determine the extent to which the total economy will be growing, stagnant, or shrinking.

Ignoring the economic activities of government and foreign trade, let the real level of gross national product be denoted as Z. If the real output of the dynamic, maturing, and declining industries is denoted respectively as x_1, x_2, and x_3, and $\dot{A}/A$ is taken to be the proportional growth rate of quantity A, then it is clear that

$$\frac{\dot{Z}}{Z} = f\left(\frac{\dot{x}_1}{x_1}, \frac{\dot{x}_2}{x_2}, \frac{\dot{x}_3}{x_3}\right)$$

The rate of growth in national output is some function of the proportional rates of growth of the dynamic, maturing, and declining industries. By definition, the following characteristics of the proportional growth rates are assumed:

$$\frac{\dot{x}_1}{x_1} > \frac{\dot{x}_2}{x_2} > 0$$

$$\frac{\dot{x}_3}{x_3} \lesseqgtr 0$$

But industrial rates of expansion do not determine $\dot{Z}/Z$ alone. An equally important influence will be that of the industrial shares of real G.N.P. If the dynamic industries, no matter how fast they are growing, account for a small proportion of the national product, the aggregate rate of growth will be relatively low. To the extent that the dynamic and maturing industries predominate in the aggregate, $\dot{Z}/Z$ will be relatively high.

Let α, β, and ϕ stand for the respective shares of real national output accounted for by the dynamic, maturing, and declining industries. If

$$\Omega = \alpha + \beta - \phi$$

then $\dot{Z}/Z$ may be reformulated as

$$\frac{\dot{Z}}{Z} = g(\Omega)$$

To the extent that the dynamic and maturing industries account for larger and larger shares of G.N.P., the aggregate rate of expansion is increased. However, so soon as Ω becomes zero or negative, the economy stagnates. Figure 1A-1 graphically depicts these conclusions.

Movements in the value of Ω are the outgrowth of those secular mechanisms that influence the growth, maturation, and decline of specific industries in the long run. The *rate of change* in the value of Ω will be determined primarily by short-run factors (and exogenous shocks) having to do with the functioning of capital markets and temporary variations in the level of effective demand.

It is now possible to analyze formally the interaction between secular and short-run factors in the determination of macroeconomic performance. Figure 1A-2 shows the archetypical movement in the value of Ω over time. The dynamic industries win ever larger shares of national output until they eventually mature and decline. Hence the concave shape of the Ω function. That function formally expresses the secular development factors that lie behind long-term growth. The rate of change in Ω expressed as $d\Omega/dt$ may be superimposed on this graph.

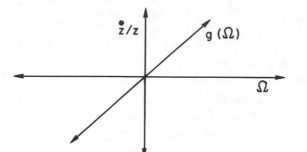

Figure 1A-1. The aggregate rate of expansion.

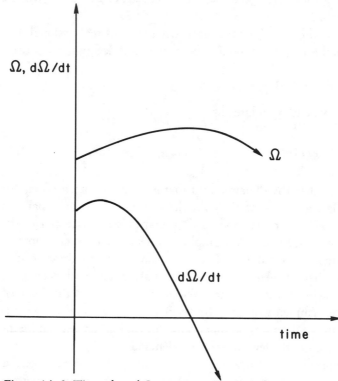

Figure 1A-2. Time plot of Ω.

At a given point in time the economy as a whole can be characterized by the level of Ω and its associated rate of change. In a long-run framework, the economy can be characterized (as in Figure 1A-3) by a succession of Ω functions (and their associated rates of change) that denote the secular rise and fall of industries – the so-called long waves in

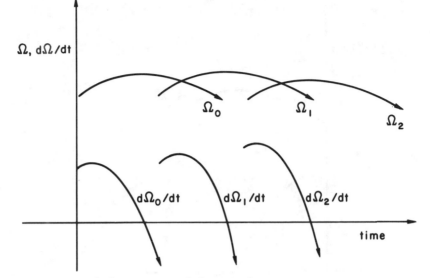

Figure 1A-3. The long-run growth framework.

economic life. Secular development factors determine the growth position of the economy along the time dimension measured on the abscissa of Figure 1A-3. Short-run events and shocks will shift the $d\Omega/dt$ function along the ordinate, thereby changing the rate of change of Ω at a given moment in time.

Alterations in the value of $d\Omega/dt$ are tied to concrete, often random, events that may aid or hinder changes in the industrial composition of the economy. Changes in the availability of capital and in the level of effective demand, in the short run, are two major examples of such concrete events. Exogenous shocks due to the impact of foreign transactions, wars, and/or natural events will also play a role.

This schema provides important insights with regard to the dramatic length of the Great Depression in the United States. By the interwar period, the American economy was about to embark on a new era of industrial expansion characterized by the emergence of a new set of industries. By the decade of the twenties, these dynamic industries were still relatively young, composing but a small share of national output and investment. Hence, Ω was fairly low, as shown in Figure 1A-4 as point B at time A. Associated with this specific position in the secular trend of development was a determinate rate of change in the value of Ω shown at point C. The aggregate economy was in a stage of transi-

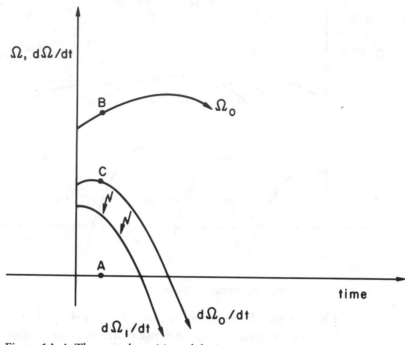

Figure 1A-4. The growth position of the interwar economy.

tion in which a new set of growing industries were gaining larger and larger shares of national output and investment activity over time. This was, in schematic form, the long-term growth position of the American economy by the interwar period.

But interacting with this secular trend were short-run factors of considerable importance, factors that, when their full force was unleashed on the economy, substantially interfered with the long-run transition in industrial composition. These contemporary mechanisms shifted the $d\Omega/dt$ function downward, as shown in Figure 1A-4. The pace with which the dynamic industries were emerging slowed greatly; the aggregate result was a reduction in the economy-wide rate of growth. Because of these obstacles to the secular transformation of industrial structure, the growth performance of the economy was seriously jeopardized.

By far the greatest hindrance to the adjustment of the industrial composition of national output was the financial collapse of 1929. The failure of the capital markets after 1929 virtually halted the transition in economic structure that had been in progress for over two decades. Poor sales and a short-run lack of investor confidence slowed the movement of capital out of old and into new industries. High rates of unemployment and of deflation, after the 1929 crash, biased effective demand so as to bolster more affluent consumption patterns and dramatically weaken middle- and low-income demand. As a result, only a small subset of national industries could maintain their expansion.

With the devastating crash of 1929, the long-term development process, which had begun to shift the focus of national economic activity in conformity with a new structure of demand, slowed to a virtual halt. In the absence of forces such as government spending that could move the economy out of this deadlock, the aggregate investment function broke down. Ten years of depression followed.[24]

24 See the extremely useful survey of the "industrial policy" and "industry aging" literature in R. D. Norton, "Industrial Policy and American Renewal," *Journal of Economic Literature*, 24 (March, 1986), 1–40.

2. The transformation of American industry in the interwar period

> There was abundant capital in the country and a mass of unemployed labor. But the markets on which they had of late depended ... were overworked and overstocked ... and capital and labor wanted "a new channel."
>
> – Benjamin Disraeli, Earl of Beaconsfield

In macroeconomic terms, the impact of the Great Depression on the United States is well known. From the stock market collapse in late 1929 until the middle of the thirties, the physical output of goods and services contracted by 33%. Almost 25% of the labor force was idled. Capital accumulation came to a standstill – one investigator has even reported a negative rate of net investment for the decade 1929–39.[1] This broad outline of the nation's worst economic misfortune has been the focus of almost all the theoretical and historical work done on the depression.

Despite the large amount of aggregate data that has been examined, there remain many unanswered questions concerning the course of the Great Depression in the United States. The differential effects of the slump on regions, on industries, and on classes of income recipients are but a few of the missing parts in the received scenario. Moreover, little attention has been paid to the experience of particular industries.[2]

Portions of this chapter have appeared in "The Response of American Manufacturing Industries to the Great Depression," in *History and Technology* 3 (1986), by Michael A. Bernstein, reprinted with permission of the publishers. Copyright Harwood Academic Publishers Gmbh and OPA Ltd.

1 See Temin, *Did Monetary Forces Cause the Great Depression?* x; and Broadus Mitchell, *Depression Decade: From New Era through New Deal, 1929–1941* (New York: Rinehart, 1955). The estimates of negative net investment are reported by Steindl, *Maturity and Stagnation in American Capitalism*, 160. Also see Lester V. Chandler, *America's Greatest Depression: 1929–41* (New York: Harper & Row, 1970).

2 See R. A. Gordon, "Business Cycles in the Interwar Period: The 'Quantitative-Historical' Approach," 47. The need for more detailed analyses of cyclical processes in general has been emphasized in debates concerning the efficacy of macroeconomic policy. See R. E. Lucas, "An Equilibrium Model of the Business

Indeed, the gaps in our empirical knowledge of the Great Depression have led to the inaccurate conclusion that the downturn left all sectors prostrate. In fact, the impact of the crash was not uniform; the variegated response to it of American manufacturing industries demonstrates this clearly.

That industries reacted in distinct ways to the instability of the thirties is hardly surprising. The hypersensitivity of durable goods sectors to the slump has been well documented, as have the particular difficulties of the construction industry.[3] But these phenomena have usually been examined only in terms of the decline in disposable income occasioned by the crash. Yet the persistent shortfall in effective demand due to the downturn must be accounted for not simply in terms of the stock market crash or the lack of consumer confidence for which it was responsible. Such a conception fails to explain the length of the depression. Explicit attention must be paid to the reasons why industries did not recover from the slump in a relatively short period of time. As for those sectors that did recover quickly, an examination must be made of the effort of firms to grow by means of technical change, product innovation, and improvements in methods of distribution.[4]

An aggregative analysis of the interwar period obscures the uneven long-term development of particular industries that played a large role in the span of the business cycle that began in 1929. The lack of recovery in the American economy of the 1930s did not result from every manufacturing sector being depressed. It was the combination of growth rates of the industries composing the national economy that

Cycle," *Journal of Political Economy*, 83 (December, 1975), 1113–44; T. J. Sargent, "A Classical Macroeconometric Model for the United States," *Journal of Political Economy*, 84 (April, 1976), 207–37; and R. E. Lucas, "Understanding Business Cycles," in K. Brunner and A. H. Meltzer, eds., *Stabilization of the Domestic and International Economy* (New York: North-Holland, 1977), 7–29.

3 See, for example, Solomon Fabricant, *The Output of Manufacturing Industries, 1899–1937* (New York: National Bureau of Economic Research, 1940); Lawrence R. Klein, *Economic Fluctuations in the United States, 1921–1941* (New York: Wiley, 1950); and Mitchell, *Depression Decade*.

4 That successful firms responded to the Great Depression in this manner for reasons other than distortions in market structure is documented in Bernstein, *Long-Term Economic Growth and the Problem of Recovery in American Manufacturing: A Study of the Great Depression in the United States, 1929–1939*, chs. 3–4.

yielded a net result of virtually no growth. Specifically, the mass of the dynamic effort emanating from those sectors least affected by the depression was insufficient to generate a broad-based advance from the trough of 1932. The aggregate impact of the 1929 slump led the overall mix of industrial growth rates to shift downward, thereby aggravating the destabilizing tendencies already present at the time.

A comprehensive study of the depression would also examine agriculture, mining, services, and the distributive trades. But by the 1930s the largest percentage of economic activity in the United States was located in manufacturing. From 1929 through 1938, adjusted annual estimates by the United States Department of Commerce show 9.3% of national income originating in agriculture; 2.1% in mining; 16.1% in the distributive trades; 11.1% in service industries; 13.1% in finance; 12.1% in activities of government; 10.6% in transportation and other public utilities; and 25.6% in manufacturing.[5] I focus on manufacturing in this study on the grounds that this is a justifiable narrowing of the evidence.

A further methodological comment is in order. Except through cartel behavior, industries as a whole do not implement recovery strategies or investment programs. Firms do. The title of this chapter notwithstanding, it is decisions made at the microeconomic level of the firm that determine the overall performance of industries and indeed of the macroeconomy. But it is industry-wide evidence that indicates to the historian the segments of the economy where dynamic firms are located. Moreover, the severe lack of firm-level data (especially concerning profit and earnings rates) for periods prior to 1945 in the United States necessitates the use of sectoral data.

The dearth of firm-specific evidence creates another difficulty for the economic historian – determining the relative success of various investment strategies and programs for economic recovery. But here industry-wide evidence once again becomes useful. Investment expenditure data by industry are available for the interwar period. They indicate which sectors expanded during the depression and which did not. Where industry net investment performance was good, it may be inferred that at least some of the firms within the industry executed successful recovery strategies.

5 See U.S. Department of Commerce, *Historical Statistics of the United States: Colonial Times to 1970* (Washington, D.C.: U.S. Government Printing Office, 1975), part 1, series F216–225, p. 238.

Table 2-1. *Net investment in equipment as a percentage of the 1929 level of net investment*

Industry	1937	1938	1939
Chemicals and allied products	369.9	256.6	401
Stone, clay, and glass products	850.3	422.9	306.3
Petroleum and coal products	131.9	50.1	21.2
Tobacco products	130.2	85.6	159.6
Food and kindred products	178.2	61.2	115.7
Nonelectrical machinery	96.9	58.5	148.9
Apparel & other textile products	32.6	Neg.[a]	114.4
Rubber and plastic products	22.2	14.8	74
Transportation equipment	34.7	8	53.2
Paper and allied products	27.4	8.6	29.5
Primary metal industries	38.6	Neg.	Neg.
Fabricated metal products	18.7	25.3	100.2
Printing and publishing	Neg.	Neg.	Neg.
Leather and leather products	19	Neg.	3.6
Lumber and wood products	Neg.	Neg.	Neg.
Textile mill products	Neg.	Neg.	Neg.

[a]Neg. indicates net disinvestment.
Source: Michael A. Bernstein, *Long-Term Economic Growth and the Problem of Recovery in American Manufacturing: A Study of the Great Depression in the United States, 1929–1939* (Ph.D. dissertation, Yale University, 1982), ch. 2, appendix C.

Table 2-1 presents data concerning net investment expenditures in major manufacturing industries. Insofar as economic recovery involves the achievement and ultimate transcendence of pre-crash peaks in output and employment, it is appropriate to note what percentage of their pre-crash peak-level net investment expenditures had attained by the late 1930s. I have chosen net investment in equipment as an appropriate proxy for total net investment. The data in Table 2-1 show that the most dynamic and successful industries of the depression decade were chemicals, building materials, petroleum, tobacco, food products, nonelectrical machinery, rubber and plastic products, transportation equipment, paper and allied products, and fabricated metal products.

This chapter documents the uneven impact of the 1929 downturn on the nation's manufacturing industries. Interindustry variations in output indicate which sectors were growing or stagnating during the interwar period. A more detailed consideration of these differences in output performance is pursued by identifying the actual markets in which industries displayed a resiliency to the crash, and those in which industries collapsed. In most cases the success or failure of an industry after 1929 was tied to development factors of a secular nature.

The chapter closes with a presentation of data concerning changes in the sectoral shares of national product before and after the depression. This demonstrates the evolutionary process at work during the interwar period that fundamentally transformed the composition of American industry. The sectors least affected by the instability of the 1930s were those that by the postwar era gained ever-increasing proportions of aggregate economic activity. By contrast, the relatively stagnant sectors of the depression era continued to shrink in size over time.

I   Interindustry variations in production

Evidence on sectoral production movements has been compiled from the monthly index of industrial production reported by the United States Federal Reserve Board and published in the *Survey of Current Business* of the United States Department of Commerce. These indices have all been seasonally adjusted.[6] The aggregate industrial index shows a steady rise from the first quarter of 1927 to roughly the second quarter of 1929. The effects of the stock market crash emerge at this point, with industrial activity showing a steady decline until the final months of 1932, when the production index hits its lowest value of the decade – a full eighty points below its pre-crash peak. A brief improvement following the inauguration of President Franklin Roosevelt is a prelude to a rather stagnant phase that lasts approximately three years. Thereafter, an anemic recovery takes place that is aborted in early 1937 – the so-called Roosevelt Recession. Manufacturing does not regain its pre-crash peak until nearly the end of 1940. Overall, the aggregate index moves from a pre-crash high of 127 to a low, just before Roosevelt took office for the first time, of 57. For manufacturing industries as a whole, the duration of the depression of the 1930s is some ten years.

Five of the time series for production in specific sectors (iron and steel; cement, brick, and glass; automobiles; rubber products; and tex-

6 Time plot diagrams of these indices are appended to this chapter. Also included in the appendix are the percentages of pre-crash output achieved in each quarter for each industry, and estimates of each industry's growth rate in output for the years 1933 to 1940.

tiles) show trends similar to that for the aggregate series. Three achieve their pre-crash output maximum in the second quarter of 1929: iron and steel at an index value of 155, textiles at 121, and automobiles at 166.[7] The rubber industry peaks a bit earlier, in 1928:3, at a level of 169; while cement, brick, and glass producers reach their zenith at 143 in 1929:3. All five of these industries reach a trough in 1932: textiles in the second quarter of that year; iron and steel; cement, brick, and glass; and rubber in the third; and automobiles in the fourth. And all experience a falling-off in their indices roughly similar to the aggregate movement, ranging from 60 points for textiles to 150 points for automobiles. In terms of the duration of depressed conditions, only iron and steel closely resembles the total index. Textiles recover pre-crash output levels as early as 1933, but fall off again until late in 1936, and do not reach full, sustained recovery until 1939. The automobile and rubber industries never recover in the time period under consideration; they had to await America's full mobilization for war. Interestingly enough, the building materials sector (cement, brick, and glass) recovers strongly in 1936, but is hit by a further downturn until 1939:4.

One industry exhibits somewhat damped behavior relative to the aggregate cycle. Food products peak early, in February of 1928, and reach bottom late – in 1935:2. But the downturn is relatively mild, a drop of only 35 points. Moreover, the industry never falls below 30% of its pre-crash high. Although full recovery does not occur until 1940, there is some justification for viewing this sector as "depression-proof."

Of the six remaining sectors, three show somewhat idiosyncratic behavior, and three exhibit virtual stagnation. The leather industry is fairly robust, starting from a peak of 118 in 1927:3 and experiencing a barely perceptible trough in the last quarter of 1931. Virtually total recovery ensues in 1935 and is slowed very little by the downturn in 1937. The duration of the depression in this sector is thus only 5½ years. Even more surprising is the behavior of the petroleum and tobacco industries. But for a slight hesitancy after the stock market's debacle, neither petroleum nor tobacco suffers a depression at all. Petroleum output almost exceeds the 1929:4 peak in early 1936 and, without significant pause, grows until the decade's end. In the tobacco industry the recovery begins in 1934, after which there is impressive output growth.

7 Hereafter, years and quarters are denoted in abbreviated fashion; e.g., the second quarter of 1929 is denoted 1929:2.

Stagnation characterizes the lumber, nonferrous metal, and paper and printing firms. Paper and printing seems the most fortunate of this group. Even so, after a boom in September of 1929, output drops continuously, with no recovery during the remaining years of the decade. Lumber demonstrates a similarly poor performance; output disappears almost altogether in 1937. This industry's misfortune begins as early as 1927:1. Finally, nonferrous metals output appears to be stagnant, although this assessment is tenuous. The incompleteness of the data makes even qualitative conclusions difficult, but it seems that after the late summer of 1929 nonferrous metal output sinks unremittingly.

II   The changing strength of markets

Interindustry variations in output performance offer an overview of the varied impact of the 1929 downturn on American manufacturing. A closer examination of the source of these variations requires explicit attention to the changing strength of particular markets during the interwar period. Such an investigation helps to show the actual shifts in patterns of consumer expenditure and sectoral investment. These alterations in the composition of economic activity had profound implications for the direction and speed of economic recovery in the wake of the crash.

Iron and steel

In the case of iron and steel firms, those least affected by the Great Depression produced for newer markets in lighter steels and in tin plate. The shift in markets experienced by iron and steel producers in the interwar period may be seen in Table 2-2. The downward trend in railway and construction demand was due to the secular decline in population growth and the slower rate of territorial expansion. Whatever strength in markets existed was found in such sectors as food containers and miscellaneous manufacturing. Indeed, once the depression occurred, steel plate and rails fell in importance, as a percentage of total industry shipments, while the rank of shipments of black plate (for tinning) rose from seventh to third, and the rank of strip steel rose from sixth to fourth. From 1925 to 1934, as plate and rail manufacturing capacity fell, sheet mill capacity rose by 44.6%.[8] Thus, profitable

8 See Carroll R. Daugherty et al., *The Economics of the Iron and Steel Industry* (New York: McGraw-Hill, 1937), vol. I, 53–4, 320, 364–5, 447; and C. H.

Table 2-2. *Percentage of total steel output consumed by major industries, 1922–39*

Industry	1922	1926	1929	1939
Railways	22	23.5	17	9.3
Construction	15	19.5	16.5	13.1
Automobiles	10	14.5	18	18.1
Oil, gas, mining	10	9.5	10.5	5.5
Export trade	7	5	5.5	6.5
Food containers	4	4	5	9.4
Machinery	NA[a]	4	3	3.8
Agriculture	4	4	5.5	1.9
Miscellaneous	28	16	19	32.4[b]

[a]Data not available.
[b]Includes pressing and stamping, and jobbers.
Sources: Homer B. Vanderblue and William L. Crum, *The Iron Industry in Prosperity and Depression*, 146; E. D. McCallum, *The Iron and Steel Industry in the United States*, 186; *Iron Age*, 117 (January 7, 1926), 7; Standard and Poor's, *Industry Surveys* (June 27, 1947), section 2, pp. s3-s6.

avenues of steel production shifted from heavy structural markets to fabricators' markets, consumer and producer hardware, and new alloys.

The investment behavior of firms serving these markets (see Table 2-1, Fabricated metal products) demonstrates their relative well-being in a time of severe economic distress. For example, rolling mills continued investment during the 1930s aimed at standardizing shapes and improving the ductility of the product. The American Steel and Wire Company spent $4.7 million in 1935 on new rod mills and wire machines; National Steel, the only firm in the industry not to run a deficit in 1932, maintained an aggressive investment policy with respect to its continuous hot-strip rolling operations and was one of the few firms to maintain a flexible pricing policy throughout the depression decade. Inland Steel Company, having served heavy-product markets throughout the 1920s, altered the focus of its investment in the 1930s in order to shift "the emphasis in production from heavy steel (rails,

Hession, "The Metal Container Industry," in W. Adams, ed., *The Structure of American Industry: Some Case Studies* (New York: Macmillan, 1961), 430–67. Nonintegrated steel producers, according to Daugherty and his associates, tended to improve their economic position in the 1930s owing to the fact that the markets in which they excelled (finished, rolled products) were far better off than those in which the large integrated producers were dominant (rails and structural shapes).

plates, structurals) for the capital goods industries to lighter steel (sheets, strip, tin plate) for the consumer industries." It is not surprising, therefore, that of the twelve largest steel companies, Inland and National secured the highest operating profits (13.1% and 9.2%, respectively, of gross fixed assets) for the period 1936–40.[9]

Tin plate was one of the most successful markets for steel producers during the 1930s. U.S. Steel earned $10 million annually in tin plate. Those firms producing for the canning industry benefited from the fact that the demand for canned food was relatively stable with respect to changes in income – making the crash in 1929 less problematic. In the latter part of the decade, the canning of beer and motor oil (for the first time) provided a further stimulus. The drop in canned food production after 1929 was only 13% at the trough of the depression. A substantial recovery in 1933 was due to both the trend in the demand for canned food products and the development of containers for products not previously packed in cans. Zinc coatings for cans made possible the sanitizing of foods that previously could not be so packaged – a major marketing success being the canned fruit cocktail of the early 1930s.[10]

A large demand emerged as well for appliances, the truly new products of the interwar period. In 1930, over 791,000 refrigerators were sold. Seven years later, annual sales rose to 2.3 million. The rise in appliance sales was linked not only with the technical development of the appliances and, thereby, with the establishment of consumer confidence in them but also with factors contributing to their use: the spread of electrification; the emergence of installment buying schemes (80% of all refrigerator sales in the 1930s were financed on credit); the articulation of retail and repair networks; and changes in the pattern and extent of domestic labor, given the secular and cyclical rise in the

9 From William T. Hogan, *Economic History of the Iron and Steel Industry in the United States* (Lexington, Mass.: D. C. Heath, 1971), vol. 3, parts IV–V, 1148, 1201, 1244, 1246, 1267; and Gertrude G. Schroeder, *The Growth of Major Steel Companies, 1900–1950* (Baltimore: Johns Hopkins University Press, 1953), 175.

10 From James W. McKie, *Tin Cans and Tin Plate: A Study of Competition in Two Related Markets* (Cambridge, Mass.: Harvard University Press, 1959), 46, 114–16; and Hogan, *Economic History of the Iron and Steel Industry in the United States*, vol. 3, parts IV–V, 1058–9, 1061–2. United States Steel built the first electrolytic tinning mill in 1937 after several years of research on the proper coatings to avoid the spoilage of canned goods. American Can pioneered the development of the beer can and the key-opening starch and oil container during the Great Depression. By 1955, this firm had acquired 845 patents in the field. In this regard, see *Tin Cans and Tin Plate*, 37, 251, 257, 260.

rate of labor force participation by women. The consumption of steel in the production of refrigerators had risen from 1,000 tons to 88,000 tons in the course of the twenties. Similarly dramatic increases were made in other appliance lines. As one historian of the iron and steel industry has written: "[During the thirties], purchases of durable goods were postponed with one notable exception, electrical appliances."[11]

With the onset of the crash, several major markets in iron and steel contracted. Automobile output fell by almost 4 million vehicles in the first three years of the downturn. Oil pipeline mileage built in the 1930s was 60% less than the 1920s total. Construction came to a halt. It was in the markets for light, flat rolled steels (sheets, strip, and tin plate) where earnings continued to grow. These steels were used in the newer appliance and canning markets; their percentage of total industry shipments rose from 25.8% to 40% later in the decade. By 1938 the railroads consumed only 6.1% of the nation's hot-rolled steel, while abandoning 11,000 miles of track by 1939. The automobile producers were similarly affected, their consumption of steel falling by close to 4 million net tons from 1930 to 1932.[12] It would take the advent of World War II to reverse this decline in the heavy-products division of the industry.

There were still other avenues of expansion available to steel producers in the depression decade. Technical developments in light alloy steels for electrified railways led in the late thirties to the electrification of the New York–Washington and New York–Harrisburg roads. Automakers, seeking to improve their sales, sought more streamlined, all-steel bodies that required alloys, such as "aluminum-killed" steel, which could withstand the stamping operations for the "turret-top" body. And hypoid transmission gears, which were more durable and dependable than earlier versions, required alloy steel. In addition, the intervention of the Public Works Administration (P.W.A.) gave some strength to the construction sector and encouraged the use of light-gauge steel and cellular flooring (which allowed space for plumbing and electrical fixtures) to reduce the deadweight loss in tall structures. P.W.A. projects included the Boulder Dam, the Overland Highway in Florida, the Williamsburg Housing Project in New York City, Rockefeller Center, and Radio City Music Hall. In addition, federal action brought about

11 See Hogan, *Economic History of the Iron and Steel Industry in the United States*, vol. 3, parts IV–V, 1069, 1081, 1119.
12 From Hogan, *Economic History of the Iron and Steel Industry in the United States*, vol. 3, parts IV–V, 1119–20, 1297–9, 1306–67.

Table 2-3. *Age composition of car stock*

Number in 1929 (in thousands)	Age of car (years)	Number in 1931 (in thousands)
1,394	>8	2,011
916	7–8	1,833
1,979	6–7	1,225
1,956	5–6	2,302
2,498	4–5	2,198
2,903	3–4	2,763
2,528	2–3	3,529
3,145	1–2	2,566
3,866	<1	1,900

Source: John W. Scoville, *Behavior of the Automobile Industry*, 3.

the construction of the Golden Gate and Oakland Bay bridges in California, along with the Triborough and Bronx-Whitestone bridges in New York. The Pulaski Skyway, Lincoln Tunnel, Belt Parkway, East River Drive, and La Guardia Field were also New Deal projects. During the depression, the "showing made by the construction industry was poor, but without the P.W.A. it probably would have been pathetic." Coupled with high rates of appliance demand, the demand for steel for electrical machinery production was also enhanced by the activities of the Rural Electrification Administration and the Tennessee Valley Authority.[13]

Automobiles

The automobile industry had two outstanding problems in the interwar period: the slowing in the absolute rate of growth of its market, due to a decrease in the growth rate of the population and a general decline in the income held by most of the nonfarm population, and the difficulty of stimulating demand for its product during a depression. In the first three years of the Great Depression the number of cars in use declined only 10%, but with the relatively large number of new vehicles on the road because of the boom of the 1920s, the amount of unused mileage per car (i.e., service life) rose 37%. Scrap rates of used cars consequently fell. Table 2-3 shows the shift in the age composition of the stock of

13 See Hogan, *Economic History of the Iron and Steel Industry in the United States*, vol. 3, parts IV–V, 1301, 1307, 1311, 1313, 1323–40.

cars owned in 1929 and 1931. An idea of the magnitude of the problem may be gained from data on replacement sales. In 1913, three out of every four cars sold in the United States were net additions to the national total; by 1924 the ratio fell to one in every three; and by 1927 replacement sales accounted for three-fourths of total production. The inevitable result occurred in 1931, when 755,000 fewer new cars were made than the total number scrapped, replaced, or stored by owners. Some firms were so concerned about the used car problem that they attempted to ship used vehicles to foreign markets (where there was no competition) and undertook payment schemes to reward dealers for each used car scrapped. During the 1930s the industry "took greater punishment than most others because a new car was not an essential in a home where the breadwinner was out of work." [14]

It is difficult to distinguish between secular and short-run mechanisms contributing to the poor auto sales performance of the 1930s. The immediate cause, namely the depressed purchasing power of the population, is obvious enough. But superimposed on this were long-term developments in automobile and tire manufacture and in road building that made cars last longer. Operating costs were also falling because of improvements in fuels, lubricants, and repair techniques. All these developments lengthened the service life of cars and increased the impact of a fall in national income on the sales of new vehicles. The "increased durability of automobiles [rendered] the industry more subject to large cyclical swings and [increased] its resemblance as regards economic position to residential building." [15]

Many automobile producers responded to the depression in classic fashion, by cutting prices. This created intense problems for independent companies producing luxury cars, such as Auburn, Duesenberg,

14 From John W. Scoville, *Behavior of the Automobile Industry in Depression* (n.p.: n.p., 1935), 19–27; Arthur Pound, *The Turning Wheel: The Story of General Motors through Twenty-Five Years, 1908–1933* (Garden City, N.Y.: Doubleday, Doran, 1934), 373–4; Philip H. Smith, *Wheels Within Wheels: A Short History of American Motor Car Manufacturing* (New York: Funk & Wagnalls, 1968), 96, 115; Harold A. Baker, *Marketing and Consumption Trends in the Automobile Industry, 1929–1933* (Chicago: n.p. 1938), 196–7; and General Motors Corporation, *The Dynamics of Automobile Demand* (New York: General Motors Corporation, 1939), 8.

15 See John W. Scoville, *The Automotive Industry*, 13–14; and General Motors Corporation, *The Dynamics of Automobile Demand* (New York: General Motors Corporation, 1939), 69–70, 88. From just over $1 billion in 1926, the national expenditure for car parts, tires, and the like fell almost 41% to $592 million in 1933. This decline was not entirely cyclical.

and Packard. Yet the price-cutting strategy was not overly successful. The Maxwell Company (later to become Chrysler) had already experienced such a problem when in 1923 it cut prices on all models by $100 and experienced no increase in sales. As a result, by 1932 many firms in the industry hesitated to make substantial price cuts when their impact on revenues was uncertain and, with lower volume obtaining, their effect could be catastrophic. Car manufacturers found that sales could be stimulated more by changes in the operating characteristics of their product than by lowering retail prices – prices that represented only one-third of the cost of using a car throughout its life.[16]

Many car manufacturers turned to style changes and technical innovation to increase sales volume. There were systematic attempts to provide "more car for less money." Vehicle weights increased, as did wheelbases and horsepower ratings. Many of the changes provided auxiliary instrumentation or minor additions. No real effort was made to develop a simple, cheap "depression car." Indeed, one such experiment was a market failure. The number of engine models and body types per make did not change. "The fact remains that instead of tending toward offering 'raw' transportation [during the 1930s], the cheaper cars of the period presented many features hitherto associated exclusively with the more expensive makes." As part of this nonprice response to poor sales performance, most automakers continued annual model design changes throughout the 1930s.[17] Special trade-in allowances on used cars and installment buying plans were also introduced.

In the absence of a constant or rising rate of durable goods purchases in the 1930s, automobile firms suffered relatively more than nondurable goods manufacturers.[18] The lessons of the depression were well learned.

16 See Baker, *Marketing and Consumption Trends in the Automobile Industry*, 200; E. D. Kennedy, *The Automobile Industry: The Coming of Age of Capitalism's Favorite Child* (New York: Reynal & Hitchcock, 1941), 229; John W. Scoville, *Reasons for the Fluctuations in Automobile Production* (Ohio State University Publications, 1938), 54; General Motors Corporation, *The Dynamics of Automobile Demand*, 31, 89, 94; and Scoville, *Behavior of the Automobile Industry in Depression*, 16.

17 See Scoville, *Behavior of the Automobile Industry*, 9; Baker, *Marketing and Consumption Trends in the Automobile Industry*, 195–6, 198; and H. B. Vanderblue, "Pricing Policies in the Automobile Industry," *Harvard Business Review*, 17 (Summer, 1939), 392. Also see Robert Paul Thomas, *An Analysis of the Pattern of Growth of the Automobile Industry: 1895–1929* (Ph.D. dissertation, Northwestern University, 1965).

18 See Kennedy, *The Automobile Industry*, 321–2; and General Motors Corporation, *The Dynamics of Automobile Demand*, 95.

After the artificial stimulus of wartime production had played out, the industry moved into a new era in the 1950s and 1960s of style development and technical change. Moreover, until the fuel embargo of the seventies, design and technical developments focused on appearance, advertising convenience, and luxury rather than on durability or efficiency.

Food products

Several factors were responsible for the dynamic behavior of food producers during the thirties. Low consumer income generated by the downturn appears to have encouraged the purchase of relatively cheap and nutritious processed foods. Government expenditures for unemployment relief may have further enhanced the demand for such foods. The depression-inspired increase in the number of homemakers holding jobs also qualitatively altered the demand for food products. And there were long-term trends, involving the increase in the spread of household appliances and automotive transportation, that increased the derived demand for and access to processed food products.[19]

As incomes fell after 1929, households appear to have purchased increasing quantities of processed (most notably canned) foods owing to their low price and high nutritional value. Direct relief employment may have played a role in this regard, because 90 percent of the persons employed in relief projects received security wages below the average manufacturing wage in the private sector.[20] Government expenditures

19 As noted in U.S. Department of Agriculture, *Technology in Food Marketing* (Washington, D.C.: U.S. Government Printing Office, 1952), 9. Also see "Statement by Surgeon General Thomas Parran, Public Health Service, before the Special Senate Committee to Investigate Unemployment and Relief" (March 16, 1938), processed. Public recognition of the nutritional value of canned foods was enhanced by the 1930 McNary-Mapes Amendment to the Food and Drug Act of 1906, which set standards for food labeling and the listing of ingredients and additives. The thirties saw the emergence of the synthetic vitamin and preservatives industry, which allowed for the maintenance of the quality of canned foods. A reliable test for milk pasteurization was introduced in 1933, and the molecular distillation of vitamins was first achieved in 1935. In general, there were important links between agricultural and nutrition science, and food storage and preservation technology, in the interwar period. See U.S. Department of Agriculture, *Technology in Food Marketing*, 31, 43, 46, 56.

20 See U.S. Department of Commerce, *Historical Statistics of the United States* (Washington, D.C.: U.S. Government Printing Office, 1975), part 1, series D85–101, p. 135; and series D794–810, pp. 169–70; and A. E. Burns and

for unemployment relief may have therefore further biased household demand toward the purchase of cheaper, standardized food products.

Short-run developments fit well with secular changes in technology (in both the plant and the home) and the rising labor force participation rate of women. It was only with improved methods of home storage and preparation that cheaper food products could be successfully marketed. In addition, the demand for appliances was directly linked with the alteration in the sexual division of labor. The increasing entrance of women into the labor force dated from the end of World War I. It was not limited to young women. While the participation rate of women twenty to twenty-four years old rose from 37.5% in 1920 to 45.6% in 1940, that of women of prime marriage age (twenty-five to forty-four years) rose even faster, from 21.7% to 30.5%. The hardship of the depression obviously encouraged greater labor force participation by women from households where the primary income earner was idle or on short time. Full-time domestic labor by women was virtually impossible in a period of massive unemployment. Consequently, demand increased for cheaper foods that could be stored and prepared more easily.[21] Food producers responded to the long-term and cyclical opportunities that the 1930s provided. These opportunities were realized by technical change, product innovation, and the development of new methods of distribution.

Important developments in the techniques of food processing dated from the end of World War I. Most involved the preparation of canned and frozen foods. By the thirties, these innovations had reached the operational stage and attenuated the impact of the 1929 downturn. Although canning output fell off from 1929 to 1931, there was a swift recovery by 1935. In 1931, output stood at 160 million cans of foodstuffs; by the end of the decade, this figure had more than doubled. At

P. Kerr, "Recent Changes in Work-Relief Wage Policy," *American Economic Review*, 31 (March, 1941), 62. Also see Donald S. Howard, *The W.P.A. and Federal Relief Policy* (New York: Russell Sage Foundation, 1943), 165–7, 532; and U.S. National Resources Planning Board, *Security, Work, and Relief Policies* (Washington, D.C.: U.S. Government Printing Office, 1942), 122, 176, 236, 341. The latter shows that while 14.9% of Works Progress Administration (W.P.A.) funds were spent on professional and service projects from 1936 to 1940, 70% of the funds went into construction projects that employed predominantly unskilled and semiskilled workers. Holding security wages below the private sector rate was a policy designed to discourage resort to relief employment.

21 See U.S. Department of Commerce, *Historical Statistics of the United States*, part 1, series D26–62, pp. 131–3.

the other end of the pipeline, retailers saw the merit of canned foods in terms of their ease of storage, reliability of supply, opportunities for advertising, and potential for customer self-service. As can shipments increased and won an ever-increasing share in the revenue of shippers, there were competitive reductions in transportation costs that further improved the canners' market. The reduction in domestic working time, which increased as the depression worsened, was compensated for by a greater reliance on canned items. This was paralleled by investment in nutrition and agricultural research (especially hybridization) and in machinery for the washing, peeling, trimming, grinding, and cutting of raw produce.[22]

Developments in frozen food processing were not as impressive as those in canning. Nevertheless, they did play a role in stimulating investment in the industry during the depression decade. Clarence Birdseye sold his patents and trademarks to the General Food Corporation in 1929 after many years of research. By 1930 the company marketed a full line of frozen poultry, meat, fish, and sixteen varieties of fruits and vegetables. Even so, the frozen foods market was initially limited by the lack of refrigeration in homes and stores, which in turn was due to technical bottlenecks and high costs.[23] Immaturity in storage technology also brought into question the quality and reliability of the product. This was especially the case with meats. The low rate of consumer acceptance also had roots in the competition of retail butchers, who provided personalized attention to customers. But there was substantial progress in expanding the frozen foods market during the thirties. In 1933, for example, only 516 stores in the country had refrigeration capacity. That number grew to approximately 15,000 by the end of the decade. As early as 1934, easily accessible freezers for use in stores were commercially developed.[24]

22 See E. C. Hampe and M. Wittenberg, *The Lifeline of America: Development of the Food Industry* (New York: McGraw-Hill, 1964), 118, 130–1.

23 This is not to say that innovation in refrigeration equipment was lacking. In 1930, tunnel air-blast freezers were developed in Canada, as were freezers using movable refrigerated plates. The fog freezer was developed in 1933, the immersion freezer in 1939. Thus, "despite the depression, the rise of the frozen-food industry began in the 1930's." See U.S. Department of Agriculture, *Technology in Food Marketing*, 11–13.

24 The full acceptance of frozen meat packing also had to await the development of effective wrapping materials – the most important (with respect to its technical superiority and inherent display characteristics) being cellophane by the DuPont Corporation. See Hampe and Wittenberg, *The Lifeline of America*,

Throughout the 1930s, a large amount of product innovation in the food industry also took place. New items were widely distributed, including fresh-pack pickles, prepackaged ice cream, ready-to-eat breakfast cereals, and margarine. From 1929 to 1939, the food industry introduced thirty-eight new primary products. For the same ten-year period, the annual rate of product addition was higher than the rate from 1939 to 1950. In addition, the food industry had one of the lowest rates of non-primary-product addition from 1929 to 1954.[25] Innovation in both processes and product lines was a powerful stimulus to this industry's performance throughout the first half of the twentieth century.

Associated with the dynamic impact of process and product innovation in food manufacture was the articulation of more efficient and sophisticated mechanisms of distribution. Improvements in packaging materials, cans, and glassware, called forth by the dynamism of firms in the food industry, allowed for the wider and more appealing distribution of the industry's products. Concentrated food retailing in the form of supermarkets increased enormously with the pressures of reduced demand in the thirties. The scale economies of supermarket retailing allowed for effective competition with the small grocery store; they were due, in part, to the greater reliability and variety of supplies that the large stores and chains developed.[26] From 1935, when there were 300 supermarkets in the nation, to 1939, when there were 4,982, the average annual increase in supermarket retailing was almost 1,200 stores. Linked with this marketing development was the increased use of advertising in various media. By 1932, the food industry ranked second among all manufacturing sectors in annual expenditures on national magazine advertisements.[27]

154–5, and ch. 7. Also see U.S. Department of Agriculture, *Technology in Food Marketing*, 20.

25 From Michael Gort, *Diversification and Integration in American Industry* (Princeton, N.J.: Princeton University Press, 1962), 42–4, 46. Gort's investigation included a sample of the top Fortune 200 companies in the food and kindred products group. A "primary" product is defined as part of the output of the dominant activity of the industry or firm in question.

26 See Alfred D. Chandler, Jr., *The Visible Hand: The Managerial Revolution in American Business* (Cambridge, Mass.: Harvard University Press, 1977), 233–9.

27 As reported in *The National Advertising Records* (New York: Denney, 1929–34). Also see Hampe and Wittenberg, *The Lifeline of America*, 273, 316, 322–4. As the chain stores quickly acquired 37% of the national market in food products by 1933, the demand by smaller retailers for antitrust action found adherents in Congress. This, along with the activist ideology of the New Deal

Petroleum and chemicals

The petroleum industry's relative success in the 1930s was largely due to long-run developments in related markets that stimulated the demand for petroleum products and spurred technical progress and product innovation. In addition, expansion in their markets encouraged aggressive marketing by oil companies, resulting in better distribution and sometimes lower prices.

The growth of automotive transportation in the thirties continued a trend dating back to the end of World War I. Coupled with this expansion was steady development in the surfaced road system that served to enhance the demand for cars. In the ten years prior to the depression, highway mileage had already doubled.[28] In the thirties, the increase was slightly more than double. In the same period, exemplifying the increasing reliance of the population on automotive transportation, the average annual consumption of gasoline per car rose from 525 to 648 gallons. One in every 5.2 people used a car in 1929; that ratio rose to one in every 4.5 by 1941.[29]

Throughout the 1920s the automobile industry had improved its product by increasing engine compression ratios and by moving up to six-cylinder design. These developments, carrying over into the depression decade, expanded the demand for gasoline both extensively and with respect to quality. Larger engines required more fuel; enhanced compression ratios required fuel with better octane ratings.[30] Refineries both expanded output during the thirties and continually revamped their cracking technologies to improve the quality of gasoline. Linked with this derived demand from automobile users was an increase in the need for lubricants that further improved refinery revenues.[31]

era, culminated in the well-intentioned but ill-conceived Robinson-Patman Act of 1936.

28 The highway construction provided a further avenue for the petroleum industry to grow, because a major by-product of crude oil refining is asphalt.

29 See H. F. Williamson et al., *The American Petroleum Industry: The Age of Energy, 1899–1959* (Evanston, Ill.: Northwestern University Press, 1963), 446, 604–5, 651–5, 694. Yet another factor in the improved market conditions facing the industry was the demand from farms. The number of tractors in use increased by about 750,000 in the 1930s.

30 The development of larger and more powerful automobile engines was linked with improvements in roads that in turn were dependent on the production of improved surfacing materials.

31 See Williamson et al., *The American Petroleum Industry*, 457, 605, 667–8. With respect to lubricants, there was a countervailing influence, that is, the

The markets in home heating, aviation, and railroading also supported the petroleum industry during the depression. The advent of the oil burner in the twenties, both in homes and in commercial establishments, generated an increased demand for refinery output. From 1929 to 1941 this trend continued as the introduction of oil heat steadily increased. The new technology was highly specialized, prohibiting shifts into cheaper fuels, such as coal or kerosene, when the price of fuel oil rose. Such inflexible demand was another factor in this industry's "depression-proof" experience. The diesel locomotive created and expanded the demand for yet another distillate product. Just over 1.7 million barrels of diesel fuel were consumed in the last four years of the depression. And by the end of the decade, an entirely new sector – aviation – made its presence felt, demanding still newer refinery products for its equipment.[32]

As in the petroleum sector, firms in the chemical industry profited from new market linkages and techniques of production during the depression. Of major importance was the drive to innovate both to cut costs and to meet the needs of downstream industries for new and better products. As a result, the focus of investment activity in this industry during the thirties was on technical innovation and product development rather than on simply seeking a rebound in standard output and sales. The bulk of the derived demand for chemical products came from the rayon and petroleum producers and, to a lesser extent, rubber, metals, and paper corporations. Radio and moving-picture production generated an increased need for chemicals. Tanners, soapboilers, paintmixers, and glassmakers also populated the chemical producers' market more than ever before. The automobile firms increased their purchase of such inputs as rubber compounds and synthetic lacquers and also stimulated more metallurgical research in order to improve chassis and engines. And the depressed conditions prevailing gave added incentive to investment to improve on output recovery rates and the utilization of the wastes and by-products of reactions.[33]

decreasing frequency of oil changes because of quality improvements in motor oils themselves.

32 See Williamson et al., *The American Petroleum Industry*, 448, 455, 642–3, 660, 663, 666.

33 See Williams Haynes, *American Chemical Industry* (New York: Van Nostrand, 1948–54), vol. 4, pp. 5–6; and vol. 5, pp. 6–7, 31, 38, 297. The soil conservation and crop restriction programs of the New Deal, created by the Agricultural Adjustment Act, also increased the demand for fertilizers and other agronomic chemicals.

In petroleum and chemical production, improvements in technology and innovation in products were intimately linked. During the thirties, efforts dating to the previous decade to achieve continuous processing came to fruition and provided a cheaper alternative to the earlier batch production of chemicals and petroleum distillates. The downturn of 1929 stimulated further efforts to reduce costs. For petroleum producers, major emphasis was placed on the development of new cracking methods; in chemicals, the concern was to automate the control of reaction temperature, pressure, volume, duration, and other attributes such as the pH level.[34]

Where the link between these two industries proved to be most important was in the movement from the thermal distillation to the catalytic cracking of crude oil. Until the 1930s the distillation of petroleum products proceeded by subjecting the large molecules of crude oil to high temperature and pressure – thereby "cracking out" lighter molecules such as those of gasoline. This method had several drawbacks: the stress it placed on equipment, the batch charging it required, and the resultant limitations imposed on the quality of its product. The second of these problems was alleviated by the introduction of fractionating towers in the twenties. Expansion in the size of thermal cracking units helped to achieve scale economies in heat generation, and thereby improved product quality by the mid-thirties. Despite the depression, chemical and petroleum companies continued the search for more efficient alternatives. Success was achieved in 1937 when catalytic cracking was commercially developed by Eugene Houdry. By means of catalysis, this process exploited the chemical characteristics of crude oil, allowing for higher yields and generating a better-quality distillate at lower temperature and pressure. The product had a higher octane rating than that achieved by any other process, thereby successfully linking advances in refining with the new engine designs of the automakers. The introduction of the Houdry process spurred efforts in the chemical industry to devise cheaper and more effective catalysts.[35]

34 See Haynes, *American Chemical Industry*, vol. 5, pp. 37, 226; and Williamson et al., *The American Petroleum Industry*, 374–5, 624–5. Also see John McLean and Robert Haigh, *The Growth of Integrated Oil Companies* (Norwood, Mass.: Plimpton Press, 1954), ch. XIX.

35 See Williamson et al., *The American Petroleum Industry*, 394–407, 603–19, 624–6; and J. Stanley Clark, *The Oil Century: From the Drake Well to the Conservation Era* (Norman: University of Oklahoma Press, 1958), viii. Overall, the number of research personnel in chemicals rose 175.5%, and in petroleum 538.7%, during the thirties. See George Perazich and Philip M. Field, *Industrial*

Product innovation was also a notable part of the behavior of producers in these two industries in the thirties. Such activity often took place on the basis of interaction between both sectors. In the 1920s, chemical producers had developed tetraethyl lead, an ingredient used for the refinement of premium motor fuel. Other chemical innovations in the thirties that were of use in the petroleum and automobile sectors were isopropyl alcohol and ethylene glycol (both antifreeze agents) and various additives to improve the viscosity and minimize the oxidation and sludge-forming hydrocarbons of engine lubricants. Corrosion inhibitors and detergent additives for motor oil were also developed as the chemical firms invested in laboratories to evaluate lubricants and their performance. There were also impressive achievements in petrochemical lines, most notably in the synthesis of toluene (made possible by the introduction of new catalysts on the market), a major ingredient in TNT.[36]

Chemical firms created several new product lines. In the twenties, new markets were created in viscose rayon yarn (1920), cellophane film (1923), synthetic ammonia (1924), photographic film (1924), industrial alcohol (1925), and seed disinfectants and acetate rayon yarn (1928). The thirties saw no slowing in this trend, but merely a change in its focus, with major advances achieved in pharmaceutical markets – most notably in sulfa drugs, vitamins, new barbiturates, and anesthetic gases.[37]

From 1929 to 1939, petroleum producers made ten primary product additions; in chemicals, the figure was fifty-three. For both industries, the annual rate of product addition in that period was higher than in the subsequent two decades. Moreover, both sectors showed some of the lowest annual rates of non-primary-product addition of all manufacturing industries.[38]

Research and Changing Technology (Philadelphia: Works Progress Administration, 1940), 19.

36 See Williamson et al., *The American Petroleum Industry*, 412, 423, 629, 631–5; and Haynes, *American Chemical Industry*, vol. 5, 208–25.

37 From Haynes, *American Chemical Industry*, vol. 4, 38; and vol. 5, 245–64. A. E. Kahn, "The Chemical Industry," in *The Structure of American Industry*, 259, points out the stimulatory impact of such product innovation, especially with regard to the search for low-priced substitutes for already existing commodities.

38 See Gort, *Diversification and Integration in American Industry*, 42–3. Gort's sample comprised 14 chemical companies (representing 45.6% of total sector assets) and 10 petroleum companies (representing 71.5% of total sector assets).

Price and nonprice competition, improvements in distribution networks, and new marketing strategies also played a role in the unique experience of the chemical and petroleum sectors during the depression. Chemical firms, during the thirties, either eliminated charges or tolerated extreme tardiness in remittance of charges on delivery containers such as carboys, steel drums, and cylinders. Depressed market conditions also encourged the granting of discounts on cash purchases and attempts to establish reciprocal buying contracts. Companies wishing to avoid price-based tactics competed through trademarks and brand names and by creating specialty lines in various industrial, agricultural, and automotive product markets.[39]

In the twenties, electrification and the development of railroad tank cars had enabled petroleum refineries to locate near concentrations of consumers rather than oil fields. Aided by the expansion of the national highways, distribution of petroleum products by trucks and filling stations began. The downturn in the industry's prices in the early part of the thirties (due to high inventories, the production of "hot oil," and depressed sales) brought an intense struggle for business. Most of the firms in the industry (with the exception of self-service independent dealers and so-called trackside operators) were loath to cut already low prices. As a result, competition for retail sales took the form of offering, in addition to gasoline at the pump, mechanical repair and car washing services. Stations of a given company became standardized in their design and endowed with a uniform color scheme – a practice that aided both motorists seeking a given company's products and dealers by increasing the salvage value of a station if it were dismantled. Distributors, eager to secure retail outlets and thereby higher volume, offered dealers free equipment and station repairs, and dealers in turn extended customer rebates, discounts, and gift premiums. Credit card systems became widespread by 1939. These sales techniques had been previously condemned in 1929 in the industry's self-adopted Code of Ethical Competition.[40]

39 See Haynes, *American Chemical Industry*, vol. 5, 43–5, 51.
40 See Williamson et al., *The American Petroleum Industry*, 467–9, 680–4, 686, 697. "Hot oil" was the name given to crude produced in excess of prorationing laws established by the states. Such laws were passed, with pressure from the oil companies, to limit output and allocate target levels; the first was Texas's Market Demand Act of 1932. Many firms shipped hot oil out of the state(s) where they had exceeded their quotas. This practice contributed to the impressive output performance in crude until 1935, when the federal Connally Act prohibited

The depression inspired greater efforts by refiners to control distribution outlets and caused an initial increase in the number of retail establishments owned, leased, operated, or controlled by the major companies. But by the second half of the decade, retail control by the majors began to slip because of continued pressure from independents and trackside operators, state chain-store taxation, and federal antitrust investigations. At the wholesale level alone, the independent ownership of bulk plants and terminals rose from 25.9% in 1933 to 36.1% in 1939.[41] Such competitive conditions were a factor in the increasing use of billboards, newspapers, magazines, and radio for advertisements. It has been estimated that by 1935, one-fifth of every penny per gallon in gasoline sales paid for advertising.[42]

Tobacco products

The thirties were exceptionally prosperous years for manufacturers of tobacco products. In itself this is not a surprising fact, because these firms traditionally enjoy a steady demand for their highly addictive product. Moreover, the cost of tobacco products as a percentage of a typical consumer's budget was fairly low throughout the first half of this century. But the success of this industry in the midst of the depression can also be traced to the exploitation of key characteristics of its product – its susceptibility to image differentiation; the multitude of opportunities it offers for alterations in its extrinsic characteristics; and thus the large extent to which its sales may be influenced by marketing techniques and strategies. The industry's remarkable performance in the thirties was the result of developments reaching back to the end of World War I.

At the time of the Armistice, two factors initiated several decades of growth in the tobacco industry. The first was the disruption of Turkish supplies of leaf, which allowed the introduction of cheaper American blends. The second was the rise of cigarettes, a process stimulated by

such interstate shipments. See John Blair, *The Control of Oil* (New York: Pantheon, 1976), 161–4.

41 See Williamson et al., *The American Petroleum Industry*, 673–5, 699, 702–9, 715–16. The majors often forced dealers to become tied agents – by discriminating against multibrand stations with high station rents and refusing to honor other brands' credit cards.

42 From Williamson et al., *The American Petroleum Industry*, 697; and *The National Advertising Records*. Cf. Walton Hamilton et al., *Price and Price Policies* (New York: McGraw-Hill, 1938), section IV.

the use of tobacco by women on a large scale for the first time. Such a new market benefited those companies ready to adapt, for cigarettes offered "opportunities for [the] utilization of a considerable variety of merchandising skill" with respect to the persuasion of tobacco users of both sexes and of all ages.[43]

From 1911 to 1941, the annual per capita consumption of all tobacco products, except cigarettes, fell. In 1911, per capita consumption was 78 cigars, 2.5 lb. of chewing tobacco, 1.7 lb. of pipe tobacco, and 0.31 lb. of snuff. By 1941, the figures were 45 cigars, 0.78 lb. of chewing tobacco, 1.46 lb. of pipe tobacco, and 0.3 lb. of snuff. Annual per capita consumption of cigarettes, in striking contrast, rose from 108 in 1911 to 690 in 1925, 972 in 1930, and 1,551 in 1941.[44] The growth in per capita consumption of all tobacco products from 1900 to 1949 was due solely to the growth in cigarette use. Such a remarkable secular trend was linked with the rise in the number of working women in the population, the increasing size of the urban population, the distribution of free and low-cost cigarettes to the military, and the "general increase in nervous tension and the quickened tempo of life."[45]

The cigarette division of the tobacco industry fared well in the depression. After a slight drop in 1932, cigarette output increased steadily. The same cannot be said for other tobacco products; their markets had been growing slowly since World War I because of the competition of cigarettes, the declining popularity of chewing tobacco and snuff, and the reluctance of women to take up cigars and pipe tobacco. The relative inflexibility of tobacco demand aided the industry during the downturn, with consumption falling proportionately less than incomes, even though prices, given the oligopolistic structure of the industry, initially held firm.[46] Demand for cigarettes through the thirties was so strong that firms could execute large sales efforts to their own advantage without necessarily taking old customers away from other firms.

43 See Reavis Cox, *Competition in the American Tobacco Industry, 1911–1932: A Study of the Effects of the Partition of the American Tobacco Company by the United States Supreme Court* (New York: Columbia University Press, 1933), 40–1, 46, 317.

44 From Joseph C. Robert, *The Story of Tobacco in America* (New York: Knopf, 1949), 224, 237–40.

45 William H. Nicholls, *Price Policies in the Cigarette Industry: A Study of "Concerted Action" and Its Social Control, 1911–1950* (Nashville, Tenn.: Vanderbilt University Press, 1951), 12; and Cox, *Competition in the American Tobacco Industry*, 40–1.

46 See Cox, *Competition in the American Tobacco Industry*, 144, 210–11.

Often these marketing strategies involved shifting consumers from other industries, as in the tremendously successful "Reach for a Lucky Instead of a Sweet" campaign.[47]

Competitive strategies during severe depression must be premised on optimistic expectations of the future. Product innovation, output expansion, and sales efforts proceed on the basis of an estimation of the potential market to be won by such actions. In the case of the tobacco industry, several decades of development, dating from the 1911 dissolution of the Tobacco Trust, had laid the basis for its dynamic behavior during the depression. The targeting of a wholly new market after the war – women – and the associated introduction of new brands and companies as a result initiated a secular upswing in the sector's fortunes in cigarettes. Low prices, consumer convenience, and a high potential for standardization made cigarettes a highly profitable product. In addition, the cigarette market provided many opportunities for differentiation and sales strategies.

The history of the 1930s in the tobacco industry is the record of a thriving sector, continuing thirty previous years of growth, confidently facing the future. Challenges by new brands were met with vigor, and new initiatives in selling, advertising, and packaging were undertaken. Such atypical behavior, relative to the manufacturing sector as a whole, was a direct result of both the characteristics of the industry's product and the stage of long-term growth that it had reached in the early twentieth century. When the crash came, these attributes of the sector enabled it to exploit to its own advantage the short-run changes in consumer behavior and to recover relatively quickly its long-term growth trend.

Stone, clay, and glass products

Building materials and glass typically exhibit a high degree of sensitivity to movements in the business cycle because the sales of the sector depend on the volume of construction activity. But from the mid-thirties on, this industry performed remarkably well. Long-term developments

47 Compare Nicholls, *Price Policies in the Cigarette Industry*, 97, 167; Cox, *Competition in the American Tobacco Industry*, 224; and G. W. Hill, "The Newer Competition," *World's Work*, 58 (June, 1929), 72ff. Hill was, in 1929, the president of the American Tobacco Company.

in market opportunities, along with the impact of government policies in the short run, made this possible.

For the glass division, secular developments were particularly important. High import tariffs, along with the inflated wages that they encouraged, aided the early development of modern glassmaking from 1880 to 1920. By 1915, the nation met its own glass needs and created a surplus for export for the first time. The rise of the automobile industry after 1900 bolstered the market for plate glass that had previously been limited to construction needs. And although Prohibition and the demise of gas lighting lowered the demand for bottles, globes, and chimneys, other markets were developed that provided further opportunities for growth.[48]

From the turn of the century, the industry embarked on an era of development based on new processes and products. Perhaps most important for this growth between 1890 and 1920 was the tenfold rise in the demand for glass in food packaging. Glass became the favored choice of food processors because of its relatively low price, its superiority in holding vacuum seals, its sanitary properties, and its virtues as a display device to aid sales. Its unique flexibility with respect to coloring, size, and shape allowed for distinctive trademark designs. The Pure Food and Drug Act of 1906 bolstered the public's confidence in the quality of prepackaged foods, and the act's insistence on specified weight tolerances (to avoid fraud) increased the demand for uniform glass containers.[49]

During the depression, the glass industry benefited from the continued growth of new markets for its output. The spread of electrification bolstered the demand for refrigerated foods, many of which were packaged in glass, and for electric bulbs – a wholly new product. The thirties saw mostly uninterrupted increases in the demand for lighting and packaging glassware. From mid-decade on, electrification (both

48 See Warren C. Scoville, *Revolution in Glass-Making: Entrepreneurship and Technological Change in the American Industry, 1880–1920* (Cambridge, Mass.: Harvard University Press, 1948), 82, 248–9, 253–5, 257–9, 261–2; Pearce Davis, *The Development of the American Glass Industry* (Cambridge, Mass.: Harvard University Press, 1949), chs. IX–X; and J. M. Hammer, "The Glass Industry," and P. A. Hughes, "The Plate Glass Industry," both in J. G. Glover and W. B. Cornell, eds., *The Development of American Industries: Their Economic Significance* (Englewood Cliffs, N.J.: Prentice-Hall, 1932).

49 See Scoville, *Revolution in Glass-Making*, 252–6; and Davis, *The Development of the American Glass Industry*, viii, 220–1.

Table 2-4. *Index of new construction,*
1929–40 (1947–9 = 100)

Year	Total	Private	Public[a]
1929	96	98	92
1930	81	72	112
1931	65	50	115
1932	41	25	96
1933	31	19	70
1934	36	21	85
1935	42	29	88
1936	62	42	134
1937	63	49	112
1938	62	44	126
1939	74	54	145
1940	78	60	137

[a]Federal, State, Local; excludes military expenditures.
Source: U.S. Department of Labor, U.S. Department of Commerce, *Construction Volume and Costs, 1915–1956,* 39.

private and New Deal-inspired) was a crucial aspect of this development – because of both its direct effect on the demand for light bulbs and its indirect effect (given the spread of refrigeration) on the demand for glass food containers.[50]

The stone, clay, and glass sector as a whole made impressive commitments to research and development throughout the depression. The number of research personnel in the industry increased 166.4% from 1927 to 1938. Thirteen primary product additions were made in the same period, along with twenty-four secondary additions.[51]

The surprisingly strong performance of the building materials division in the latter half of the thirties relied on government expenditures on residential and public-facility construction. Table 2-4 provides data on public and private construction. The Works Progress Administration

50 Glass production in the thirties may also have been bolstered by the increasing use of glass for windows and other fixtures in automobiles. Automobile producers may have used more glass per car in an effort to improve sales (by image differentiation) during the depression years.
51 See Gort, *Diversification and Integration in American Industry,* 42–3; and Perazich and Field, *Industrial Research and Changing Technology,* 19.

alone built or renovated 2,500 hospitals, 5,900 school buildings, 1,000 airfields, and 13,000 recreation sites.[52]

It appears, therefore, that the relative success of this industry was due to a combination of factors. Development of new consumer markets provided a secular stimulus to the glass division. Government stabilization and relief policies during the depression bolstered the building materials producers. Both secular mechanisms and the intervention of government lent this industry a dynamism that served it well during the crisis of the thirties.

Textile products

For the textile industry, the Great Depression was almost fatal. In the wake of the 1930s, fundamental alterations took place not only in the sector's geographic location within the United States and around the world but also in its role within American manufacturing. By the postwar period, textiles no longer occupied a central place in American manufacturing. Mass-market fabrics were increasingly produced by low-cost foreign industry, and the American sector shrank in size and came to rely on the production of style fabrics, some cheap-grade garments, and industrial goods. This structural transformation began in the twenties and thirties.

Textiles, like most nondurable goods, did better in output terms during the depression than major durable goods industries. But the economic performance of the sector was nevertheless quite poor. Profit margins had been squeezed since the 1920s by excess capacity and extremely volatile prices for raw cotton.[53] With the crash of 1929, industrial demand for textiles fell, and the purchasing power of consumers was insufficient for a profitable garment market. Over half of the firms in the industry managed to report a positive net income in 1929; one year later, less than one-fourth did so.

Although the corporate economy as a whole suffered net losses in income from 1931 to 1933, the textile industry ran deficits in 1924, 1926, 1935, and 1938. This economic misfortune was uneven in its impact. The New England branch of the sector was most negatively

52 See William E. Leuchtenburg, *Franklin D. Roosevelt and the New Deal, 1932–1940* (New York: Harper & Row, 1963), 125–6.

53 See H. E. Michl, *The Textile Industries: An Economic Analysis* (Washington, D.C.: The Textile Foundation, 1938), chs. 9–10.

Table 2-5. *Percentage of installed spindles idle, by region, 1920–40*

Year	U.S. (total)	North	South
1920	0.84	1.1	0
1921	1.67	1.6	1.26
1922	3.25	5.3	1.24
1923	2.94	4.23	1.21
1924	5.29	8.06	1.74
1925	7.65	12.6	1.7
1926	7.45	13.4	1.68
1927	6.27	11.2	41.65
1928	5.35	11.	1.08
1929	6.9	13.8	1.6
1930	8.24	15.6	2.62
1931	11.31	20.5	5.24
1932	13.92	4.6	10.5
1933	12.94	24.1	6.3
1934	10.36	19.8	4.15
1935	11.31	9.6	5.7
1936	12.12	4.7	6.32
1937	5.93	11.1	3.7
1938	6.06	13.2	3.72
1939	6.32	11.5	3.3
1940	4.45	10.2	2.8

Source: Jules Backman and M. R. Gainsbrugh,
Economics of the Cotton Textile Industry, 173;
computations by the author.

affected[54] (Table 2-5). By the trough of 1932, two-thirds of the mills in New Bedford, a long-time center of textile production in North America, were shut down. And in the winter of that year, the city of Fall River, Massachusetts, went into receivership – 50% of its spindles were liquidated, 17 mills permanently closed, and 21,000 persons idled. Of the boom before October 1929, Walker D. Hines, president of the Cotton Textile Institute, had said: "Everyone in America seemed to be making money except the cotton manufacturers." Even the prospect of eventual recovery held little promise for the old centers of the industry.

54 It should be noted that insofar as exports amounted to only 6.7% of total production in 1929, the shrinkage of the foreign market (to a low of 2.3% of annual output in 1936) was not a significant factor in the distress of the textile industry. See Jules Backman and M. R. Gainsbrugh, *Economics of the Cotton Textile Industry* (New York: National Industrial Conference Board, 1946), 181, 210–1.

New mills had emerged in the South, and an upturn would only spur them to produce more. It "would do nothing for the companies [to the North] which had sold their machinery, emptied their granite-walled mills, and offered their property for rent."[55]

Data from the *Census of Manufactures* on changes in the level of physical output for the various categories of textile products show the wide diversity in the depression experience of firms in the industry. With reference specifically to performance in the late thirties and from 1929 to 1937 overall, the evidence indicates that the producers of cotton goods were especially unfortunate in the 1930s. The product lines most unaffected by the downturn were those linked with clothing and style fabrics, namely, lace goods, silk and rayon goods, women's clothing, corsets, and hats. Other commodity groups that recovered well were asphalted, felt-base floor covering, jute goods, and some specialty lines such as knit goods, artificial leather, and wool shoddy. Whatever strength the industry had in the face of the Great Depression was found in the style fabrics category. By the thirties the textile industry experienced a major shift in its markets. The difficulty lay in the fact that the predominant share of the productive capacity of the industry was concentrated in product lines that showed little growth potential.

Contrasting with the disappointing performance of most of the textile industry in the 1930s was the good fortune of the rayon producers. Despite downturns in physical output in 1932 and 1937, rayon production rose overall in the interwar period. Profit rates in the thirties ranged from 1.5% to 12%. Output rose from 36,000 to 1 billion pounds from 1925 to 1947; in the same time period, employment tripled to 60,000 persons. Such success was linked with the fact that because of chemical research and development, technical change, the introduction of mass production strategies, and tariff protection, the price per pound of rayon fell from five dollars in 1919 to fifty-four cents in 1941.[56]

The key to understanding the Great Depression in the American

55 From Louis Galambos, *Competition and Cooperation: The Emergence of a National Trade Association* (Baltimore: Johns Hopkins University Press, 1966), 134, 139, 171–2. Also cf. Backman and Gainsbrugh, *Economics of the Cotton Textile Industry*, 175ff.; and Seymour L. Wolfbein, *The Decline of a Cotton Textile City: A Study of New Bedford* (New York: Columbia University Press, 1944), 12.

56 See Jesse W. Markham, *Competition in the Rayon Industry* (Cambridge, Mass.: Harvard University Press, 1952), 6–7, 124, 193–4, 224, 227.

textile sector lies in appreciating the extensive shift in demand patterns that had begun in the 1920s. Despite low rates of net investment in textiles in general, in apparel and other style lines economic activity remained relatively strong. In addition, some spinning and weaving mills benefited from the emergence of new markets in tire cord, brake lining, automobile upholstery and cushions, and electric wire insulation. But the most potential lay in garments, and attendant upon that the most risk. For as styles changed and market opportunities emerged, the producer faced a dilemma. If one style was produced for stock, the risk of price changes in both the input and final markets emerged; yet if the producer delayed the production of a given design, he incurred high overhead costs and found it subsequently difficult to meet an order in time.[57]

The interwar period witnessed significant changes in the product mix of the industry. Ginghams, drills, and table damask virtually disappeared from production by the 1930s. While there was no major shift into luxury fabrics, there was a dramatic increase in the output of print cloth. By 1939 such cloth accounted for over one-third of cotton textile manufacture. The combined share of fine goods and narrow sheetings fell to approximately 30%. The problem for cotton goods producers lay in the fact that by the mid-thirties the use of cotton in industrial commodities and clothing lines fell; in household items its use fluctuated throughout the decade. In sum, the percentage of textile output made from cotton and its mixtures fell from 71% to 39% from 1927 to 1939.[58]

Even though there was surprising strength in apparel markets (especially women's clothing) during the depression, this did little to help the cotton textile manufacturers. Consumer preferences clearly leaned toward garments made from wool, silk, and rayon. In addition, a change in style from large cotton dresses to short skirts further limited the market. Cotton hosiery was a particularly unfortunate enterprise. In the twenties, despite a price differential favoring cotton over silk

57 See Michl, *The Textile Industries*, 59, 168–9. It must be borne in mind, however, that unlike the woolens producer (who had to incorporate color changes at the weaving stage), finished cotton textiles could be altered in color relatively easily at the finishing stage. See Backman and Gainsbrugh, *Economics of the Cotton Textile Industry*, 32, 131.
58 See Gordon Donald, *The Depression in Cotton Textiles, 1924 to 1940* (Ph.D. dissertation, University of Chicago, 1951), 95; and Backman and Gainsbrugh, *Economics of the Cotton Textile Industry*, 28–9, 41, 62.

hose of close to 475%, silk hosiery output rose over eight times while cotton hose production fell by 79%. Competition in apparel markets was most difficult for cotton mills insofar as in these markets, "style and design, color and texture may [have] outweigh[ed] price, durability, and launderability."[59]

Increasing inroads were made by rayon in cotton markets during the interwar period. The tire cord market was almost wholly usurped because of rayon's technical superiority. Silk and rayon were easily interchangeable on looms, facilitating the access of rayon producers to markets previously limited to silk. In New Bedford alone the proportion of total textile employment committed to silk and rayon production rose from 5% to 22% in the latter half of the 1930s. At the same time, the share of the total capital invested in the city's textile manufactories that were linked with cotton goods fell from about 75% to 50%. To add to these woes, the cotton goods producers saw major markets lost to paper mills, which started to produce cheaper handkerchiefs, towels, napkins, and (with a price differential enhanced by superior guarantees of sterility) surgical dressings and bandages.[60]

Rubber products

At the onset of the depression in 1929, the rubber industry faced three major problems. First, declining turnover sales had already emerged as a result of the improved quality of the sector's major product – automobile tires. Second, the decline in disposable income occasioned by the crash reduced tire sales as consumers postponed expenditures on durables. And finally, there was a dramatic rise in foreign competition in the late twenties and early thirties. It is not surprising, therefore, that the most severe losses for rubber producers were in the standard markets: footwear, tires, and tubes. The Great Depression had less of an impact on newer markets, some of which were just developing their

59 From Backman and Gainsbrugh, *Economics of the Cotton Textile Industry*, 59, 62.
60 See Wolfbein, *The Decline of a Cotton Textile City*, 23–6, 100, 120, 123; and Backman and Gainsbrugh, *Economics of the Cotton Textile Industry*, 54–5, 68. Jesse W. Markham points out, in *Competition in the Rayon Industry*, p. 33, that the relative success of the rayon industry "[was] attributable to the fact that the rayon industry [was] a relatively new and rapidly expanding one, whereas the silk, cotton, and woolen industries [were] considerably more mature."

potential, such as conveyors, communication and electrical equipment, landscaping materials, and sporting goods.[61]

By 1932, tire manufacturers were operating at 49% of capacity; they did not achieve their pre-crash peak in capacity utilization until World War II. As operating rates fell, prices weakened; the wholesale price index for tires (1914 = 100) stood at a low of 23.7 in 1932 and managed to reach 35 only by the end of the depression. Per tire-mile, the price index fell even faster because of quality improvements. Although the output of pneumatic tire casings fell throughout the first half of the thirties, the amount of crude rubber consumed steadily rose – a lower number of better tires were produced in the depression years. The result was a continuing weakness in the net growth of tire sales while renewals remained only somewhat steady. As a result, industry profits were quite poor in the initial stages of the downturn.[62]

The poor economic performance of the rubber manufacturers during the 1930s had both short-run and secular causes. The short-term fall in disposable income and the skewed concentration of purchasing power after the crash had a serious impact on the producers of such durable products. Secular causes were more varied in their effects, but overall also served to shrink the markets for rubber products. These long-term factors were (1) improvements in the quality of tires, motor vehicles, and roads; (2) the emergence of foreign competition; (3) the deleterious effects (to 1928) of the International Rubber Regulation Agreement of the British Rubber Growers' Association, which forced up the price of crude rubber; and (4) the slow development of new uses for rubber and its products.[63]

Ironically, the 1930s penalized the industry for the excellent job it had done in developing its product in the 1920s. Whereas in 1916 the average auto used 8 tires per year, by 1936 the average annual use per car was 1.2 tires. Replacement sales accounted for 70% of all tire sales

61 See William C. Geer, *The Reign of Rubber* (New York: Century, 1922), passim, and P. Schidrowitz and T. R. Dawson, eds., *History of the Rubber Industry* (Cambridge, Mass.: W. Heffer, 1952), 334.

62 See John D. Gaffey, *The Productivity of Labor in the Rubber Tire Manufacturing Industry* (New York: Columbia University Press, 1940), 36, 60, 131, 135, 163; and L. G. Reynolds, "Competition in the Rubber Tire Industry," *American Economic Review*, 28 (September, 1938), 463–5.

63 See P. W. Barker, *Rubber Industry of the United States, 1839–1939* (Washington, D.C.: U.S. Government Printing Office, 1939), 11–12; and Howard Wolf and Ralph Wolf, *Rubber: A Story of Glory and Greed* (New York: Covici, Friede, 1936), 465.

Table 2-6. *Average mileage and weight of tire casings for selected years, 1905–37*

Year	Average mileage	Average weight (lb.)	Average life (years)
1905	2,000		
1910	3,000		0.73
1915	3,500	12.8	0.77
1920	5,000	15.3	1.28
1925	10,000	17.3	1.58
1930	15,000	22.9	2.47
1937	20,000	26.1	2.69

Source: John D. Gaffey, *The Productivity of Labor in the Rubber Tire Manufacturing Industry*, 39.

and just over half of all the crude rubber used by 1932. Improvements in equipment to retread tires only made the situation worse. Table 2-6 shows the dramatic increase in the service life of tires. Table 2-7 documents the shift in the industry's markets that took place. The condition that created tremendous difficulties for tire producers – technical change – also made the achievement of stability all the more problematic. Yet tire producers throughout the thirties tended to await the impact of stimuli from outside the sector to generate a sales recovery. Harvey Firestone, one of the most outspoken members of the industry, said at the time: "If in lengthening the life of its product the tire industry seemed to be improving itself out of a market, the economics of the business pointed to greater and greater production of motor vehicles." [64]

Lacking an exogenous mechanism to improve sales, the rubber sector needed to diversify product lines and lessen its dependence on soft markets. The shift from solid to pneumatic tire production after World

64 From Alfred Lief, *Harvey Firestone: Free Man of Enterprise* (New York: McGraw-Hill, 1951), 202; and see David M. Beights, *Financing American Rubber Manufacturing Companies* (Urbana, Ill.: n.p., 1932), 3; Hugh Allen, *The House of Goodyear* (Akron, Ohio: n.p., 1936), 344; Walton Hamilton et al., "The Automobile Tire – Forms of Marketing in Combat," in W. Hamilton et al., *Price and Price Policies* (New York: McGraw-Hill, 1938), 89; and Gaffey, *The Productivity of Labor in the Rubber Tire Manufacturing Industry*, 32, 38, 40, 42, 187–8. The industry was hit in the 1930s by a decline in aggregate demand at the same time that a "learning curve" effect took hold in the development of its new products. Product prices thus quickly fell. Cf. A. M. Spence, "The Learning Curve and Competition," *Bell Journal of Economics*, 12 (Spring, 1981), 49–70.

Table 2-7. *Analysis of principal markets for pneumatic tires, 1910–36*

| Year | Number of tires (in thousands) | | | | |
	Original equip-ment	Renewal sales	Inven-tory exports	Renewal sales change	Tires per car
1910	724	1,525	51	+100	5.0
1911	797	2,031	72	+100	4.4
1912	1,424	2,971	105	+500	4.8
1913	1,846	4,022	132	—	0.5
1914	2,175	6,008	139	−300	5.0
1915	3,584	7,871	495	+50	4.8
1916	6,139	10,782	644	+1,000	4.7
1917	7,086	16,754	496	+1,500	5.1
1918	4,046	20,494	460	−1,000	4.4
1919	7,249	23,373	964	+1,250	4.1
1920	8,472	20,565	1,543	+1,820	2.9
1921	6,299	1,973	649	−1,620	2.6
1922	10,113	28,477	1,438	+900	2.9
1923	16,409	27,796	1,489	−270	2.4
1924	14,645	33,728	1,389	+1,240	2.4
1925	17,212	39,288	1,770	+540	2.3
1926	17,548	39,200	1,654	+1,740	2.0
1927	14,001	46,888	2,811	−140	2.2
1928	18,019	52,303	2,689	+2,520	2.3
1929	22,067	45,471	2,979	−750	1.9
1930	13,970	37,231	2,684	−2,270	1.4
1931	10,429	37,983	1,959	−980	1.4
1932	6,246	33,474	1,095	+100	1.3
1933	9,464	33,699	1,239	+990	1.4
1934	13,510	31,869	1,289	+570	1.3
1935	19,435	30,091	1,100	−2,130	1.2
1936	21,921	31,353	1,077	+3,790	1.2

Sources: U.S. Bureau of Foreign and Domestic Commerce, *United States Renewal Tire Market Analysis*, 14; and Automobile Manufacturers Association, *Automobile Facts and Figures*, 16.

War I had proceeded smoothly enough, but during the 1930s similar adjustments were not easy. Financial requirements for product and process innovation were hard to meet because of the severely constrained revenues of firms and incomes of potential stockholders. For many corporations, the prospect of changing plant and equipment before they had been completely amortized was unacceptable. This, of course, merely intensified the excess capacity problems of the industry. Firms moving into new investments (such as the production of new varieties of tires or the manufacture of improved cotton twist cord for tire casings) tended to be highly integrated.[65]

Some diversification did occur. While pneumatic tires and tubes still accounted for 85% of the rubber industry's output in 1931, the proportion of non-tire production rose steadily thereafter. Rubber tubing, belting, hoses, washers, gaskets, and engine mounts were manufactured with greater frequency. Firestone was the leader in the diversification movement, adding close to 500 mechanical rubber goods to its line during the 1930s. The company also was the first to develop special tires for farm machinery, earth-moving equipment, and power shovels. One such tire was 6.5 feet high and 20 inches wide and weighed 1,000 lbs. This unique firm also experimented with liquid latex in the mid-thirties and developed the first foam cushioning material from rubber. But such activities were more the exception than the rule; World War II revitalized the industry and spurred the development of synthetics and new products in a way that one or two enterprising companies could not.[66]

Lumber and paper products

Almost every category of lumber product showed output declines during the thirties. Losses were greatest in the major product categories. Table 2-8 documents the major weakness in construction. Many sawmills went into receivership and closed. In 1929, over 4,000 lumber corporations had reported a positive net income to the Internal Revenue Service. By 1932, only 541 did. Between 1926 and 1932, over 1,000

---

65 See Hamilton et al., "The Automobile Tire – Forms of Marketing in Combat," 91; and Allen, *The House of Goodyear*, 75ff., 156, 319. It is curious that the textile firms, almost without exception, made no attempts to move into the relatively new field of tire cord manufacture. Faced with difficulties in their own traditional markets, it seems remarkable that these firms did not take action. Indeed, as early as 1916 the Goodyear Tire and Rubber Company, exploring the possibility of joining with a textile firm to produce tire cord, "found a lack of receptiveness to its ideas. . . . They [the textile companies] didn't seem to speak the same language." (From Allen, *The House of Goodyear*, 156.)

66 Consider Gaffey, *The Productivity of Labor in the Rubber Tire Manufacturing Industry*, 51–2, 191–2; Alfred Lief, *The Firestone Story: A History of the Firestone Tire and Rubber Company* (New York: Whittlesey House, 1951), 209, 218–19, 245; Lief, *Harvey Firestone*, 279–80, 283; and P. T. Bauer, *The Rubber Industry: A Study in Competition and Monopoly* (Cambridge, Mass.: Harvard University Press, 1948), 196.

Table 2-8. *Indices of construction activity,*
1920–34 (1923–5 = 100)

Year	Lumber output	Residential contracts	Industrial contracts
1920	86	30	90
1921	72	44	65
1922	87	68	88
1923	101	81	86
1924	98	95	94
1925	101	124	120
1926	98	121	135
1927	92	117	139
1928	91	126	142
1929	91	87	142
1930	64	50	125
1931	41	37	84
1932	25	13	40
1933	32	11	37
1934	32	12	48

Source: J. P. Barry, "The Marginal Utility of Lumber
and Lumber Substitutes," *The Timberman*, 37 (February, 1936), 18.

firms left the industry.[67] With per capita lumber consumption on a
downward trend, and "forested lands . . . a drug on the market," the
price structure broke down. Russian dumping of pulpwood did not
help matters. Immigration restrictions and a lower overall rate of
population growth further compounded the weakness of the construction market as the demand for new homes fell. Changes in the techniques of marine design and manufacture lowered the demand for
traditional naval stores. Price differentials between grades of wood
quickly narrowed as producers sought out profitable markets.[68]

Papermaking and related activities, however, showed surprising
strength in the face of the downturn. The extent of unutilized capacity
rose until 1932, when it stood at 42%. Capacity utilization then rose as

67 See Nelson C. Brown, *Lumber: Manufacture, Conditioning, Grading, Distribu-*
tion, and Use (New York: Wiley, 1947), 19; W. L. Compton, "The Lumber
Industry Is Not Defeated," *American Lumberman* (June 11, 1932), 1; and Peter
A. Stone et al., *Economic Problems of the Lumber and Timber Products Indus-*
try. U.S. National Recovery Administration, work materials no. 79, 1936, 81.

68 From Arthur N. Pack, *Forestry: An Economic Challenge* (New York: Macmillan, 1933), 15, 26, 38, 42–3, 79; and Nelson C. Brown, *The American
Lumber Industry* (New York: Wiley, 1923), 135.

papermakers took action to improve their performance. But nonetheless, output fell 29% from 1929 to 1932, in large part because newspaper circulation fell 11% at the same time. Forty percent of the productive capacity of the industry went bankrupt during the depression years. Prices of domestic spruce pulpwood (f.o.b. mill) fell from $17.57 per peeled cord in 1929 to $8.91 in 1934. The National Recovery Administration (N.R.A.) code bolstered prices thereafter. In 1933 the net return on capital invested in this sector was effectively zero.[69]

By the 1930s, 60% of the output of the paper industry was accounted for by printing grades, 30% by converting grades (for boxes, posters, and coatings), and 10% by writing grades. In the buyer's market of the Great Depression, special quality and delivery demands were made that stimulated process and product innovation, product line diversification, and grade shifting. Paper producers became more and more adept at changing their output – a suitable antidepression strategy insofar as the need to locate with respect to pulp, water, and power supplies prevented any relocation to low-wage areas such as the South.[70] Such timely innovation served to make paper manufacturers relatively well-off in an industry generally doing very poorly. And it provided a reserve of knowledge for the future when major opportunities emerged with the birth of the computer, fast food, photography, and xerography industries. The 1930s instructed papermakers in ways of becoming less dependent on external demand stimuli and encouraged the anticipation of market changes.

Lumber and timber product manufacturers faced many of the same problems in the 1930s as other durable goods firms. The postponement of durable purchases, especially in the housing market, and the deferment of replacement expenditures hurt the lumber industry a great

69 See Lockwood Trade Journal Company, *250 Years of Papermaking in America* (New York: Lockwood Trade Journal Company, 1940), 70; News Print Service Bureau, *The Story of News Print Paper* (New York: News Print Service Bureau, 1936), 60–1, 69; John A. Guthrie, *The Newsprint Paper Industry* (Cambridge, Mass.: Harvard University Press, 1941), 97, 144, 234, 247–8; and Louis T. Stevenson, *The Background and Economics of American Papermaking* (New York: Harper & Bros., 1940), 86, 210, 220.

70 See Groundwood Paper Manufacturers Association, *Ten Year Trends in the Groundwood Paper Industry, 1935–1944* (New York: n.p., 1945), 3; and Avi J. Cohen, *Technological Change in the North American Pulp and Paper Industry* (unpublished manuscript, Stanford University, 1981), 5, 9, 81–2. Also see his "Technological Change as Historical Process: The Case of the U.S. Pulp and Paper Industry, 1915–1940," *Journal of Economic History*, 44 (September, 1984), 775–99.

Table 2-9. *Percentage consumption of major building materials (by tonnage)*

Year	Lumber	Steel	Cement	Brick	Stone
1919	59.7	10.8	11.8	15.7	2.0
1920	52.6	13.6	14.9	16.4	2.5
1921	56.4	5.9	17.2	17.3	3.2
1922	50.8	11.8	15.6	18.4	3.4
1923	50.6	11.9	15.3	19.2	3.0
1924	48.7	12.2	16.8	18.9	3.4
1925	49.1	12.2	16.3	19.1	3.3
1926	47.2	13.5	16.8	18.9	3.6
1927	45.4	13.8	18.0	19.0	3.8
1928	48.3	14.2	16.8	17.2	3.5
1929	44.1	17.2	17.3	17.4	4.0
1930	40.4	17.1	20.6	17.1	4.8
1931	44.0	14.6	21.2	14.3	5.9
1932	46.0	11.8	21.4	12.1	8.7

Source: Peter A. Stone et al., *Economic Problems of the Lumber and Timber Products Industry*, 203.

deal. By the time of the Great Depression, 40% of the sector's output was devoted to construction materials. But even aside from the softness of the housing market, the lumber sector was suffering a long-term shift in markets linked with (1) the rising price of wood relative to other building materials and (2) the increasing use of nonflammable materials to meet building code requirements (Table 2-9). Indeed, concrete and fabricated steel had begun cutting into lumber markets as early as 1920. Similarly, a declining trend was evident well before the crash in the use of wood in ships, tank cars, and other rolling stock. From 1930 to 1934, the slump accelerated the increase in the share of housing that was accounted for by multiple-family units. Other things being equal, this lowered per capita (and per family) lumber consumption. Finally, the development of creosote allowed for the production of railroad cross-ties and telephone poles with far greater endurance than simple wood. Whereas half the cross-ties in use in 1920 were creosoted, by 1940 close to 90% had been so treated.[71] As a result, while 7.3

71 See Brown, *Lumber*, 283; Brown, *The American Lumber Industry*, 18, 27–8, 264–7; Brown, *Timber Products and Industries: The Harvesting, Conversion, and Marketing of Materials other than Lumber, including the Principal Derivatives and Extractives* (New York: Wiley, 1937), 15, 68; Israel I. Holland, *Some*

million new cross-ties were sold in 1929, just under 1 million were sold in 1935. In the same years, the sale of replacement ties declined by over 30 million units.

There were some new markets ready for exploitation by lumber producers, but movement into them was slow and required the stimulus of war in the 1940s for their potential to be fully realized. Rayon and cellophane production was the most important of these. Other opportunities lay in derivatives of wood such as adhesives, turpentine, rosin oil, acetic acid, and wood gas. Home decorating contractors created new markets for flooring materials (derived from sawdust and wood shavings), plywoods, and veneers. But again lumber firms were slow to make new investments, as evidenced by the fact that in the early 1930s, 60% of the output of lumber mills was remanufactured and/or dressed by *other* industries.[72]

More inclined to innovate because of the high turnover and special requirements of their markets, papermakers experimented widely in the 1930s. The use of pulp in plastics, textiles, and rayon production began, and major efforts were made in developing new paperboard containers, most notably the thirty-dozen egg case. Cheaper grades of book and writing paper were developed, although the decline in newsprint sales could not be overcome. New product lines were opened in the health and beauty fields – paper towels, handkerchiefs, tissues, plates, cups, and sanitary napkins. Some attempts were made to develop paper and pulp products for use in wire insulation and tire carcasses.[73]

   Factors Affecting the Consumption of Lumber in the United States with Empha-sis on Demand (Ph.D. dissertation, University of California, Berkeley, 1955); 24–7, 30–1, 42, 45; Stone et al., *Economic Problems of the Lumber and Timber Products Industry*, 198, 200; and Pack, *Forestry*, 43–7. Pack notes the indifferent attitude of lumber producers to the change in demand patterns. As urban, vertical construction turned increasingly to steel, many lumber firms were confident that the demand for wood would remain high because of the need for scaffolding on construction sites. But within a short time, steel scaffolding also became preferred.

72 From Pack, *Forestry*, 49–50, 52–3; Brown, *Timber Products and Industries*, 5, 13, 15, 101–2; and Brown, *The American Lumber Industry*, 1, 190–2.

73 See Lockwood Trade Journal Company, *250 Years of Papermaking in America*, 71; Alling and Cory Company, *One Hundred and Twenty-Five Years in the Paper Business, 1819–1944* (Rochester, N.Y.: Alling and Cory Company, 1944), 71; Groundwood Paper Manufacturers Association, *Ten Year Trends in the Groundwood Paper Industry*, 8, 14–15; Stevenson, *The Background and Economics of American Papermaking*, 142, 156, 163, 231; and Cohen, *Technological Change in the North American Pulp and Paper Industry*, 4–5, 16.

In the years ahead, paper firms found an almost limitless market in the sterile medical products field.

Perhaps the most remarkable aspect of the behavior of paper producers was their willingness to shift grades of production in the face of long-term and cyclical alterations in their markets. Although newsprint producers suffered a bit during the early years of the downturn, many paper firms shifted grades and began to expand the variety of products and their characteristics, focusing on color, sizing (which affected stiffness and rattle), absorbency, and opacity. In the first five years of the depression, 800 tons of daily capacity were shifted in terms of grades in New York State alone.[74]

III   Alterations in the sectoral composition of national output, 1910–72

Differences in the performance of American manufacturing industries during the Great Depression show that long-term shifts in the strength of markets played a crucial role in determining the rate and extent of recovery. These shifts were the outward expression of the process of secular growth and development in the interwar American economy. And they were reflected in the changing sectoral composition of national output, especially later in the twentieth century. In this context it becomes clear that the changes in product mix experienced by American industry throughout the thirties were the result of trends in development and not simply the result of cyclical events. Just prior to World War I, the ten largest American industries, in declining order of value added, were machinery, lumber, printing and publishing, iron and steel, malt liquors, men's clothing, cotton goods, tobacco manufactures, railroad cars, and boots and shoes. By 1960, the ten largest industries by value added were nonelectrical machinery, electrical machinery, motor vehicles, steel, aircraft, basic chemicals, beverages, dairy products, structural metal products, and newspapers.[75]

---

74 See Cohen, *Technological Change in the North American Pulp and Paper Industry*, 18; and Guthrie, *The Newsprint Paper Industry*, 9, 13, 70–1, 101.

75 As shown in U.S. Bureau of the Census, *Thirteenth Census of the United States: 1910* (Washington, D.C.: U.S. Government Printing Office, 1913), vol. 8, p. 40; and U.S. Bureau of the Census, *Annual Survey of Manufactures: 1959 and 1960* (Washington, D.C.: U.S. Government Printing Office, 1962), 28–47. "Value added" is the difference between the final value of output and the cost of materials used in its production.

Evidence on the percentage change in industry shares of national income provides another demonstration of the structural transformation of the American economy that began during the interwar years. Between 1929 and 1972, government enterprise increased its share of national income by 174%. Communications industries expanded their portion of national income by 75%, and service industries did so by 26.7%. Contract construction and durable goods manufacturing grew, as indexed by their share of national income, approximately 25%. And electric, gas, and sanitary service sectors won a 5.6% rise in their share of aggregate output. Such sectors as wholesale and retail trade, finance, insurance, real estate, transportation, agriculture, forestry, fisheries, and mining declined in importance during this forty-three-year period.[76]

The industries that fared relatively well during the thirties were in most cases the same ones that secured larger and larger shares of national income in the postwar era. In the case of durable goods manufacturing and contract construction, the stimulus of war and the release of pent-up demand after war appear to have outweighed a secular decline in their importance as constituent parts of national value-product. The "baby boom" and cold war of the fifties also clearly played an important role. The evidence indicates that the growing sectors of the interwar period were benefiting from secular development factors as well as responding to cyclical forces. The following chapters of this investigation make more explicit the causes and consequences of these cyclical and secular mechanisms.

Statistical appendix to Chapter 2

Time plots of industrial output, 1927–40

The time plots were generated by monthly output data (Figures 2-1 through 2-12).

76 This information was computed on the basis of data reported in U.S. Department of Commerce, *Survey of Current Business* (Washington, D.C.: U.S. Government Printing Office), August, 1965, 42–5; July, 1966, 15; July, 1970, 21; July, 1973, 22.

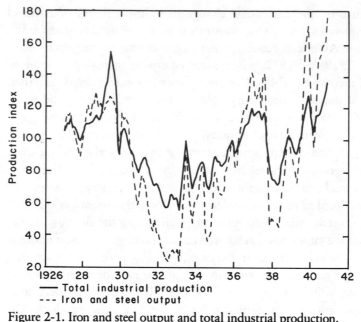

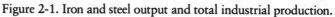

Figure 2-1. Iron and steel output and total industrial production.

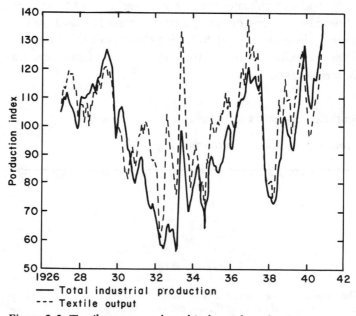

Figure 2-2. Textile output and total industrial production.

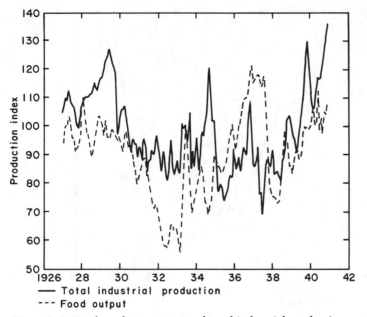

Figure 2-3. Food products output and total industrial production.

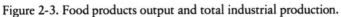

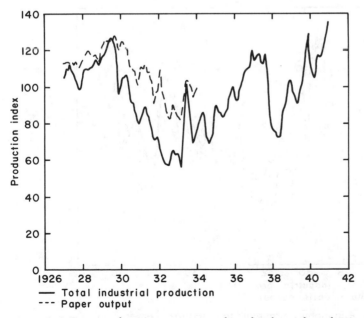

Figure 2-4. Paper and printing output and total industrial production.

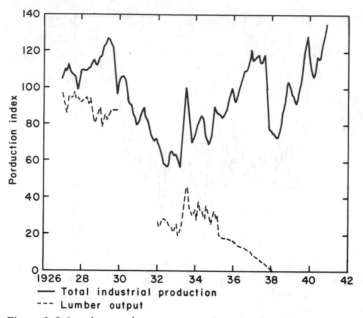

Figure 2-5. Lumber products output and total industrial production.

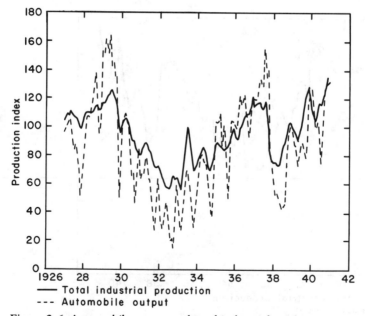

Figure 2-6. Automobile output and total industrial production.

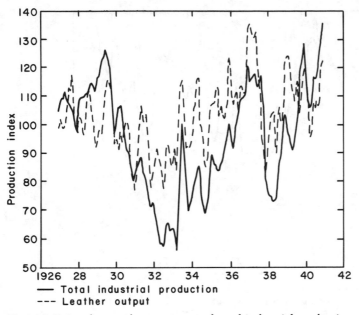

Figure 2-7. Leather products output and total industrial production.

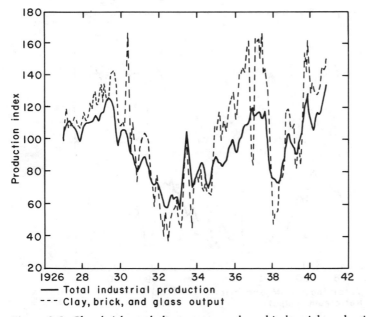

Figure 2-8. Clay, brick, and glass output and total industrial production.

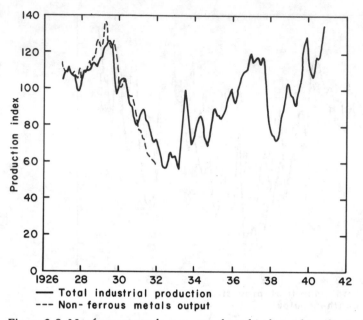

Figure 2-9. Nonferrous metals output and total industrial production.

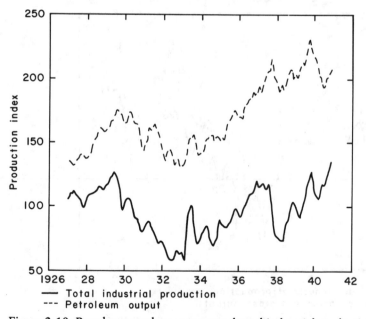

Figure 2-10. Petroleum products output and total industrial production.

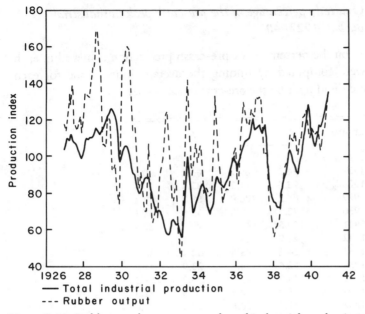

Figure 2-11. Rubber products output and total industrial production.

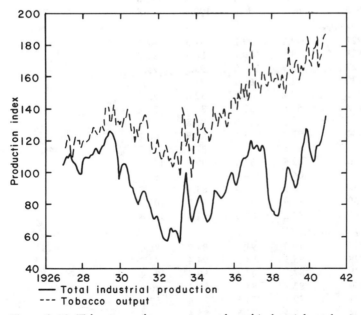

Figure 2-12. Tobacco products output and total industrial production.

Quarterly percentage of the pre-crash peak in industrial output, 1927–40

The tables on the percentage of pre-crash production achieved in each quarter were computed by finding the average index value for each quarter and dividing it by the pre-crash peak value.

Quarter	1	2	3	4
1. Iron and steel				
1927	74.2	69.7	63.2	60.6
1928	73.5	74.2	82.6	79.4
1929	85.2	100.0	89.7	58.1
1930	72.3	71.0	55.5	38.1
1931	50.3	41.3	29.7	27.1
1932	21.9	16.1	18.1	18.1
1933	14.2	46.5	42.6	38.7
1934	42.6	54.8	23.9	41.9
1935	46.5	42.6	54.2	66.5
1936	53.5	72.9	76.8	92.3
1937	81.3	76.8	80.6	31.6
1938	31.6	29.7	49.0	65.2
1939	53.5	57.4	78.1	111.6
1940	66.5	96.1	102.6	113.5
2. Textiles				
1927	94.2	99.2	97.5	87.6
1928	69.0	69.7	88.4	91.7
1929	95.9	100.0	95.9	79.3
1930	81.0	69.4	72.7	71.9
1931	80.2	80.2	82.6	72.7
1932	68.6	52.1	86.0	75.2
1933	62.8	110.0	81.8	64.5
1934	77.7	63.6	52.9	80.2
1935	81.0	82.6	87.6	91.7
1936	82.6	88.4	99.2	114.9
1937	106.6	104.1	89.3	63.6
1938	66.9	71.9	85.1	96.7
1939	90.9	91.7	100.0	101.7
1940	80.2	86.0	93.4	112.4
3. Food products				
1927	90.9	91.8	82.7	86.4
1928	95.5	84.5	96.4	94.5
1929	87.3	87.3	89.1	86.4
1930	82.7	84.5	87.3	80.9
1931	79.1	75.5	83.6	88.2
1932	76.4	75.5	86.4	76.4
1933	76.4	90.9	95.5	78.2

Quarter	1	2	3	4
1934	76.4	87.3	109.1	92.7
1935	70.0	67.3	70.9	75.5
1936	79.1	80.0	81.8	90.0
1937	80.9	70.0	79.1	78.2
1938	75.5	73.6	89.1	78.2
1939	80.9	79.1	90.9	90.0
1940	99.1	101.8	89.1	98.2

4. *Paper and printing*

	1	2	3	4
1927	88.3	88.3	89.1	87.5
1928	92.2	92.2	92.2	89.1
1929	97.7	98.4	100.0	93.8
1930	96.9	91.4	85.2	78.9
1931	85.9	84.4	81.3	75.8
1932	77.3	69.5	67.2	67.2
1933	64.1	78.9	78.9	75.8
1934	78.1	47.4	44.7	41.6
1935				
1936				
1937				
1938		Not available.		
1939				
1940				

5. *Lumber products*

	1	2	3	4
1927	94.8	96.9	101.0	95.9
1928	96.9	93.8	84.5	89.7
1929	85.6	87.6	90.7	90.7
1930		Not available.		
1931		Not available.		
1932	27.8	28.9	24.7	23.7
1933	22.7	39.2	37.1	33.0
1934	39.2	32.0	33.0	29.9
1935	30.9	19.3	18.5	18.0
1936	15.1			
1937		Not available.		
1938				
1939				
1940				

6. *Automobiles*

	1	2	3	4
1927	62.7	56.0	48.8	34.3
1928	66.9	70.5	83.7	62.0
1929	98.2	100.0	81.9	29.5
1930	65.7	59.0	41.0	51.2
1931	40.4	39.2	24.1	39.8
1932	16.9	28.3	14.5	36.1
1933	16.3	39.8	34.9	27.1
1934	47.0	49.4	30.7	53.0

Quarter	1	2	3	4
6. Automobiles (continued)				
1935	63.9	60.2	30.1	64.5
1936	64.5	71.1	64.5	73.5
1937	72.9	78.3	81.3	47.0
1938	32.5	27.7	27.7	59.6
1939	54.8	48.8	51.2	76.5
1940	71.7	63.3	65.1	80.1
7. Leather products				
1927	83.1	89.8	100.0	82.2
1928	86.4	91.5	93.27	8.0
1929	83.9	93.2	97.5	78.8
1930	77.1	85.6	84.7	68.6
1931	78.0	85.6	82.2	69.5
1932	78.0	69.5	78.0	72.0
1933	71.2	96.6	78.0	79.7
1934	91.5	84.7	73.7	89.0
1935	91.5	87.3	86.4	105.1
1936	90.7	86.4	94.1	113.6
1937	111.9	100.0	82.2	72.9
1938	88.1	76.3	86.4	104.2
1939	102.5	91.5	88.1	101.7
1940	89.0	92.4	90.7	103.4
8. Cement, brick, and glass				
1927	83.9	76.2	79.0	74.1
1928	78.3	86.0	90.9	90.9
1929	94.4	88.1	100.0	79.0
1930	77.6	116.4	77.6	51.7
1931	69.9	71.0	52.4	55.6
1932	35.0	38.5	34.6	40.2
1933	32.9	59.1	52.1	49.7
1934	50.3	47.2	46.9	64.7
1935	80.4	76.9	79.0	91.3
1936	84.6	102.1	110.5	62.9
1937	112.6	116.8	95.1	62.6
1938	37.4	52.1	61.5	82.2
1939	77.3	71.0	85.0	114.7
1940	95.8	89.5	101.4	106.3
9. Nonferrous metals				
1927	79.6	78.8	77.4	81.0
1928	78.8	83.9	85.4	93.4
1929	94.2	92.0	92.0	83.2
1930	75.9	71.5	70.1	62.0
1931	56.2	49.6	45.8	
1932		Not available.		
1933				
1934				
1935				

Quarter	1	2	3	4
1936		Not available.		
1937				
1938				
1939				
1940				

10. Petroleum products

1927	76.7	76.1	79.0	77.8
1928	80.1	86.9	92.0	90.3
1929	90.9	95.5	98.9	94.3
1930	95.5	96.6	93.2	84.7
1931	86.4	91.5	91.5	84.7
1932	77.3	83.0	75.6	75.0
1933	76.7	87.5	89.2	78.4
1934	81.3	87.5	86.4	87.5
1935	86.9	94.3	97.7	98.3
1936	95.5	102.8	105.7	108.5
1937	108.0	114.8	117.6	114.2
1938	108.5	109.1	117.0	114.2
1939	114.8	122.2	125.6	125.6
1940	119.9	114.8	114.8	118.8

11. Rubber products

1927	72.2	82.8	67.5	66.9
1928	79.3	84.6	100.0	84.6
1929	89.9	94.1	69.2	47.3
1930	62.1	70.4	56.8	43.2
1931	58.0	74.6	46.7	52.1
1932	43.2	63.3	37.9	39.6
1933	24.3	68.0	60.9	63.9
1934	62.7	49.7	46.7	78.7
1935	55.0	46.7	49.1	58.6
1936	50.3	76.9	70.4	72.8
1937	78.1	72.8	60.4	39.1
1938	36.7	42.6	56.8	66.3
1939	67.5	66.3	72.8	65.1
1940	66.9	66.3	68.6	79.3

12. Tobacco products

1927	81.1	80.4	85.3	79.7
1928	83.9	87.4	89.5	88.8
1929	88.1	97.2	100.0	93.0
1930	89.5	98.6	87.4	89.5
1931	91.6	93.0	82.5	79.0
1932	76.2	82.5	77.6	78.3
1933	69.2	94.4	80.4	86.0
1934	83.2	92.3	87.4	100.0
1935	90.9	96.5	90.2	102.8
1936	97.9	109.8	109.8	128.0
1937	107.0	104.9	113.3	118.9

Quarter	1	2	3	4
12. Tobacco products (continued)				
1938	111.9	107.7	111.9	125.2
1939	114.7	118.9	114.7	130.1
1940	116.8	130.1	122.4	129.4

Source: U.S. Department of Commerce, *Survey of Current Business*; computations by the author.

Estimates of industrial growth rates in output, 1933–40

A more rigorous assessment of sectoral performance requires the estimation of rates of growth in output and of output elasticities for each industry in the wake of the crash. Some notion of the potential for full recovery in each industry may thereby be established. These statistical objectives do not involve behavioral or structural hypotheses; the primary task is one of de-trending the production time series and calculating sectoral growth rates and output elasticities. Sectoral production may be regarded as a simple function of aggregate economic performance and a time trend. In order to fit the time series more closely, a double-log transformation of the data was employed. For the purposes of statistical estimation, the following relationship was used:

$$\ln(S_{it}) = \sigma + \pi_i[\ln(X_t)] + \Gamma_i[\ln(Z)] + \epsilon_t$$

$$(i=1,\ldots,12; \ t=1,\ldots,68)$$

where S_{it} represents the output of the ith sector in month t, X_t is total manufacturing output in month t, and Z is a time trend.

The coefficient π_i indicates the percentage response of output in sector i (at time t) to a unit increase in the aggregate industrial index, X_t specifically, π_i is the output elasticity of the ith sector. Γ_i is the percentage growth rate per unit of time in the relevant sector. Because of the characteristics of the data used to generate X_t there is no need to impose an adding-up constraint on S_{it}. The total production index is not the weighted sum of the twelve sectoral indices examined. It also contains information on other manufacturing and service industries, as well as mining sectors not included in this analysis. Potential problems concerning simultaneous-equations bias and spurious correlations between S_{it} and X_t are, therefore, legitimately ignored.[77] Regressions for

77 See United States Federal Reserve Board, "New Index of Industrial Production," *Federal Reserve Bulletin*, 13 (March, 1927), 170–7; and Jan Kmenta, *Elements*

Table 2-10. *Annual growth rates and output elasticities for selected U.S. manufacturing industries, 1933–40*

Sector	Growth rate	Output elasticity	R^2
Iron & steel	−4.8	2.39	0.92
	(−1.36)[a]	(27.7)[b]	
Textiles	−11.35	0.925	0.92
	(−2.7)[b]	(10.35)[b]	
Food products	1.32	0.121	0.88
	(0.216)	(1.09)	
Paper and printing	NA[c]	NA	
Lumber products	NA	NA	
Automobiles	−16.08	1.99	0.64
	(−1.29)	(8.21)[b]	
Leather products	−6.84	0.577	0.92
	(−1.49)	(6.57)[b]	
Clay, brick, and glass	−5.94	1.59	0.70
	(−0.692)	(8.3)[b]	
Nonferrous metals	NA	NA	
Petroleum products	21.6	0.142	0.98
	(5.85)[b]	(3.42)[b]	
Rubber products	−14.64	1.28	0.81
	(−2.04)[b]	(9.3)[b]	
Tobacco products	20.28	0.205	0.86
	(9.98)[b]	(3.85)[b]	

[a] *t* statistics are in parentheses.
[b] Significant.
[c] Data not available.

the sample period 1933–40 were run using a generalized least-squares technique.[78] The results are presented in Table 2-10.

Of those sectors for which data are available, five endure continuous declines in output and exhibit the high output elasticity characteristic of such durable goods producers in a downturn: iron and steel, automobiles, cement, brick, and glass products, and rubber products. To

of Econometrics (New York: Macmillan, 1971), 517–18. Because the objective of the statistical analysis solely concerns interindustry comparisons, the problem of spurious correlation is relatively insignificant.

78 See D. Cochrane and G. H. Orcutt, "Application of Least-Squares Regressions to Relationships Containing Auto-correlated Error Terms," *Journal of the American Statistical Association*, 44 (1949), 32–61; and J. Durbin and G. S. Watson, "Testing for Serial Correlation in Least-squares Regression," *Biometrika*, 37 (June, 1950), 409–28; and 38 (June, 1951), 159–78.

some extent the same is true of textiles and leather products, but the relevant elasticities suggest that, as semidurable goods industries, their sensitivity to the trade cycle is less.

A moderate, positive rate of growth for food product output and dramatic expansion in petroleum and tobacco products are the most striking results of this statistical analysis. Output elasticities for these enterprises are sufficiently small to suggest that such behavior is due to forces that did not affect other industries. These same industries were the only manufacturing sectors to report a positive net income as a percentage of capitalization in 1932, the worst year of the depression.[79]

79 As reported in S. Fabricant, "Profits, Losses and Business Assets, 1929–1934," National Bureau of Economic Research bulletin 55.

3. A reassessment of investment failure in the interwar economy

> While the profits of stock are high, men will have a motive to accumulate.
>
> – David Ricardo

A radical shift in the industrial composition of final demand played an important role in delaying a complete recovery from the trough of 1932. This shift in the composition of demand made full employment virtually impossible to achieve after the crash of 1929. Complete recovery required a mass of interrelated new techniques and human and physical capital that, in the timid financial environment prevailing after the crash (and given the uncertainties of the New Deal), could not be organized on the necessary scale by private investment markets.

Investment behavior has been the least examined aspect of the depression, yet it holds the key to understanding cyclical instability. The persistent currency of the "overproduction" (or its mirror image, "underconsumption") theory of the Great Depression is based on the idea that massive overaccumulation of output in the late 1920s left American industry saddled with enormous inventories that depressed investment for almost a decade below its full-employment level. Although this argument may have some legitimacy for the agricultural sector, it is not supported by the limited available evidence on inventories in major industries.[1]

An inventory-based view of the business cycle also suffers from theoretical inadequacies.[2] One problem concerns the model's characterization of the relevant planning horizon for investment decisions. The model implies that the horizon is relatively short, with modifications in expenditure decisions quickly and easily made. But capital com-

---

1 See, for example, Erik Lundberg, *Instability and Economic Growth* (New Haven, Conn.: Yale University Press, 1968), 74–6.
2 See D. P. Levine and Nai Pew Ong, "Competition and Economic Fluctuations" (unpublished paper, Yale University and University of California, Riverside, 1979); and Robert T. Averitt, *The Dual Economy: The Dynamics of American Industry Structure* (New York: Norton, 1968), 4–21.

mitments are by their nature often large and long-lived. Such pledges become fixed in equipment and plant that, because of both size and technical specificity, are not easily or quickly liquidated or retooled. As a result, short-run fluctuations in sales (i.e., inventories) may have little impact on decisions that are long-term in nature.

Another weakness of the inventory argument concerns the explanation of the clustering of investment during the cycle. It has traditionally been argued that such clustering derives from a behavioral connection between sales levels and producers' confidence. Yet this notion ignores the impact of changes in the short-run availability of discretionary funds for investment. In an upturn, such funds are more easily obtained than in a slump. Moreover, during an upswing, the costs of initiating a major project or of bringing forward its date of completion are outweighed by the costs of postponement, which include the likelihood of being preempted in the relevant market by a competitor. The opposite is true of a downturn. Thus, an inventory model tends to obscure some of the very aspects of the investment process that are important for explaining the absence of recovery during the 1930s.[3]

Functional relationships between sales and investment also obscure the influence of secular changes in the mix of industries constituting the national aggregate. Long-range prospects for expansion underlie the decision making associated with large investment obligations. The size and rate of growth of the relevant market are of primary concern. To the extent that firms in an industry during a trough phase of the business cycle have pessimistic expectations regarding their markets, a revival becomes dependent on either the creation of wholly new, promising markets (i.e., products) or the stimulus of new expenditures arising outside the industry. Increasing concentration in the mature sectors bolsters the potential for stagnation. The reluctance to compete and expel excess capacity in these markets intensifies the gloom of the environment in which plans are formulated, besides contributing to the state of depressed sales and net revenues that makes investment upturns more and more difficult.

Product innovation requires large net revenues or adequate access to external sources of funds – both of which are less available in a downturn. External stimuli must be sufficiently large to have an adequate effect. Secular changes in the growth performance and potential of

3 See David P. Levine, *Economic Theory: The System of Economic Relations as a Whole* (London: Routledge & Kegan Paul, 1981), 243–55.

various industries must offset declines in certain groups with rises in others.[4] The chance that such changes in sectoral performance will proceed smoothly is small.

Secular transitions in development involve the decline of old and the rise of new industries. These alterations in the composition of national output tend to be discontinuous and disruptive not because of imperfections in markets but rather because of forces inherent in the accumulation of capital over time. First, the ongoing expansion of the capitalist economy is coterminous with the advance of scientific and technical knowledge that transforms production technique, cost structures, and the availability of raw materials and creates entirely new inputs and outputs. Consider, for example, the emergence of fossil fuels, the replacement of natural fibers with synthetics, and the rise of internal combustion as a means of locomotion. Entire industries are made obsolete or virtually so, while new ones are created.[5] Second, the structural milieu in which product and technical changes take place is itself in part a product of economic growth.

As neoclassical economic theory attempts to show, in perfectly competitive markets changes in output mix and technique proceed smoothly, with the eventual transference of labor and capital to sectors where they are most highly valued.[6] But this theory is inadequate to the task of explaining structural change, for such change is assumed either not to exist or in aggregate terms to have no net effect. Even Keynesian analysis is flawed in this regard. A recessionary gap is examined in terms of a shortfall in the level of real national output relative to a full-employment (or minimum-unemployment) target. Little attention is given to the consequences of changes in the composition rather than the level of real national output.

Indeed, the concentration and increasing specificity of capital may interfere with the movements of inputs required for smooth transitions

4 See E. Lederer, "The Problem of Development and Growth in the Economic System," *Social Research*, 2 (February, 1935), 20–38; and Averitt, *The Dual Economy*, 38–41.

5 Some reflections on the disruptive impact of shifts in industrial life cycles are offered in M. Abramovitz, "Welfare Quandaries and Productivity Concerns," *American Economic Review*, 71 (March, 1981), 1–17.

6 Moreover, the orthodox theory of the firm asserts that in the face of a decline in the demand for its product, the firm alters the level of output so that marginal cost and marginal revenue remain equal. Little attention is paid to the conditions that will encourage (and indeed enable) a firm to shut down, leave the industry, or alter its product or process of production.

in sectoral activity. The decline in competitive pressure in the concentrated industries not only makes entry difficult, because of pricing strategies, but also exit. Large amounts of capital are fixed in plant and equipment, their liquidation not encouraged by a competitive environment, nor practical if the industry is in long-run decline. The hesitancy of large firms to liquidate in depressed times may also be due to a reluctance to relinquish goodwill and the technical specialization of labor and organization, and to uncertainty as to the growth potential of new markets.[7]

Concentration of capital leads to unequal access to investment funds, which obstructs further the possibility of smooth transitions in industrial activity. Because of their past record of profitability, large enterprises have higher credit ratings and easier access to credit facilities, and they are able to put up larger collateral for a loan. Equity issues by such firms are more readily financed and sold, and such firms can avoid takeovers more easily than small firms. Large firms, too, may have commonalities of interest with financial institutions through interlocking directorates. All these factors may impede the flow of capital out of old and into new sectors.[8]

In the American economy of the thirties, these potential discontinuities in the transition process were intensified by the exceptional severity of the crash in 1929. The massive euphoria of the stock market

7 Further expansion under these circumstances may take place by means of diversified mergers, with the exhaustion of opportunities for horizontal and vertical integration. Diversified integration, of course, provides no net expansion for the economy as a whole, although possibly improving the firm's individual profitability. Should such a form of investment predominate in a time of depression, there will be no stimulus to general economic activity. The causes of such investment behavior are still poorly understood, but conditions in the capital markets and in the treatment of depreciation for tax purposes would seem to be of overriding importance. Even so, such merger activity seems insignificant in the interwar period; it has become much more of a factor in the American economy of the late twentieth century.

8 However, combinations of financial and manufacturing interests need not necessarily reduce capital movements. The experience of the German cartels in the late nineteenth and early twentieth centuries is a case in point. See E. Maschke, "Outline of the History of German Cartels from 1873 to 1914," in F. Crouzet, W. H. Chaloner, and W. M. Stern, eds., *Essays in European Economic History: 1789–1914* (London: Edward Arnold, 1969), 226–58. But also see L. Davis, "The Capital Markets and Industrial Concentration: The U.S. and U.K., a Comparative Study," *Economic History Review*, second series, 19 (August, 1966), 255–72, which examines the impact of capital concentration on the mobilization of funds for new industries in Britain and the United States in the nineteenth century.

of the 1920s, the large amounts of banking funds tied up in the call market, and the questionable sales practices engaged in by brokerage houses meant that the number of individual incomes affected by the downturn was very large. And the devaluation of holdings was singularly steep. Coupled with the almost total destruction of consumer confidence, these events left the markets for industrial products extremely soft. Such an environment was hardly conducive to new ventures by old industries, large commitments of capital to new customers, or long-term planning in general.

Investment varied widely among industries in the wake of the 1929 downturn, as previous chapters have shown. Net investment expenditures on plant and equipment grew throughout the 1930s in the chemical industry, for example, and remained fairly stable in food products, tobacco manufactures, petroleum products, and certain branches of the machine tool and building materials industries. Net expenditures exhibited a downward trend in textiles, lumber and paper products, leather products, rubber manufactures, transportation equipment (including automobiles), iron and steel products, and nonferrous metals.[9]

Such industrial variation in investment commitments in the wake of the crash was due to a weakening of confidence or a deterioration in the availability of credit or both. "But whereas the weakening of either [was] enough to cause a collapse, recovery require[d] the revival of both. For whilst the weakening of credit [was] sufficient to bring about a collapse, its strengthening, though a necessary condition of recovery, [was] not a sufficient condition."[10]

Investors' perceptions of the future played an important role in the recovery process. There is ample evidence that American manufacturing industries differed in their attitudes about future prospects and strategies. Some firms and sectors accurately forecasted the development of new markets and technologies.[11] Others did not. Interindustry variation in investment recovery after 1929 was therefore a far more complicated

9 See the statistical appendix to this chapter for data on net investment in manufacturing industries during 1927–40.
10 From Keynes, *The General Theory*, 158.
11 Interestingly enough, the relative success of German cartels during the late nineteenth and early twentieth centuries was in part due to their accurate perceptions of shifts in market strength between intermediate and finished goods. See L. L. Peters, "Cooperative Competition in German Coal and Steel: 1893–1914," *Journal of Economic History*, 42 (March, 1982), 227–30; and S. Webb, "Tariffs, Cartels, Technology, and Growth in the German Steel Industry, 1879 to 1914," *Journal of Economic History*, 40 (June, 1980), 309–29.

affair than an inventory model would imply. Investment behavior during the depression years was determined by a combination of cyclical and secular factors. The financial determinants of investment spending also had both short-run and long-run components.

I   The performance of the capital markets

The investment performance of American manufacturing industries in the wake of the 1929 downturn was critically influenced by the performance of capital markets and by the impact of the slump on firms' funding decisions and behavior. The monetary history of the thirties is well known, and there is no need to repeat or embellish it here. But for the focus of this investigation – the real determinants of macroeconomic performance – further attention must be given to the financial impacts of the depression and their consequences for investment behavior and the actions of firms.[12]

The main financial problems restricting recovery were (1) the disruption of securities markets by the stock market crash and the concomitant difficulties for firms in floating new equity; (2) massive reductions in internal funds due to low earnings; (3) a low supply of aggregate savings, also due to the downturn; and (4) corporate tax surcharges (particularly the undistributed profits tax) later in the decade that may have impaired firms' ability to raise internal funds for investment commitments. A 1938 study of ninety-three durable goods companies showed that from 1927 to 1930, $674 million was saved out of profits. By 1934 these same firms had a total deficit of $55 million. By 1936, their savings from profits had reached only $129 million, or less than 20% of the 1930 figure.[13]

The deflationary actions of the monetary authorities made matters worse. The 50% increase in reserve requirements, the gold sterilization policy that was zealously pursued, and the resulting high "liquidity preference premium" made access to capital extremely difficult and hardly straightforward. In the face of monetary stringency, firms considered equity financing as a possible alternative in order to accumulate

---

12 The comprehensive monetary history for the interwar period is found in Friedman and Schwartz, *A Monetary History of the United States*, chs. 6–10; and see Bernanke, "Nonmonetary Effects of the Financial Crisis in the Propagation of the Great Depression."

13 See A. Sachs, "Summary of a Comprehensive Financial Analysis of the Causes of the Slump," *The Annalist*, 51 (January 14, 1938), 35–6.

funds for maintenance and expansion. Whereas in 1928 the average dividend yield (as a percentage of the issue price) was 5.24%, as compared with 5.71% for a Baa bond, in 1936 the respective rates were 8.65% and 4.07%. Equity financing was thus very expensive, and companies therefore found it less attractive.[14]

The disruption of equity markets confronted firms with a financial environment very different from the one to which they had grown accustomed in the years preceding the crash. Since the end of World War I, businesses had generally shunned loans from banks and sought to finance their commitments through the flotation of stock. There were several reasons for this tendency. Large firms in the prosperous 1920s found it easier to issue stock when the costs of flotation were often less than the bank rate. Stocks and bonds had become increasingly desirable assets since the Great War, even for small investors, because of their experience with War Bonds and the ease of margin buying. What is most interesting in this regard is that certain sectors had unusually high rates of growth in equity issues. Firms in public utilities, miscellaneous manufactures, petroleum, real estate, merchandising, chemicals, and food products issued securities at an average annual rate of 14.3% during the twenties. This was a substantially higher rate than the 5.5% average characteristic of all other sectors. There were also very high rates of equity issue in new fabricated product sectors such as aluminum manufacturing, electrical machinery, and certain appliance lines. Companies in these industries enjoyed higher earnings rates and were often larger than those firms that issued less equity and relied relatively more on bank loans to finance their funding commitments.[15]

Thus, the newer industries of the interwar period that had the potential to withstand the crash of 1929 and that might have led the economy out of depression were precisely those sectors that, in the years preceding 1929, relied most heavily on the securities markets for their growth. Disruption in those markets after 1929 had disastrous consequences for the economy as a whole and provides an important part of the explanation for the duration of the depression.

14 See A. Sachs, "The Financial Dynamics of the Recovery since 1933 and Latest Constriction Phase in Capital Flow," in *Corporate Finance and Taxation*, Financial Management Series number 53 (New York: American Management Association, 1938), 13, 17, 23–4, 27–9.

15 See P. T. Ellsworth, "The Output of New Corporation Issues," *Review of Economics and Statistics*, 14 (November 15, 1932), 195–200; and L. Currie, "The Decline of the Commercial Loan," *Quarterly Journal of Economics*, 45 (August, 1931), 698–709.

After 1929, firms definitely preferred debt financing to equity financing. Securities market conditions were highly unfavorable. Moreover, and perhaps most important, the costs of flotation rose after 1933 with the imposition of securities and exchange regulation. A further constraint on the role equity issues might have played in securing recovery was the tendency for the proportional costs of flotation to fall as the size of issue increased. This placed smaller (or more timid) firms at a profound disadvantage when considering the desirability of securities-financed expansion. With internal funds inadequate because of the depression itself, and by 1936 with the imposition of corporate tax surcharges, most businesses turned increasingly to term loans as a means for expansion. Short-run loans were shunned because of the lessons of the depression.[16]

Borrowing funds was not easy. Restrictive monetary policy seriously limited the access of firms to adequate financial resources at rates encouraging investment. As a consequence, a dual tendency emerged: Larger firms relied more and more on internal funding; small firms were forced into increasingly exposed and illiquid positions. The financing of asset expansion by income retention became a dominant trend in the behavior of American manufacturing in the period 1900 to 1950. In the interwar period, funds retained as a share of gross corporate savings rose from 30% in the twenties to 58% between 1930 and 1933, and reached 78% between 1934 and 1937. The attractiveness of internal funding clearly had to do with the absence of the need to negotiate with outside agencies, make debt maintenance payment commitments, accept time constraints on the use of the funds, and issue statements regarding the company's financial and competitive position.[17]

16 See U.S. Securities and Exchange Commission, Research and Statistics Section of the Trading and Exchange Division, *Cost of Flotation for Small Issues: 1925–29 and 1935–38* (Washington, D.C.: n.p., 1940); U.S. Securities and Exchange Commission, Research and Statistics Section of the Trading and Exchange Division, *Cost of Flotation for Registered Securities: 1938–39* (Washington, D.C.: n.p., 1941); and Neil H. Jacoby and Raymond J. Saulnier, *Term Lending to Business* (New York: National Bureau of Economic Research, 1941).

17 See Sergei P. Dobrovolsky, *Corporate Income Retention: 1915–43* (New York: National Bureau of Economic Research, 1951), 15–18, 35–6; Daniel Creamer et al., *Capital in Manufacturing and Mining: Its Formation and Financing* (Princeton, N.J.: Princeton University Press, 1960); Albert R. Koch, *The Financing of Large Corporations: 1920–1939* (New York: National Bureau of Economic Research, 1943), 5–7, 76–7, 79–80, 105; W. L. Stoddard, "Small Business Wants Capital," *Harvard Business Review*, 18 (Spring, 1940), 265–74; and H. M. Hunter, "The Role of Business Liquidity during the Great Depres-

Whether firms sought to invest by means of securities flotation, debt financing, or internal funding, the availability of credit (directly to firms or individual investors) was a critical determinant of the pace and pattern of recovery after 1932. The thirties, for obvious reasons, witnessed a "deep and extended trough" in aggregate savings.[18] Ultimately the source of the financial derangement of the thirties that interfered with recovery was the collapse of the banking system and the imposition of monetary stringency in the wake of the stock market collapse of 1929.

From 1929 to 1933, loans and investments of the Federal Reserve member banks fell from \$35.7 to \$24.8 billion; loans fell \$12.8 billion alone − 31% and 50% declines, respectively. During the same period the number of banks in the United States, exclusive of mutual savings banks, fell by approximately 10,500. Member bank borrowing from the Federal Reserve was negligible from 1933 to 1938. Indeed, member bank excess reserves rose dramatically in the years after the trough of 1932. What is most remarkable is that low money market rates prevailed from 1933 to 1938 primarily because of gold inflows from troubled overseas economies and the decline in money demand after 1929. In New York City alone, the prevailing loan rate stood at a nominal level of 4.02% in 1933 and fell to 2.4% by 1938. Bankers nonetheless maintained high excess reserves and claimed there was an abject scarcity of safe investments. Critics charged that the banks were overly cautious. A 1939 study of the availability of bank credit during the depression found that loan refusals and restrictions were not functions of the particular industries that sought funding. The timidity of the banking system appears to have been general and widespread. Indeed, the 1939 survey found that over half of the reasons given for credit refusals by banks were "bank policy"; only a third were because of "the condition of the borrowing concern."[19]

The restrictive policies pursued by the monetary authorities after the crash arose from a fear of an external drain after Britain's departure

    sion and Afterwards: Differences between Large and Small Firms," *Journal of Economic History*, 42 (December, 1982), 883–902.

18 See Raymond W. Goldsmith, *A Study of Saving in the United States* (Princeton, N.J.: Princeton University Press, 1955), vol. 1, pp. 5, 7.

19 See Charles R. Whittlesey, *Banking and the New Deal* (Chicago: University of Chicago Press, 1935), 1, 6; Lewis H. Kimmel, *The Availability of Bank Credit: 1933–1938* (New York: National Industrial Conference Board, 1939), 16–24, 37, 87–90; and U.S. Board of Governors of the Federal Reserve System, *Banking and Monetary Statistics* (Washington, D.C.: National Capital Press, 1943), 18–21, 283, 368, 441–2, 464, 477, 489–94.

from the gold standard in 1931. They were also implemented because of a failure to appreciate the linkage between the presence of an internal drain (or "panic") and the absence of a systematic open market purchasing policy. Hence, the stock of money fell by 33% by 1933, and bankers generally felt pressure to liquidate old loans and avoid past errors. It appears that there was a palpable demand for loanable funds after 1933, but firms' requirements were left unsatisfied.[20]

Although financial constraints impinged on all industries during the depression decade, some industries did expand their borrowing. Petroleum companies, which had borrowed a total of $125 million in 1929, secured funding of $220 million in 1938. Industry-specific factors played an important role in determining the potential for recovery after 1932. As other parts of this study show, these included the extent to which the levels of existing demand and productive capacity were equalized, the development of new products and productive techniques, and the overall level of firms' income. The interindustry differences illustrate the general point that raising "the supply of credit funds and the sources through which they are available is meaningless unless there is an active or latent demand for them."[21] The financial parameters of recovery in the American economy of the interwar period can tell only part of the story. Real determinants involving the extent of opportunities were crucial.

II   The attenuation of the accelerator mechanism in the interwar period

Another factor interfered with recovery during the depression years. The impact of the accelerator mechanism itself was weakened by trends in the magnitude of the capital-output ratio. As a result, despite dynamic behavior in certain industries, the extent to which an upturn in any sector of the economy could spark a general recovery was reduced.

The accelerator mechanism is based on the idea that there is a functional relationship between changes in output and changes in invest-

20 See Friedman and Schwartz, *A Monetary History of the United States*, 299; and C. O. Hardy and Jacob Viner, *Report on the Availability of Bank Credit in the Seventh Federal Reserve District* (Washington, D.C.: U.S. Government Printing Office, 1935).

21 See G. A. Eddy, "The Present Status of New Security Issues," *Review of Economics and Statistics*, 21 (August, 1939), 116–21; and Kimmel, *The Availability of Bank Credit*, v.

ment. As output expands and inventories are reduced, net business investment will rise. For any given annual change in output, net investment will rise by a proportionate amount. That amount is indexed by the coefficient in the functional form that has been dubbed "the relation." It can be shown that "the relation" is the capital-output ratio; as it falls, the accelerator mechanism is reduced.[22] In the interwar years, the capital-output ratio fell. As output rose in some industries in the wake of the crash of 1929, the impact on net investment economywide of any given increase in output was consequently less than previously had been the case. Thus, qualitative, long-term changes in the American economy made a full recovery from the downturn of 1929–32 more difficult to achieve.[23]

Financial factors and changes in the accelerator mechanism form part of the explanation of weak recovery. A more complete analysis, however, must include assessments of both the process of technical innovation and the effective demand problem, rooted in secular economic transformation, that interfered with the economy's capacity to rebound quickly from the panic of 1929.

Statistical appendix to Chapter 3

Net investment expenditures for selected manufacturing sectors, 1927–40

In the following tables, all data are in millions of 1972 dollars. N = net investment expenditures. 1929-P = net investment expenditures as percentages of their 1929 levels.

Sources and methods of estimation: Industrial classifications are based on the 1972 Standard Industrial Categories, with appropriate concordances used for the 1930s. Investment figures include expenditures by corporate and noncorporate firms and expenditures by new firms even if actual production has not yet begun. They are also establishment-based rather than company-based. Costs of land are excluded.

22 See the seminal article by P. A. Samuelson, "Interactions between the Multiplier Analysis and the Principle of Acceleration," *Review of Economics and Statistics*, 21 (May, 1939), 75–8.

23 Results of an estimation of a simple accelerator model for the interwar period are reported in this chapter's appendix. They confirm that there was a statistically significant decrease in the capital-output ratio during the interwar years.

For the purpose of deriving net figures from extant gross investment data, physical depreciation is defined as the decline in the productivity of a capital asset at a given level of output. This technique avoids problems associated with the use of book-value figures, primarily distortions in asset valuation arising from tax rules. A "perpetual inventory" technique is used that traces an industry's investment in a capital asset by estimating the annual decline in the asset's productivity from time of purchase to time of scrapping. Service life is estimated from relevant engineering data. The technique also assumes that at the starting point of the investment series, no initial capital stock exists. The series from which the following data are taken commences in 1921, so this assumption is not overly problematic. The assumption that an asset, once classified, remains in the given industry until scrapped abstracts from changes in output mix. But at the two-digit classification level used here, this problem also can be safely ignored. The data are taken from the following sources: U.S. Bureau of Labor Statistics, *Capital Stock Estimates for Input-Output Industries: Methods and Data*, Bulletin 2034 (Washington, D.C.: U.S. Government Printing Office, 1979); U.S. Bureau of the Census, *Census of Manufactures*, relevant years; U.S. Bureau of the Census, *Annual Survey of Manufactures*, relevant years; U.S. Office of Internal Revenue, *Statistics of Income*, relevant years; L. Chawner, "Capital Expenditures for Manufacturing Plant and Equipment – 1915 to 1940," *Survey of Current Business* (March, 1941), 9–14; L. Chawner, "Capital Expenditures in Selected Manufacturing Industries," *Survey of Current Business* (May, 1941), 17–56; L. Chawner, "Capital Expenditures in Selected Manufacturing Industries – Part II," *Survey of Current Business* (December, 1941), 14–23.

	Food and kindred products				Tobacco manufacturers			
	Equipment		Plant		Equipment		Plant	
	N	1929-P	N	1929-P	N	1929-P	N	1929-P
1927	200616.8		451699.8		3911.5		829.2	
1928	232271.6		572640.8		10485.5		7097.8	
1929	134152.4	100	506770.9	100	7506.4	100	5294.3	100
1930	259183.2	193	612160.9	120.8	4560.2	60.8	1371.5	25.9
1931	138401.1	103.2	217436.8	42.9	3116.1	41.5	−809.1	
1932	−31332.2		−28996.5		−637.4		−2801.8	
1933	181572.4	135.3	380252.1	75	−2001.8		−2605.5	
1934	73519.2	54.8	208907.3	41.2	2773.6	36.9	242.5	4.6
1935	−59175.1	54.8	208907.3	41.2	257	3.4	−2063.3	
1936	133903.3	99.8	69370.7	13.7	935.9	12.5	−1471.3	
1937	238994.4	178.2	229418.1	45.3	9773.5	130.2	3886.4	73.4
1938	82123.3	61.2	21867	4.3	6425	85.6	1072.7	20.3
1939	155188.5	115.7	97914.5	19.3	11980.1	159.6	185.5	116.8
1940	19420.9	14.6	31595.6	6.2	−4470		−2593.8	

	Textile mill products				Apparel and other textile products			
	Equipment		Plant		Equipment		Plant	
	N	1929-P	N	1929-P	N	1929-P	N	1929-P
1927	117709.9		−15381.9		13700		7959.4	
1928	57677.1		−51667.8		12222.1		7644.9	
1929	−49354.1	100	−117019.7	100	16581.3	100	18340.3	100
1930	−70125.7		−144935.6		6835.6	41.2	1379.4	7.5
1931	−39086.2		−135622.4		−84.6		−8573.9	
1932	−110023.6		−173711.3		4919.5	29.7	−7718.7	
1933	−80551.5		−133067.3		−484.6		−5802.4	
1934	−102605.4		−144346.2		18609.2	112.2	10444.3	56.9
1935	−48356.9		−145154.8		37712.8	227.4	9692	52.8
1936	−68565.7		−144070.4		23170.2	139.7	5466.7	29.8
1937	−89767.2		−142522.2		5413.1	32.6	−1507.5	
1938	−53229.3		−137773.9		−1529.3		−7121.2	
1939	6420.8		−116795		18971.5	114.4	4734.6	25.8
1940	−123784.8		−168369.6		19246.2	116.1	9540.1	52

	Lumber and wood products				Paper and allied products			
	Equipment		Plant		Equipment		Plant	
	N	1929-P	N	1929-P	N	1929-P	N	1929-P
1927	74662.4		14681.3		94521.2		16246.5	
1928	72990.3		34698.4		179830		97917.4	
1929	78484.3	100	67891.1	100	208291.8	100	150493.7	100
1930	−26855.2		−91817.9		33518.1	16.1	−24690.9	
1931	−46561.5		−126471.4		−31012.4		−73918.8	
1932	−57266.6		−138806.5		28233	13.6	−59071.3	
1933	−54575.3		−121650.4		−35947.4		066938	
1934	−45355.1		−116175.4		−2667.3		−44714	
1935	−43818.8		−130061.1		−15020.8		−62958.2	
1936	−7729.2		−108283.9		7121.7	3.4	−50128.3	
1937	−45541.3		−122850.9		57005.1	27.4	−14659.4	
1938	−41996.1		−126683.8		17813.3	8.6	−39875	
1939	−12024.1		−82258.8		61444.4	29.5	6867.5	4.6
1940	−48710.1		−115977.8		−28668.9		−32733.2	

	Printing and publishing				Chemicals and allied products			
	Equipment		Plant		Equipment		Plant	
	N	1929-P	N	1929-P	N	1929-P	N	1929-P
1927	471207.8		102896.5		14268.5		3423.1	
1928	525944.3		148801.2		16480.6		8169.9	
1929	822974.9	100	246471.4	100	54967.4	100	73385.8	100
1930	338179.5	41.1	−20790.4		25359.6	46.1	19363.6	26.4
1931	94043.9	11.4	−102565.9		82072.1	149.3	49237.6	67.1
1932	−109302.2		−142982.9		33402.2	60.8	−3880.6	
1933	−121834.7		−135004.2		16696	30.4	18032.7	24.6
1934	−261615.5		−132434.4		13421.7	24.4	−2778	
1935	−218517.9		−136263.9		37865.8	68.9	−3900.3	
1936	−47418.7		−94736.6		130964.1	238.3	36321.1	49.5
1937					203314.7	369.9	115773.6	157.8
1938	−237541.7		−89652.8		140983	265.5	58262.8	79.4
1939	−306269.7		−66820.4		220423.9	401	122059.8	166.3
1940	93800.2	11.4	107521.1	43.6	299095.4	544.1	319674.4	435.6

	Leather and leather products				Stone, clay, and glass products			
	Equipment		Plant		Equipment		Plant	
	N	1929-P	N	1929-P	N	1929-P	N	1929-P
1927	23224.2		10116.9		65215.6		48867.7	
1928	14046		2806.9		108793.6		119342.3	
1929	45762.7	100	46420.1	100	23874.4	100	8833.4	100
1930	4126.7	9	−6961.6		36985.5	154.9	32089.1	363.3
1931	−4633.7		−16359.2		17345.3	72.7	−26915.4	
1932	1702.9	3.7	−14682.4		−30076		−63673.5	
1933	18849	41.2	6446.5	13.9	−10066.7		−38120.8	
1934	13352.4	29.2	503.6	1.1	−13688.4		−40525.4	
1935	9524	20.8	−9700.7		−9781.9		−50254.1	
1936	1905.4	4.2	−11095.5		69755.8	292.2	372042.1	
1937	8690	19	−4202.1		202998.6	850.3	119238.6	1349.9
1938	−1288.6		−11390.8		100954.5	422.9	18348.9	207.7
1939	1637.8	3.6	−7441.5		73126.2	306.3	43753.1	495.3
1940	15620.7	34.1	4264.2	9.2	24795	103.9	26697.8	302.2

	Petroleum and coal products				Rubber and miscellaneous plastics products			
	Equipment		Plant		Equipment		Plant	
	N	1929-P	N	1929-P	N	1929-P	N	1929-P
1927	47666.4		89823.6		34552		9131.7	
1928	87640.5		474209.4		55743.4		25999.3	
1929	82150.5	100	574623.1	100	70142.2	100	53100	100
1930	19102.6	23.3	−63137.7		22651.3	32.3	6909.8	13
1931	23449.3	28.5	−166914.1		11171.1	15.9	−8741.4	
1932	−6454.8		−335116.2		−10573.2		−12306.9	
1933	28179.1	34.3	−34213.9		−11396.4		−17949.5	
1934	−29672.3		−350180.1		−1178.8		−11446.3	
1935	24408.3	29.7	−214639.1		8951.9	12.8	−11390.4	
1936	76873.3	93.6	−107.1		−4964.9		−13999.3	
1937	108364	131.9	27434547.4		15559	22.2	−1932.4	
1938	41181.9	50.1	−85668.2		10387.3	14.8	−9056.5	
1939	17419.3	21.2	−82813		51934.3	74	−1985.1	
1940					4738	6.8	−8760.8	

	Primary metal industries				Fabricated metal products			
	Equipment		Plant		Equipment		Plant	
	N	1929-P	N	1929-P	N	1929-P	N	1929-P
1927	872647.6		642376		90344.6		46721.4	
1928	635721.9		378683.7		84725.5		48445.7	
1929	598503.4	100	605360.1	100	100698.7	100	98528.7	100
1930	765135.5	127.8	630258.7	104.1	41161.6	40.9	6886.57	
1931	356914.1	59.6	−284439.9		4984.4	4.9	−41923.7	
1932	31894	5.3	−671721.5		−19602.1		−59648.2	
1933	−277588.6		−704737.8		−21141.9		−10727.3	
1934	457738.2	6.4	−200870.7		−28864.5		−51197	
1935	429249.4	71.7	−345831.6		−20017.6		−52382.7	
1936	240547.5	40.2	−360142.1		26568.3	26.4	−26648.6	
1937	231053	38.6	−163468.8		18792.6	18.7	−18607.1	
1938	−216509.2		−601633.9		25503	25.3	−20464.6	
1939	−438665.5		−656079.8		100921.8	100.2	−1411.6	
1940	−238478.5		−699677.7		200453.5	199.1	128613.8	130.5

	Nonelectrical machinery				Transportation equipment			
	Equipment		Plant		Equipment		Plant	
	N	1929-P	N	1929-P	N	1929-P	N	1929-P
1927	77303.1		35516.2		199686.3		154724.6	
1928	70799.4		35110.5		222768.7		211835.5	
1929	89462	100	79641.8	100	207832	100	269449.3	100
1930	37787.4	422.4	9242.4	11.6	23862.4	11.5	−51134.9	
1931	−1306		−34169.7		−11878.9		−113375.7	
1932	−25106.2		−47936.2		−36380.4		−14302.1	
1933	−7571.5		−17912.1		−82285.9		−149341.6	
1934	−38416.3		−48221.2		−34506.8		−68690.9	
1935	7546	8.4	−24283.9		−61157.5		−144544.3	
1936	65498.7	73.2	15385.5	19.3	32300.9	15.5	−74093.8	
1937	86677.2	96.9	53316.4	66.9	72202.3	34.7	−42759.8	
1938	52296.8	58.5	11856.1	14.9	16709.5	8	−96182.5	
1939	133186.3	148.9	28477.9	35.8	110660.7	53.2	−50921.8	
1940	85790.8	95.9	54774.3	68.8	535924	257.9	434472.9	161.2

A simple accelerator model of investment in the American economy, 1900–50

In order to test for a statistically significant shift in the capital-output ratio and therefore in the accelerator during the interwar years, a simple accelerator model was estimated using annual observations for 1900 to 1950. War years were excluded. The model was derived from the stock adjustment equation in Michael K. Evans, *Macroeconomic Activity*. Data are taken from John W. Kendrick, *Productivity Trends in the United States*. The test was run as follows: Let I_t = gross investment in time t. Then

$$I_t(\text{net}) = \mu(K_t^* - K_{t-1})$$

where K_t^* = desired capital stock. If $K_t^* = \alpha Y_t$, where Y_t = output at time t, then

$$I_t(\text{net}) = \alpha\mu Y_t - \mu K_{t-1}$$

Let δ = rate of depreciation. Gross investment at time t then will be

$$I_t = \alpha\mu Y_t - (\mu - \delta)K_{t-1}$$

The accelerator may be expressed as

$$I_t = \beta_1 Y_t - \beta_2 K_{t-1}$$

Test model:

$$I_t = \alpha_1 + \beta_1(Y_t) + X\beta_2(Y_t) + X\beta_3(K_{t-1}) + \epsilon_{t-1}$$

$$t = 1900–1950$$
$$X = 1; \{1929–1939\}$$
$$\quad 0; \{1900–1913, 1919–1928, 1946–1949\}$$

Ordinary least-squares results:

	Parameter estimate	t ratios
α_1	302.35	0.652
β_1	0.128	4.54[a]
$X\beta_2$	−0.0094	−1.47[b]
β_3	−0.03	−0.683

Notes: $R^2 = 0.46$; Durbin-Watson statistic = 2.15; estimate of serial correlation = −0.09; $\hat{\beta}_1 + X\hat{\beta}_2 = 0.119 \Rightarrow \hat{\beta}_1 > \hat{\beta}_1 + \hat{\beta}_2$; estimated standard error of $(\hat{\beta}_1 + \hat{\beta}_2) = 0.04$; t ratio $= 0.119/0.04 = 2.98$.

a. Significant.   b. Significant, one-tail test.

These regression results show a significantly smaller capital-output ratio during the interwar years. This implies that the accelerator mechanism was similarly dampened. Note that $\beta_1 + X\beta_2$ is the value of the capital-output ratio during 1929–39 (i.e., when $X = 1$). In the other years of the sample, β_1 is the value of the ratio (i.e., when $X = 0$), a value greater than that in the depression years.

4. Technical change during the interwar years

> Be not the first by whom the new are tried,
> Nor yet the last to lay the old aside.
> – Alexander Pope

For "Schumpeterian pessimists" such as Hansen, Kalecki, and Weintraub, a lack of technical innovation explains the length of the depression of the 1930s. More recent scholarship argues that technical developments provided the only means of "escape from depression."[1] Lacking in much of this literature, however, is an explicit consideration of how and why technical innovations succeeded or failed. Moreover, little attempt has been made to assess the macroeconomic implications of microeconomic evidence on technical change in the United States during the interwar years. Studies of the depression in other nations provide a somewhat more systematic consideration of the role of technical change.[2]

1 See the Introduction to this book and Gerhard Mensch, *Stalemate in Technology: Innovations Overcome the Depression* (Cambridge, Mass.: Ballinger, 1979). Also see the extremely interesting piece by C. D. Blachly, "Some Technological Changes for the Consideration of Planners," *Plan Age*, 1 (May, 1935), 13, in which it is argued that the problem for the American economy during the thirties was not a lack of technical change but rather a scarcity of "immense aggregates of capital" needed to implement new processes of production. And cf. E. Fano, "Instability, Increasing Productivity and Unemployment in the Great Depression" (unpublished paper, May, 1985, Dipartimento di Economia Politica, University of Rome I, "La Sapienza").

2 See Svennilson, *Growth and Stagnation in the European Economy*; Safarian, *The Canadian Economy in the Great Depression*; and Erik Dahmén, *Entrepreneurial Activity and the Development of Swedish Industry*. Also see Derek H. Aldcroft, *From Versailles to Wall Street: 1919–1929* (London: Allen Lane, 1977). Reflecting on technical change during the interwar years, Aldcroft writes, on p. 301: "Thus in Canada, for example, the emphasis shifted away from wheat and railways towards newsprint, metals, electric power and developments related to the spread of the motor car. Rapid growth in these and the service industries gave a significant boost to investment and determined to a significant degree the nature of the development after 1929. . . . The most advanced stage was of course reached in the United States where the boom of the 1920s was based on the products of a high-income society, motor cars, other consumer

As Chapter 2 demonstrated, there were wide disparities in investment and output growth in U.S. manufacturing industries during the Great Depression. Certain industries, such as petroleum refining and tobacco manufactures, recovered quickly after the trough of 1932 and even managed to expand in net terms before 1940. Others, such as lumber products, remained virtually stagnant until war orders came from Europe in 1939.

The industries least subject to large decreases in revenues and therefore least prone to terminate net investment expenditures were those making food products and consumer nondurables such as tobacco and petroleum distillates. The relative good fortune of these sectors depended on active innovation in technique, product characteristics, and mechanisms of distribution, innovation that reinforced the latent strength of demand in these industries. The more stagnant industries prone to reduce net investment expenditures were those committed to the production of durable goods whose markets were shrinking. Within these sectors, only limited efforts were made to innovate in product characteristics or distribution methods, though process innovation (alteration in production techniques and productivity through mechanization and labor stretch-outs) was widespread. This disparity seems to have been due less to financial constraints imposed by poor sales than to characteristics of durable goods that made them less amenable to product innovation. Larger commitments were made to research and development, and higher rates of technical change occurred in industries producing nondurables and services. There were some exceptions, but overall it appears that innovations were concentrated outside the sectors producing capital goods.

Throughout the 1930s, the industries most active in technical change were those best able to influence demand for their product through sales efforts and the creation of new products or new uses for existing products. The ability to manipulate demand "endogenously" derived from the nature of the product in question and the technique of its production. By contrast, in industries where sales depended almost entirely on general business conditions, especially those in their customers' markets, a revival in activity could not be secured by their own strategies. Their economic fortunes depended entirely on recovery initiated in other sectors of the economy. Therein lay a paradox: To the

durables, residential building and industries involving highly complex technologies such as chemicals."

extent that these industries could not help to initiate a general resurgence in economic activity, their own prospects for recovery were correspondingly reduced.

I   Technical change in interwar American industries

Widespread innovative activity formed part of the response of American manufacturing firms to the Great Depression. This suggests that the relative failure of an industry after the crash was not solely due to a lack of ideas or of technical dynamism. On the contrary, technical change was a major component of the interwar history of American industry. But such innovative activity was a necessary, not sufficient, condition for economic recovery during the 1930s.

Food products

At the onset of the Great Depression, several technical improvements in food processing came on line. The handling of inputs, estimated in 1930 to be 30% of total labor cost in the industry, was made more efficient by the introduction of hydraulic dumpsters and hydroconveying. The use of pallets and forklifts became widespread. In 1935, flash pasteurization of fruit juices was initiated, signifying the industry-wide transition from batch to continuous processing. Two years earlier, continuous refinement of cooking oils had emerged. By mid-decade, continuous processes were used in the deaeration of ice cream, the steam deodorization of oils and fats, and the starch-settling of prepackaged potatoes. Bulk selling of bread, crackers, and cookies gave way to family-size packaging that encouraged investment in continuous ovens, mechanical slicers, and more sophisticated wrapping equipment.[3]

Improvements in the nation's transportation network and facilities extended the market for food products in depressed times. As the movement of the industry's inputs and outputs became more efficient, costs and food prices fell. Diesel trucking and refrigerated trailers and boxcars (as well as gondola and stock cars) were more available in the thirties, as were more sophisticated mechanisms of traffic control for

3 See U.S. Department of Agriculture, *Technology in Food Marketing*, 36–40; and Hampe and Wittenberg, *The Lifeline of America*, 193–4. From 1927 to 1938 the total number of research personnel in the industry rose 255.1% (compared with a 133.3% increase for manufacturing as a whole). See Perazich and Field, *Industrial Research and Changing Technology*, 19.

Table 4-1. *Data on soft drink production, 1923–40*

Year	Number of plants	Value of production[a]	Total cases	Million bottles	Consumption per capita (bottles)
1923	6,818	153,729,867	195,331,227	4,688	41.1
1925	7,326	167,652,098	213,039,079	5,113	44.1
1927	7,630	185,633,446	235,923,072	5,662	47.6
1928	7,800	199,409,372	253,475,746	6,083	50.5
1929	7,920	214,322,238	272,428,486	6,538	53.1
1930	7,646	207,815,353	252,570,921	6,062	49.0
1931	7,592	172,574,269	197,784,584	4,747	38.3
1932	7,537	120,671,139	141,020,384	3,385	27.1
1933	6,728	144,815,583	173,120,843	4,155	33.1
1934	6,460	138,192,088	168,116,896	4,035	31.9
1935	6,092	159,939,553	196,859,084	4,725	37.1
1936	6,035	229,768,450	293,221,605	7,037	54.9
1937	6,056	278,616,036	362,796,882	8,707	67.5
1938	6,121	311,713,267	411,774,461	9,883	75.4
1939	6,155	361,690,917	482,995,676	11,592	88.6
1940	6,118	411,699,200	550,400,000	13,210	100.1

[a]Data in historical dollars.
Source: J. J. Riley, *A History of the American Soft Drink Industry*, 275.

the nation's railway network. In the ten-year period preceding 1929, an additional 3.5 million trucks went into service, with improvements in hydraulic mechanisms for loading and in tankers for the shipment of grains and liquid products. Trucks increased their share of the country's freight ton-miles from just under 1% in 1920 to 4.1% in 1930 and on to 10% by 1940. The greater speed and versatility of trucking helped to further the efficient marketing of food products. Spurred by the relief employment efforts of the Civil Works Administration, the federal highway system increased from approximately 185,000 miles in 1926 to 233,000 miles in 1939.[4] Such infrastructural developments mitigated the impact of the Great Depression on this sector.

For the nonalcoholic beverage branch of the industry, the evidence in Table 4-1 indicates that after a fall of 50% in production between 1929 and 1932, dramatic growth took place during the 1930s. Low prices and the popularity of soft drinks were major factors in this

4 From Hampe and Wittenberg, *The Lifeline of America*, 222–38; and U.S. Department of Commerce, *Historical Statistics of the United States*, part 2, series Q64–68, p. 711. The figures on federal highway mileage include resurfacing and multilane improvement projects.

performance. Of even greater importance, however, were improvements in product image achieved by (1) the adoption of an industry-wide sanitation code in 1929 and (2) the 1934 revision of the Food and Drug Act that established standards for bottled carbonated beverages and placed them "in a firm position as an important part of the nation's diet."[5] There were also important innovations in processing, products, and delivery systems during the first half of the century.

From 1900 to 1905, mechanical improvements were made in carbonating and bottle-cleaning equipment. Shortly thereafter, semiautomatic fillers were introduced, along with labeling machines for the new machine-made bottles first marketed by the Owens Company. By 1920, hand feeds for filling machines were replaced by conveyors, and five years later the automatic vending of soft drinks appeared for the first time. In the thirties, stainless-steel tanks and pipelines were introduced to improve product quality, along with continuing innovation in carbonaters, filling machines, and automated temperature control.[6]

During the Great Depression, several new products were marketed, including four new varieties of root beer and seven of chocolate drink alone. Ginger ale had entered the American market in 1922, and seven types of grape drink were introduced in the same year. At the time of the crash, such brands as Dr. Pepper and Seven-Up were only one or two years old. Royal Crown Cola emerged in 1935, and in 1936 a large line of orange drinks made their way onto the market as improvements in pulp reduction overcame problems of spoilage and filling-equipment breakdowns.[7]

Although the industry was hurt somewhat by the 1933 modification of the Volstead Act, which allowed the sale of 3.2% beer, innovations in distribution and some tough-minded competition during the thirties helped ensure expansion. In the early 1900s, steel six-packs were developed, but for obvious reasons met with little success. The Coca-Cola Company pioneered the use of reusable paperboard six-packs in 1923. These did not displace home shipping crates until 1929, but 2 million

5 From J. J. Riley, *Organization in the Soft Drink Industry: A History of the American Bottlers of Carbonated Beverages* (Washington, D.C.: American Bottlers of Carbonated Beverages, 1946), 133, 183–4. The alcoholic beverages industry must be excluded because of the statistical distortions created by Prohibition.

6 See John J. Riley, *A History of the American Soft Drink Industry: Bottled Carbonated Beverages, 1807–1957* (Washington, D.C.: American Bottlers of Carbonated Beverages, 1958), 259–68.

7 See Riley, *A History of the American Soft Drink Industry*, 139, 143–6, 267.

six-pack cartons were in use by 1932. The number increased to 70 million by 1939. A further stimulus to the marketing of beverages was provided by the development in 1937 of an automatic applied color-label bottle machine (by the Owens-Illinois Company), as well as by distinctive proprietary bottle design itself. There were also several improvements made in refrigerated storage and vending technology in the mid-twenties. Most notable was the introduction of the dry-cooler, which was found to have excellent sanitary features.[8]

Competition in the industry became fairly keen after the Pepsi Corporation issued a twelve-ounce bottle at the same price as the standard eight-ounce container in 1934. Continuing its farsighted conduct four years later, Pepsi launched a skywriting and radio advertisement campaign that was one of the most successful campaigns in the history of the industry. Coca-Cola had in some respects set the tone for such aggressive sales efforts with its 1929 slogan: "The Pause That Refreshes." A requirement in the industry code of the National Recovery Administration (N.R.A.) that deposits be taken on bottles helped to establish a national container deposit system for the first time, thereby reducing bottling costs.[9]

That the food industry suffered little during the Great Depression was the result of several influences, some secular, others contemporary, and a few simply fortuitous. But the overwhelming majority of these forces were long-term ones dating back a half century or more. Technological developments and innovations in products allowed for dynamic behavior that contrasted sharply with the experience of other sectors. These were also the foundation of competitive developments in distribution that stabilized and expanded the industry's market. Moreover, trends in technical development, product innovation, and distribution provided a stimulus for dynamic investment behavior. It was precisely because of the nature of this sector's products – that they were non-durable and easily susceptible to differentiation and image creation – that these opportunities for stability and growth were present.

Petroleum and chemicals

The relative success of the petroleum and chemicals industries was a function of several forces, both secular and short-term. Demand pat-

8 See Riley, *A History of the American Soft Drink Industry*, 141, 144–5, 147.
9 See Riley, *A History of the American Soft Drink Industry*, 143, 147–8, 265; and Riley, *Organization in the Soft Drink Industry*, 140.

terns were altered by cyclical impacts dating from 1929 that increased the consumption of leisure goods and thereby stimulated the petroleum markets. But primary attention must be given to long-term developments in products, technology, and sales networks in order to understand these industries' atypical performance in the 1930s. As in food products, the character of the products and technology of these sectors enabled rapid advances through the depression years.

Developments dating from World War I in other industries and in the nation's infrastructure created powerful derived demands for chemical and petroleum products, and these industries quickly recovered from the crash. The developments were part of the advance in consumer product and service-oriented industries characteristic of American economic development at this stage in its history. Chemicals and petroleum products were situated at an advantageous spot in that matrix of secular growth. In addition, a large potential for growth in the thirties was exploited by these two sectors precisely because of their confidence in their long-term prospects for accumulation.[10] Impressive efforts in marketing, technical change, product innovation, and price rivalry were undertaken at a time when other industries were awaiting some external stimulus to overcome their pessimistic assessment of the future.

Tobacco products

Technical change was a major component of the tobacco industry's excellent performance in the thirties. Consistent advances in output per person-hour were achieved, as shown in Table 4-2. An average of nearly twenty-three patents per year was awarded in the industry from 1929 to 1939.[11] There were improvements made in the mechanization of stemming and cleaning; cigarette rolling (on the Bonsack machine, invented in 1884) was speeded up by the introduction of ball bearings in 1931. Movement of materials was made more efficient by the use of conveyors. Improvements in the packaging and, thereby, the quality of

10 Such confidence characterized primarily the larger firms in these sectors. Smaller refiners, for example, had to slow their rates of technical change in the thirties owing to the financial pressures created by the downturn. See George B. Galloway et al., *Industrial Planning Under Codes* (New York: Harper & Bros., 1935), 191.

11 This excludes patents on pipes or other smoking equipment. See U.S. Patent Office, *Index of Patents* (Washington, D.C.: U.S. Government Printing Office, 1929–40). Because patents are listed in the *Index* alphabetically, this average may be biased downward.

Table 4-2. *Index of output per person-hour, tobacco products, 1929–40 (1947 = 100)*

Year	Index
1929	52.5
1930	52.7
1931	58.5
1932	56.1
1933	61.3
1934	60.3
1935	69.4
1936	75.0
1937	73.1
1938	76.1
1939	80.0
1940	80.8

Source: U.S. Department of Commerce, *Historical Statistics of the United States,* part 2, series W30–54, pp. 950–1.

cigarettes were achieved in 1930 when the Reynolds Company began to use new wrapping products introduced by DuPont.[12]

Glass industry

Technical developments in glass manufacture proceeded quickly after 1890. By the end of the twenties the hand-blowing of sheet glass had been completely displaced by cylinder and sheet machines. Michael J. Owens succeeded in fully mechanizing the production of bottles at the end of World War I. By 1929, 1,109 of his machines were in use. Improvements in kilns, shop tools, and feed mechanisms punctuated the development of plate glass factories in this period. Automatic light bulb production was perfected in 1916 (with 95% of such output automated by 1927), along with the machine production of window sheet and glass tubing. As the data in Table 4-3 show, the mechanized sheet-drawing of windows was universal by the mid-1930s. Electrification

12 See Robert, *The Story of Tobacco in America,* 243; and Nicholls, *Price Policies in the Cigarette Industry,* 83. Robert comments, on p. 243: "The most important general changes in factory management consisted of the expanding use of labor-saving machinery and the continual adoption of simplified processes."

Table 4-3. *Approximate percentages of total amount of window glass produced in the United States by various manufacturing processes for specified years*

Year	Hand cylinder process (%)	Machine cylinder process (%)	Sheet drawing process (%)
1900	100	0	0
1904	95	5	0
1916	40	60	0
1919	25	65	10
1923	10	52	38
1926	2	59	39
1929	0	20	80
1932	0	5	95
1935	0	0	100

Source: Warren C. Scoville, *Revolution in Glass-making*, 194.

provided an important linkage in this technical advance. All improvements enhanced productivity and enabled the industry to exploit fully the market opportunities that secular trends in other markets provided.[13]

The building materials sector, of which glass producers were a part, made impressive commitments to research and development throughout the depression. Research personnel in the industry increased 166.4% from 1927 to 1938. Thirteen primary product additions were made in the same period, along with twenty-four secondary additions.[14]

Textiles

By the early 1920s, textile manufacturers, sensing the growing weakness in their major markets, introduced methods of scientific management.

13 See Davis, *The Development of the American Glass Industry*, 174, 189, 211, 214, 238, 250-7; and Scoville, *Revolution in Glass-making*, 131, 156-7, 165-9, 188, and ch. VII. Also see Thomas P. Hughes, *Networks of Power: Electrification in Western Society, 1880-1930* (Baltimore: Johns Hopkins University Press, 1983).

14 See Gort, *Diversification and Integration in American Industry*, 42-3; and Perazich and Field, *Industrial Research and Changing Technology*, 19.

Two major goals were pursued: to increase output per worker by speedup and automation, and to improve the quality and uniformity of yarn, lowering breakage rates and thereby increasing production speeds. Better yarns also allowed for more opportunities to mechanize and overcome bottlenecks in manufacture.[15]

Throughout the 1930s there were dramatic increases in output per worker due largely to mechanization and stretch-outs – an increase in the number of machines tended by each worker. Cotton consumption per spindle-hour rose 20% in the interwar period; average annual hours of spindle operation rose from 2,945 to 4,183 between 1923 and 1937. Output per worker rose 82.4% from 1919 to 1940.[16] Such a classic response to a downturn in profits merely intensified the difficulties facing the industry as a whole. What was required was not an increase in output or even productivity but rather, as the more successful branches of the industry proved, a change in product mix. The response of cotton textile firms is easy to understand, however, given that wages accounted for more than half of the value added. As Table 4-4 shows, this high labor cost component placed the producers in a unique situation relative to other manufacturing industries by the late thirties. Unfortunately, the incentives it created with regard to technical change were not necessarily in the producers' aggregate best interest.

Another indication of the efforts made in technical development in the textile industry during the Great Depression may be found in data on research and development personnel. From 1927 to 1938 the number of such employees in textile production rose 252.9%. In the worst depression years, 1930 to 1932, 2,605 patents for capital goods inventions were granted in that industry alone.[17] Yet despite this major innovative effort, it appears that some firms in the industry were well aware

15 See Stephen J. Kennedy, *Profits and Losses in Textiles: Cotton Textile Financing Since the War* (New York: Harper Bros., 1936), 162. The use of long-staple cotton would have improved productivity and hastened mechanization, but the cost was too high.

16 See Donald, *The Depression in Cotton Textiles, 1924 to 1940*, 5–6, 102, 117; and Backman and Gainsbrugh, *Economics of the Cotton Textile Industry*, 189. Even so, the textile industry in New England was burdened throughout the thirties with outdated equipment. In 1937 the average age of textile machinery in New England was fifty years, compared with five to ten years of age in the South and two years in Japan. See the special issue on "The Textile Industry in the United States of America," *Plan Age*, 3 (May-June, 1937).

17 See Perazich and Field, *Industrial Research and Changing Technology*, 19; and Jacob Schmookler, *Invention and Economic Growth* (Cambridge, Mass.: Harvard University Press, 1966), 153.

Table 4-4. *Wages as percentage of value added for manufacturing, 1939*

Sector	Wage (%)
Cotton manufacturing	51.1
Transportation equipment, except automobiles	50.7
Leather products	50.4
Lumber products	50.2
Textile mills and other fibers	49.9
Automobiles	48.9
Apparel	47.4
Iron and steel	44.4
Furniture	43.8
Rubber products	39.7
Nonelectrical machinery	38.0
Miscellaneous manufacturing	37.2
Nonferrous metals	36.3
Stone, clay, and glass products	36.2
Paper products	33.6
Electrical machinery	35.6
Printing	27.9
Petroleum and coal	25.7
Food products	25.7
Tobacco products	19.6
Chemicals	19.0

Source: Jules Backman and M. R. Gainsbrugh, *Economics of the Cotton Textile Industry*, 99–100 [from *Census of Manufactures*, (1939)].

that continued prosperity lay in diversification, not in older markets. A sample of four major textile firms shows that from 1929 to 1939, only two product lines were added within the textiles classification, while sixteen new lines were undertaken in other industries.[18]

Iron and steel

Although iron and steel showed one of the lowest percentage increases in research and development personnel for the 1930s (189.4% versus 538.7% for petroleum and 255.1% for food products, for example),

18 See Gort, *Diversification and Integration in American Industry*, 42–3. On pp. 46–7, Gort also shows that after World War II the rate of non-primary-product additions in textiles still exceeded that for new primary products, despite the introduction of new synthetic fibers.

the index of output per person-hour in steel production rose steadily from 1920 to 1940. In addition, forty-one product additions were made in the primary metal industries from 1929 to 1939, though only ten were made by fabricated metal producers in the same period.[19]

Along with improvements in materials handling and continuous processing, the development of the by-product coke oven and the means to utilize waste heat and gases in blast furnaces was of major technical importance in the interwar period. Integration and rationalization of production methods meant that where the operation of four fifty-ton blast furnaces required 142 workers before World War I, 58 employees sufficed by 1920. Electrification, especially in rolling mills, had a similarly dramatic effect, enabling 20 persons to produce the same tonnage in eight hours as 360 people using hand-mill techniques.[20]

During the depression, the pace of innovation fell, with the major exception of the electrification of steel manufacture. Innovative effort, in line with the qualitative changes in the consumption of iron and steel products discussed in Chapter 2, focused on product development. The normal incentives to develop labor-saving technology generated in a depression were blunted by the N.R.A. industry codes, which sought to bolster employment and raise operating rates.[21]

Product development in the interwar period was oriented toward meeting the special needs of the electric power sector (for silicon steel) and the automakers (for chromium and vanadium and other hard alloys). But the major focus came to be the creation of new sheet and plate steels for auto bodies, appliances, and steel containers. The efforts were most intense in tinning. Indeed, a historian of the tin division of the industry argues that "[t]in plate was the aristocrat of the steel

19 See Perazich and Field, *Industrial Research and Changing Technology*, 19; U.S. Department of Commerce, *Historical Statistics of the United States*, part 2, series W30–54, p. 951; Gort, *Diversification and Integration in American Industry*, 42–3; and Folke W. Sundblad, *The American Steel Industry: At the Cross-Roads of Progress and Reaction* (Philadelphia: Dorrance, 1938), 105. Sundblad points out that few steel companies had engineers or scientists in major management positions and that scrap steel and iron were normally shipped abroad rather than recycled.

20 See Quincy Bent, *75 Years of Steel* (n.p.: The Newcomen Society, 1939), 22; and E. D. McCallum, *The Iron and Steel Industry in the United States: A Study in Industrial Organization*, 220–1.

21 See Daugherty et al., *The Economics of the Iron and Steel Industry*, 330, 895–8; and Hogan, *Economic History of the Iron and Steel Industry in the United States*, vol. 3, parts 4–5, 1344. The consumption of electricity by the steel industry rose from 54 to 82 billion kilowatt-hours during the 1930s.

industry. There was no other steel product produced in sizable volume on which so much research and development effort was lavished in recent times."[22]

Overall, the iron and steel industry, as with any durable producer's good sector, was hard hit in the thirties. But compounding this difficulty were secular transformations in the role of the traditionally large iron and steel markets. New markets in light rolled products and tin plate were the only avenues of escape from stagnation. Yet this meant little to large firms with enormous commitments in heavy product lines, and to the iron and steel workers whose prospects for employment were shrinking both extensively in the production of rails, heavy sheet, and structural shapes and intensively in the more mechanized tinning and rolling mills. Although World War II delayed the full impact of these changes in markets, the postwar era nevertheless offered the same problems – problems intensified by the emergence of foreign competition in the older standard product categories.

Automobiles

Commitments to research and development in automobiles were fairly impressive before the Great Depression, but from 1927 to 1938 the number of research personnel in the industry rose only 190.2%, a low rate compared with several other sectors. Process innovation was relatively weak, except for refinements during the 1920s producing larger engines, better lighting systems, and the like, but several firms did diversify their product lines. During the thirties, five times the number of primary product additions were made in nonprimary lines. General Motors moved into both diesel engine manufacture and aircraft engine production during the depression years, pioneering in the latter field. As early as World War I, General Motors had established the Frigidaire Corporation to produce refrigeration equipment, and the Ford Motor Company had invested in farm tractor assembly lines.[23]

The 1920s were important years in the technical development of the

22 From McKie, *Tin Cans and Tin Plate*, 40; and cf. Hogan, *Economic History of the Iron and Steel Industry in the United States*, vol. 2, part 3, 714.

23 See Perazich and Field, *Industrial Research and Changing Technology*, 19; Gort, *Diversification and Integration in American Industry*, 42–3; John B. Rae, *American Automobile Manufacturers: The First Forty Years* (New York: Chilton, 1959), 154, 198; and John B. Rae, *The American Automobile: A Brief History* (Chicago: University of Chicago Press, 1965), 107–8, 118–19.

automobile industry. Fred and Charles Fisher spearheaded the development of one-stamp metal bodies with enclosed cabs. New paints and lacquer finishes were introduced along with safety plate glass developed by Ford. The electric starter motor was perfected, which made motoring accessible to a larger segment of the population. Mechanical windshield wipers and foot-controlled headlamp dimmers also became standard equipment. Chrysler introduced rubber engine mounts to reduce noise and vibration, as well as crank-type window lifts. The engine-driven fuel pump and Cadillac's synchromesh transmission were also developed before the crash. Technical standardization in the industry progressed.[24]

Innovation continued in the 1930s, although not at the same rate. The saleability of cars increased with alterations in external characteristics and improvements in passenger comfort. Automatic transmissions, power steering, and brake controls were developed, along with radios and heaters. Oldsmobile created an automatic choke in 1932, and new ventilation systems and shock absorbers were widely marketed in 1933 and 1934. In the worst year of the depression, 1932, Ford produced the first V-8 economy car by casting the engine block and crankcase as one unit. The thirties saw automobile producers avoid high-pressure selling of fairly primitive vehicles and move into more sophisticated marketing of cars produced with consumer amenities in mind.[25] This shift in marketing strategy, linked primarily with long-term developments, was reinforced by the cyclical concentration of purchasing power in the hands of more affluent consumers during the thirties.

The automobile industry presents a classic example of the characteristics that made certain sectors extremely sensitive to the downturn of 1929 and devoid of autonomous mechanisms powerful enough to generate recovery. The durability of the industry's product, which improved with innovation, made sales volatile in the face of income fluctuations. As a result, the prior emphasis on the production of simple standardized vehicles and competitive pricing strategies had to be aban-

---

24 See Smith, *Wheels Within Wheels*, 88, 108; C. B. Glasscock, *The Gasoline Age: The Story of the Men Who Made It* (New York: Bobbs-Merrill, 1937), 166 and ch. XV; Rae, *American Automobile Manufacturers*, 155; Pound, *The Turning Wheel*, 268–9; and G. V. Thompson, "Intercompany Technical Standardization in the Early American Automobile Industry," *Journal of Economic History*, 14 (Winter, 1954), 1–20.

25 See Pound, *The Turning Wheel*, 268–9, 427; and Rae, *The American Automobile*, 106, 116. Also see J. S. Peterson, "Auto Workers and their Work, 1900–1933," *Labor History*, 22 (Spring, 1981), 214.

Table 4-5. *Data on productivity*
for selected manufacturing sectors,
1914–27

Sector	Percentage increase in person-hour productivity
Rubber tires	292
Automobiles	178
Petroleum refining	82
Flour milling	59
Iron and steel	55
Cement	54
Leather tanning	41
Paper and pulp	40
Cane sugar refining	33
Slaughtering and meat packing	26
Boots and shoes	24

Source: John D. Gaffey, *The Productivity of Labor in the Rubber Tire Manufacturing Industry,* 81 [from U.S. Department of Labor, "Productivity of Labor in Eleven Manufacturing Industries," *Monthly Labor Review,* 30 (March, 1930), 501–17].

doned. Future revenue performance depended on design changes and the introduction of new commodity characteristics, many of which were irrelevant to the transportation function of a car. Such external qualities could be changed from one model year to the next, making the product less "durable" and thus less subject to market saturation. It is not accurate, therefore, to describe the motor vehicle industry of the 1930s as stagnant. It was in fact undergoing a transition from standard durable goods production to the manufacture of commodities frequently redesigned and made obsolete. In this respect the car industry could escape the fate of other producers whose output, by its nature, was less amenable to such alteration.

Rubber products

Although advances were made, the rubber industry's commitment to technical change faltered in the 1930s after several decades of intense activity. Table 4-5 shows that from 1914 to 1927 the rubber tire industry almost tripled its worker productivity, an extremely impressive performance relative to other industries. On average, until the Great

Table 4-6. Index of capital assets
(less depreciation) in tire manufacturing, 1925–35 (1925 = 100)

Fixed capital assets	1925	1929	1932	1935
Per tire	100	125	197	146
Per pound	100	120	165	108
Per worker	100	135	222	164
Per person-hour	100	134	305	225
Total assets	100	138	122	115

Source: John D. Gaffey, The Productivity of Labor
in the Rubber Tire Manufacturing Industry, 86.

Depression, the tire manufacturers showed 30% higher productivity per person-year than all other manufacturing in terms of both value added and value of output. In value added per person-hour, the productivity differential between this industry and total manufacturing was about 40%. Most of these productivity advances were linked with process innovations, notably the introduction of continuous processing and watchcase vulcanizers that streamlined one of the major bottlenecks in tire production. Conveyor belt systems in rubber product factories and new equipment that mechanized almost all facets of production dramatically increased the capabilities of the work force. The innovations also cut down waste, allowed for finer tolerances and more uniform product characteristics, and decreased spoilage arising from contamination with grease or dirt. By the 1930s, one worker could make ten rubber tires in the time it had taken to make one by hand methods of operation.[26] After 1932, advances in productivity in tire production lagged behind other industries. Data on capital assets presented in Table 4-6 show that the crash slowed the rate of technical change in the sector. As a result, the trend in labor productivity fell during the 1930s.[27]

26 See Gaffey, The Productivity of Labor in the Rubber Tire Manufacturing Industry, 78, 92–6, 101–2. Gaffey estimates that the installation of automatic stops on rubber cutting machines alone saved fifty-six person-hours per day. Also see Lief, Harvey Firestone, 201, 287; Lief, The Firestone Story, 171, 191, 194–5; Harvey S. Firestone, Men and Rubber: The Story of Business (New York: Doubleday, Page, 1926), 153; and Wolf and Wolf, Rubber, 366. It is interesting to note that as concentrated a sector as it was, the rubber industry could not capture all the economic gains of its technical progress.

27 See Gaffey, The Productivity of Labor in the Rubber Tire Manufacturing Indus-

The percentage increase in research and development personnel in the rubber industry from 1927 to 1938 was far less than that in other, more prosperous industries such as petroleum and food products. Yet once innovations were introduced in the industry by one or more firms, the remaining firms tended to imitate the new processes or products quickly. And important technical developments did take place, particularly the commercial introduction of synthetics such as chemigum and neoprene by DuPont and Goodyear in the early 1930s.[28]

Although the evidence shows a moderately high rate of non-primary-product additions in the industry during the thirties, such antidepression efforts tended to take place in only a few firms, notably Firestone. Firestone developed wholly new product lines during the depression, such as waterproof brake linings and spark plugs, farm tractor tires, and even stainless-steel beverage containers – an outgrowth of its operations in tire drum manufacture. Major innovations were made in distribution, providing the basis of its depression sales strategy. Firestone's advertising expenditures rose throughout the 1930s, and retail networks, which combined all facets of automobile and tire service, were subsidized. This marketing effort was quite different from those of Goodyear and other companies that relied exclusively on large wholesalers such as Sears and Montgomery Ward. Such arrangements gave Firestone better control over the quality and availability of its products. But unfortunately for the industry as a whole, these activities, aimed at generating recovery and continued accumulation in difficult times, were more the exception than the rule.[29]

Lumber and paper products

Neither forest products firms nor paper manufacturers made ambitious commitments to research and development during the 1930s. The number of research and development personnel in lumber and timber product firms rose 190.9% during the Great Depression; in paper and

try, 18, 69, 77, 87, 177–8; and W. Bowden, "Labor in Depression and Recovery, 1929 to 1937," *Monthly Labor Review*, 45 (November, 1937), 1045–81.

28 See Perazich and Field, *Industrial Research and Changing Technology*, 19; L. G. Reynolds, "Competition in the Rubber Tire Industry," *American Economic Review*, 28 (March, 1938), 463; Josephine Perry, *The Rubber Industry* (New York: Longmans, Green, 1946), 22; and David Dietz, *The Goodyear Research Laboratory* (Akron, Ohio: Goodyear Tire and Rubber Company, 1943), 45.

29 See Gort, *Diversification and Integration in American Industry*, 42–3; Lief, *Harvey Firestone*, 263; and Lief, *The Firestone Story*, 178–9, 195–7, 214–15.

allied products the figure was only 177.5%. Even so, the number of patents granted in paper and forest product manufacturing was quite high throughout the interwar period. But the bulk of the patented innovations were for new types of equipment rather than new products. The more dynamic segments of the industry, however, were in paper production, where the rate of new (primary) product addition was greater for the depression years.[30]

In forestry products, technical innovations were sporadic after World War I. Circular and band saws, the mainstays of the industry, had been developed in the last half of the nineteenth century. Schools of forestry emerged at the turn of the century (the first at Cornell University in 1898), although it was nearly fifty years before the industry ceased to be dominated by the " 'hairy-chested' school of foresters whose only measure of forest values [was] the board foot." In the 1930s, major efforts were made to develop new products in tree by-product lacquers and adhesives and in arboreal genetic research. In sawmills and lumber-yards, improvements in materials handling were secured by the intro-duction of the forklift, motor truck, tractor, and electricity.[31]

As previously discussed, paper manufacturing offered many oppor-tunities for technical change, and its record in this regard was more impressive than that of the foresters. In some cases this was fortuitous, as newspaper publishers, beset with poor circulation during the depres-sion, experimented with color printing, electrotyping, and rotary power presses, all of which placed special requirements on newsprint pro-ducers. Basic improvements, linked especially with the use of electric power, were made. But most productivity gains were due to locational shifts of plants to resource-rich areas, the forced exit of inefficient firms, and improvements in labor and management skill.[32]

Process innovation in paper production from 1920 to 1940 focused on increases in machine speeds, achievement of continuous processing, and broadening the number of timber species that could be utilized for pulping. Fourdrinier machine speeds doubled from 700 to 1,400 feet per minute in the 1920s and 1930s. Higher speeds required new tech-

---

30 See Perazich and Field, *Industrial Research and Changing Technology*, 19; Schmookler, *Invention and Economic Growth*, 153, 225; and Gort, *Diversifi-cation and Integration in American Industry*, 42–3.

31 See Pack, *Forestry*, 53, 57, 109; and Brown, *The American Lumber Industry*, 47, 55.

32 See Guthrie, *The Newsprint Paper Industry*, 8; and Cohen, *Technological Change in the North American Pulp and Paper Industry*, 10–1, 50–1.

niques of sheet formation, felting, and water removal. The new processes were made possible mainly by the use of electric power and automated instrumentation. The response of the electrical machinery sector was important in developing better gears, lubrication systems, and clutches. And aluminum machine construction became more common, the resulting weight reduction allowing for faster operation.[33]

Paper companies recognized the opportunities inherent in new product and resources development. Use of southern pine for pulpwood began in the late thirties. Further profitability was realized through improvements in the brightness, color variety, strength, and uniformity of paper products. These advances were essentially tied to the continuing improvement of the Fourdrinier machine. Moreover, chemical and machinery firms focused their innovative efforts to meet the special needs of paper producers. All of these developments were symptomatic of the shift during the 1930s "in the form of innovative effort. Instead of seeking technological changes that increased throughput, quality improving innovations came to the fore."[34] Paper manufacturers found in the Great Depression a strategy that greatly aided them in the postwar era: the sustained creation of new product lines by which the rate of accumulation could be maintained. For lumber and timber product producers, primarily dependent on producer and consumer durable markets, such a response to secular and short-run changes in demand was more difficult to undertake and long in coming.

II   Technical change and the problem of recovery

It is inappropriate to speak of economic stagnation in the interwar American economy. Rather, the 1930s brought a period of profound adjustment problems inherent in the shift from heavy production to nondurable goods and a services-oriented economy. Structural change in economic development is normally viewed as a policy issue that in theoretical terms may be ignored. Yet for the historian (and the theorist looking to history for empirical guidance and support) it is the very heart of the process of growth.

During the thirties themselves and for several preceding decades, all

33 See Cohen, *Technological Change in the North American Pulp and Paper Industry*, 51–8.
34 See Cohen, *Technological Change in the North American Pulp and Paper Industry*, 16, 54–8, 63–71, 82, 87.

manufacturing industries experienced moderate to high rates of technical change and product innovation. Improvements in techniques of
production were especially pronounced in the food, petroleum, chemical, and glass industries. Innovations in products were relatively more
important in the tobacco and automobile sectors. In some cases, most
notably petroleum and chemicals, process innovation and product development were intimately linked owing to the nature of the sector's
output – the use of new techniques often generated new commodities.

To some extent the impressive performance of these industries in
process and product innovation was due to characteristics of their
products and the general state of relevant scientific knowledge. But the
dynamic performance of these industries up to and through the 1930s,
despite the depressed market conditions that interfered with the incentives for innovation, had other roots as well. These involved the particular position of the dynamic sectors in the economy's input–output
matrix and the stage of long-term development achieved by the macroeconomy at the time of the stock market crash.

Steady growth in the food and kindred products industry throughout
the interwar period, based on new techniques and new products such
as canned and frozen foods, was primarily a function of the extension
of electrification making refrigeration possible, automotive transport,
and the decreasing percentage of the population engaged in domestic
activity. Such changes in the economy's infrastructure and labor force
participation rate had emerged at the turn of the century. In addition,
related developments in the glass and chemical industries made possible
the processing and packaging of new food products.

In petroleum refining and chemicals manufacturing, several secular
events made growth possible during the thirties. Primary among these
was the rise of the automobile. The development of various grades of
gasoline, lubricants, and antifreeze solutions was linked to innovations
in the auto industry and their special requirements. During the interwar
years, heating came to be based on oil rather than coal or wood; this
also bolstered the demand for petroleum products. The advances in
cracking technology and by-product retrieval must be situated in the
context of the long-term growth in these related markets. Associated
with the technical improvements of the period was the creation of new
product lines in pharmaceuticals and explosives.

From the end of World War I, the tobacco industry engaged in fairly
continuous product innovation and in systematic efforts to distribute its

product in an entirely new market – to women. The proliferation of brands and types of cigarettes, coupled with major sales efforts and attempts to achieve product differentiation, was dependent on and indeed hastened by changes in consumption habits tied to alterations in the role of women in the labor market and in the home.

The relatively superior performance of the building materials industry during the thirties was primarily due to the vigorous behavior in the production of glass products. This is not surprising given the derived demand from the food industry for packing materials. There was also a direct stimulus to glass production from the spread of electrification, which generated demand for an entirely new glass product, the light bulb. Another important linkage for this industry was the derived demand for bottles from the beverage producers, but this was due more to exogenous forces set in motion by the repeal of the Volstead Act than to secular mechanisms.

Stable or growing industries in the Great Depression exhibited several common characteristics. All the relatively successful sectors produced at least some consumer products. Most engaged in active product innovation throughout the interwar period. As argued in Chapter 1, the incentives and potential for such innovation tended to be greater in consumer than in producer products. All these industries exhibited steady rates of technical change and moderately to intensely aggressive marketing policies. During the depression decade itself, the demand for these industries' products was not severely curtailed. The competitive practices employed were clearly a factor, but of major importance was the small share of a total consumer budget that these industries' products individually occupied.

Firms producing food products, beverages, petroleum, and tobacco also found themselves positively affected by the transformation of consumer expenditure patterns set in motion by the crash of 1929 and the enormous unemployment and deflation left in its wake. The normal floor to consumption provided by the general decline in prices created by a slump did not take hold in a broad-based fashion because of the high unemployment that arose out of the crash. Relief recipients and workers on short time tended to concentrate their purchases in ways that benefited producers of cheap standardized nondurable items.[35]

35 By the mid-thirties, close to 77% of the families and unattached individuals in the American economy were earning less than $2,000 per year. A further 19% earned annual incomes between $2,000 and $5,000. The remainder earned

Cyclical mechanisms did, therefore, play a role in the differing industry responses to the Great Depression. But they were not more important in either a quantitative or a temporal sense than long-term trends that influenced sectoral performances before, during, and after the crash.

The active sectors were located in a particularly advantageous position to exploit long-term developments in the structure of the nation's economy and the composition of its output. Image differentiation, new products, and new methods of distribution were relatively easily introduced. As a consequence, the thirties were not a stagnant period for these industries. Indeed, to the extent that the long-term focus of capital accumulation in the United States shifted from the intensive development of existing markets to the extensive creation of new markets, these industries were the sole benefactors and beneficiaries of the process.

The hardest-hit sectors also shared common attributes. These industries faced limits to their recovery and expansion that were linked both to the characteristics of their output and to the position in the economy's input–output matrix that they occupied. In some cases such barriers to continued accumulation were exacerbated by the decline in disposable income generated by the 1929 collapse of financial markets. For producers of consumer durables and luxuries this was clearly the major issue. In other cases, such as wooden construction materials, woolen goods, and wrought-iron shapes, industries were directly confronted by a secular decline in the economic importance and role of their product. Still others were locked into producers' goods markets that by their nature admitted little chance for the changes in product characteristics, packaging, and advertising that had been used to such good effect by some of the consumer goods sectors.[36] This was the unfortunate position

from $5,000 to over $50,000. See U.S. Department of Commerce, *Historical Statistics of the United States*, part 1, series G269–282, p. 299.

36 Objections might be raised from a neoclassical perspective to the dichotomy drawn here between producers' and consumers' goods markets. Indeed, one could construct a utility function for a producer (analogous to that for a consumer) that might have as one of its arguments some extrinsic quality of a input such as color, packaging, service dependability, or finance terms. Yet in the final analysis it is the input's impact on the cost structure of the buyer that decisive. A steel ingot or a lathe is never sold because it comes packaged in wrapper of a given color. It is sold because of its low price relative to those of competitors. And although it may also be sold because of its greater dependability of delivery (or, in the case of the lathe, repair service), these attributes ultimately reduce to indices of cost for the buyer. Consumer goods, by contra

tion of industries such as iron and steel and rubber products.

Evidence on manufacturing industries demonstrates that the interwar period was not lacking in technical dynamism and aggressiveness. Important variations existed in the extent to which different sectors innovated in techniques and product lines. Overall, however, a Schumpeterian pessimism seems unwarranted. Indeed, many of the products and processes developed in the interwar period came to dominate the composition of American output in the postwar period. Lack of technical change cannot, therefore, be taken as the primary cause of the depression's length.

Rejection of the Schumpeterian thesis does not, however, imply an acceptance of the opposite argument, that innovations brought the economy out of the slump. The advent of war in Europe and Asia did. This fact suggests that regardless of the technical vigor of the interwar American economy, the essential ingredient for recovery was a sufficient increase in demand to allow new techniques and products to reach the stage of profitable production. A full consideration of the effective demand crisis of the 1930s is therefore the next task of this investigation.

have many characteristics that can be exploited in a successful sales effort. Thus, two identical cars may be more or less attractive to a buyer because of color, even though their costs and their intrinsic qualities as a means of locomotion are identical. Cf. F. Machlup, "Theories of the Firm: Marginalist, Behavioral, Managerial," *American Economic Review*, 57 (March, 1967), 1–33; and William J. Baumol, *Business Behavior, Value and Growth* (New York: Harcourt, Brace & World, 1967), chs. 5–6.

5. The effective demand problem of the interwar period. I: Cyclical and structural unemployment

> The outstanding faults of the economic society in which we live are its failure to provide for full employment and its arbitrary and inequitable distribution of wealth and incomes.
> – John Maynard Keynes

Although precipitated by a collapse of financial markets, the Great Depression was prolonged by a persistent shortfall of demand. As incomes fell and employment declined, a vicious circle of excess capacity and low sales was created. An investigation of the reasons for the extended slump must therefore pay close attention to the roots of the demand problem. This chapter analyzes the contribution of persistent structural unemployment to inadequate demand. Chapter 6 considers the changes in consumer expenditure patterns that exacerbated the demand problem.

Persistent unemployment thwarted recovery of the American economy. Inadequate demand crippled both new and old industries. It also seriously depressed investor confidence. Mature industries saw their markets shrink cyclically as well as secularly. Newer, dynamic industries found it impossible to establish the broad-based markets that their full emergence required. Lowered sales led to layoffs. The resulting unemployment served to maintain the depressed level of effective demand economy-wide.

The fact that certain industries actually prospered and recovered quickly after the trough of 1932 does not mean that demand could be quickly or easily restored. The lower firm incomes and sales that resulted from the crisis of 1929–32 made the more dynamic industries incapable of growing quickly enough to absorb the unemployed from the mature and declining industries. A generally low level of G.N.P. thus limited the impact that the more vibrant sectors could have on aggregate investment and employment. Hence recovery was delayed.

There were also structural aspects to the effective demand crisis, more serious and troublesome than the cyclical ones. Whereas cyclical unemployment could be overcome by a number of exogenous stimuli,

144

the long-term problems of maintaining (and indeed increasing) manufacturing employment required more lasting and radical adjustments. There was a profound structural difficulty associated with the new skills and greater capital intensity of the production processes of several of the newer dynamic industries. This further complicated the absorption of unemployed workers from the older industries. The evidence suggests there was a secular transformation in employment patterns and opportunities dating from the Great War that hampered recovery. Such a transition in the nation's employment requirements meant that simply raising G.N.P. would not solve the problem of unemployment in structural terms.[1] The problem was twofold: Newer industries were not growing fast enough to provide employment opportunities for those laid off in the older sectors; but even if higher growth rates had been achieved, the newer industries required different amounts and kinds of labor for their production. Structural unemployment was the troubling and persistent consequence.

Total industrial employment attained a pre-crash peak early in 1929 after limited and erratic growth dating from 1927. A sharp descent to a minimum point in December of 1932 was followed by improvement (interrupted by a brief hesitation in 1933:4) until virtual recovery was attained in mid-1937. But the sluggishness of the economy turned the series downward again – to a perigee in 1938:4 that left employment at its 1930 level. Thereafter came an upswing, which brought a partial recovery yet again in late 1939.

> 1 In the late thirties, Henry A. Wallace, then secretary of agriculture and eventually vice-president, succinctly explained the unique employment problem of the decade: "New jobs have not been created as the old jobs disappeared." He went on to say: "The production of our factories is nearing normal, but the number of unemployed remains unusually large. It is apparent that many of our unemployed may never get jobs again. Machines and younger people have taken their places." See Henry A. Wallace, *Technology, Corporations, and the General Welfare* (Chapel Hill: University of North Carolina Press, 1937), 19–20. Also see Fano, "Instability, Increasing Productivity and Unemployment in the Great Depression," which notes the structural difference between "full employment" in 1929 and in the late thirties. Fano cites, on p. 8, a 1937 report by the National Resources Committee, *Technological Trends and National Policy, Including the Social Implications of New Inventions* (Washington, D.C.: U.S. Government Printing Office, 1937), in which it was argued that "it would not have been possible to go back to the 1929 level of employment in 1935 unless the amount of goods and services produced was 40% greater than that produced in 1935 – or, 10% greater than that produced in 1929. The growth of the employable population over the period made it necessary to reach even higher levels of production in order to go back to the *unemployment* level of 1929."

Most manufacturing industries experienced movements in employment that coincided with the aggregate cycle.[2] Six sectors (textiles, iron and steel, leather products, paper and printing, nonferrous metals, and automobiles) recovered and sometimes exceeded pre-crash levels by mid-decade or so. Lumber products, building materials, and all other manufacturing (which by census classification rules was mostly rubber products) showed somewhat damped oscillations in employment, with improvement just short of full recovery in 1937. Food products and chemicals (predominantly petroleum products and refining) showed dramatic growth throughout the decade. As far as employment is concerned, these industries were indeed impervious to the depression. Tobacco products demonstrated surprising employment weakness. There was a rather steady decline in this industry's work force from 1929 to 1936 that leveled off at an index value close to 40 points below its pre-crash high.[3]

Recovery from the Great Depression required investment expenditures large enough to provide not only replacements but also net additions to productive capacity – and thereby increase output and employment. But in the American economy of the interwar period, secular trends in employment opportunities made this extremely difficult. In sectors where net investment took place, the demand for labor was not large enough to absorb workers idled in other industries. The only sectors capable of leading the nation's economy in recovery were constrained in the extent to which they could bolster general purchasing power by offering adequate employment. As a result, the effective demand failure of the depression decade was extended by the structural unemployment that arose out of the differential performance of the nation's industries.

The subset of the nation's manufacturing industries that rebounded quickly after the 1929 downturn centered in the nondurables and services markets. As a result of long-term shifts in the pattern of industrial activity, these sectors had encountered a secular upswing in their market opportunities dating from the end of World War I. The particular

2 See this chapter's statistical appendix, where the employment time series are plotted. Also included in the appendix are the percentages of pre-crash employment achieved in each quarter in each industry.

3 It is interesting to note that whereas tobacco workers were particularly unfortunate, the output of the industry consistently grew throughout the depression decade. The data support the finding of the last chapter that technical change in the tobacco industry generated large increases in output per worker.

characteristics of the commodities and services that offered at that time the best opportunities for continued accumulation required technically advanced and capital-intensive methods of production. In many cases the most profitable scale of activity necessitated the introduction of continuous processing, which increased mechanization and reduced the number of employees per machine or process.[4] The net result was an unbalanced adjustment between declining and expanding industries. Changes in the role and ranking of sectors with respect to growth and output did not produce equivalent alterations in the demand for labor.

To the extent that the recovering sectors could not absorb the unemployed, the economy as a whole remained trapped at a low level of aggregate demand. This intensified the extent to which investment expenditures remained limited. Low levels of consumption dampened the incentives for bold projects that would have made large net additions to capacity and created jobs. As more time passed with consumption remaining depressed, the business community's evaluation of the feasibility of new projects became increasingly pessimistic.[5] A breakout in net investment spending was more and more difficult to achieve. The traditional mechanism of cyclical recovery was lacking – that is, an

4 It may appear that I am trying to resurrect the notion of "technological" unemployment. But no presumption is made here that the capital intensity of the newer industries of the interwar period had a *permanently* negative impact on employment. Rather, a *short-run* impact left large pockets of structurally unemployed persons, who did not necessarily have the skills or training to fill the new positions that the new techniques created. In some respects the experience of the unemployed in Great Britain during the interwar period was similar. See Carol Heim, *Uneven Regional Development in Interwar Britain* (Ph.D. dissertation, Yale University, 1982), and her "Structural Transformation and the Demand for New Labor in Advanced Economies: Interwar Britain," *Journal of Economic History*, 44 (June, 1984), 585–95. Also see H. T. Oshima, "The Growth of U.S. Factor Productivity: The Significance of New Technologies in the Early Decades of the Twentieth Century," *Journal of Economic History*, 44 (March, 1984), 161–70, concerning the displacement of American workers by new technologies.

5 Business confidence may have been further depressed by an expectation that the government would increase deficit spending to augment consumption. Of course, the federal government did not engage in the kind of bold spending (and borrowing) policies that could have "crowded out" private investment. See E. C. Brown, "Fiscal Policy in the 'Thirties: A Reappraisal," *American Economic Review*, 46 (December, 1956), 857–79. As pointed out by Alvin Hansen, aggregate public works expenditures during the 1930s (for federal, state, and local governments combined) did not equal their pre-crash levels until 1938. See A. H. Hansen, "Was Fiscal Policy in the Thirties a Failure?" *Review of Economics and Statistics*, 45 (August, 1963), 320–3.

increase in investment in the capital goods sectors, once inventories had been sufficiently run down, which would have bolstered effective demand by absorbing the unemployed.

A major aspect of the effective demand failure of the 1930s was the changing distribution of employment. Interindustry variations in rates of recovery generated an aggregate result of virtual stagnation during the 1930s. What was happening in labor markets? Certain sectors expanded after 1932, but nonetheless failed to absorb the unemployed from the declining industries. In tobacco products, petroleum, and chemicals, the relative capital intensity of new production methods was a factor. In other recovering sectors, rates of expansion were not sufficient to overcome the rate at which unemployment in others was (and had been) generated.

The sectors that grew the fastest and that recovered most quickly after 1932 had meager shares of total employment throughout the 1930s. The chemical industry by the mid-1930s ranked twenty-fifth among all industries in its share of national employment; petroleum, twenty-first; tobacco, sixty-seventh; food products, fourteenth. By contrast, the sectors hit hardest by the crash and slowest to recover accounted for much larger shares of national employment in 1935. Primary metals producers ranked first; textile mills, second; lumber mills, third.[6] Without general investment recovery there was little absorption of unemployment, even by growing sectors. With the persistence of unemployment, the effective demand problem was aggravated. This was the basis of a pernicious combination of idle plant and weakened sales that was, in essence, the economic calamity of the 1930s.

Thus, a massive structural unemployment problem characterized the 1930s that in the absence of an exogenous shock such as war would have taken many more years to solve. But the problem had actually emerged prior to 1929. Throughout the 1920s (and continuing well into the postwar era) there had been a steady decline in the percentage of national employment accounted for by manufacturing and construction sectors. The same was the case for agriculture and mining. Service industries (transportation, trade, finance, selected services, and government operations) increased their share (Tables 5-1 and 5-2).

6 See U.S. Department of Commerce, Bureau of the Census, *Biennial Census of Manufactures, 1921–37* (Washington, D.C.: U.S. Government Printing Office, 1924–1939); and John P. Henderson, *Changes in the Industrial Distribution of Employment*, Tables 5 and 6.

Table 5-1. *Percentage distribution of employment by major groups, 1919–59*

Year	Primary industries[a]	Secondary industries[b]	Service industries[c]
1919	28.5	29.4	42.1
1920	28.9	28.6	42.5
1921	30.2	25.1	44.7
1922	28.9	26.8	44.3
1923	27.6	28.2	44.2
1924	27.3	27.3	45.4
1925	26.8	27.7	45.5
1926	26.3	27.8	45.9
1927	25.5	27.7	46.8
1928	25.4	27.5	47.1
1929	25.1	28.1	46.8
1930	25.8	26.6	47.6
1931	27.1	24.5	48.4
1932	28.7	22.5	48.8
1933	30.1	22.7	45.2
1934	27.0	24.8	48.2
1935	26.6	25.5	47.9
1936	25.3	26.6	48.1
1937	24.0	27.6	48.4
1938	24.5	25.5	50.0
1939	23.6	26.8	49.6
1940	22.6	27.6	49.8
1941	20.1	31.0	48.9
1942	19.1	33.5	47.4
1943	18.3	36.0	45.7
1944	18.1	34.5	47.4
1945	17.8	32.4	49.8
1946	16.8	31.2	52.0
1947	16.2	32.3	51.5
1948	15.5	32.1	52.4
1949	15.8	30.6	53.6
1950	14.8	32.5	52.7
1951	13.3	33.1	53.6
1952	12.6	33.2	54.2
1953	11.9	34.0	54.1
1954	12.0	32.7	55.3
1955	12.0	32.9	55.1
1956	11.5	32.9	55.6
1957	10.9	32.6	56.5
1958	10.5	31.1	58.4
1959	10.3	31.5	58.2

[a]Agriculture and mining.
[b]Contract construction and manufacturing.
[c]Transportation, trade, finance, selected services, and government.
Source: U.S. Department of Labor, Bureau of Labor Statistics, *Employment and Earnings*, vol. 7, no. 1, p. 11, as cited in John P. Henderson, *Changes in the Industrial Distribution of Employment: 1919–59*, 10.

Table 5-2. *Agricultural labor force as a percentage of the total labor force*

Year	Percentage
1919	28.6
1920	25.3
1921	24.9
1922	24.9
1923	24.4
1924	24.0
1925	23.6
1926	23.4
1927	22.7
1928	22.3
1929	22.1
1930	21.3
1931	20.8
1932	20.2
1933	19.8
1934	19.3
1935	19.3
1936	19.0
1937	18.6
1938	18.0
1939	17.6
1940	17.1
1941	16.3
1949	12.6
1950	11.6
1951	10.7
1952	10.2
1953	9.7
1954	9.6
1955	9.8
1956	9.3
1957	8.8
1958	8.2
1959	8.1

Source: G. Smiley, "Recent Unemployment Rate Estimates for the 1920's and 1930's," *Journal of Economic History*, 43 (June, 1983), 490.

Data from the *Census of Manufactures* concerning the relative importance of manufacturing industries demonstrate the uneven development that was a major factor in the prolongation of the depression.[7] The evidence in censuses spanning 1909 to 1937 indicates the following:

1. The industries most seriously affected by the depression ranked relatively high in employment. Despite a progressive weakening in their economic position during these years, these sectors continued to play a dominant role in providing work for the available labor force. Just as secular trends began to shift the focus of expansion in the American economy away from these industries, their importance as employers was at an all-time high.

Lumber product manufacturing was one of the nation's most important employers throughout the interwar period, but it held an increasingly tenuous position in the economy as a whole. In iron and steel production the movement in rankings paralleled long-term alterations in demand patterns. Foundries fell in the employment rankings by the late 1920s with the declining economic importance of wrought structural shapes. Similarly, the share of employment in blast furnaces declined, although here the trend seems to have been due both to a long-run decline in heavy production and to labor-saving technical change. Only in the rolling mills producing light, flat rolled products was the share of national employment rising.

Textile production also exhibited varying patterns of employment shares. In clothing and woolen lines, the opportunities for employment shrank steadily, while in silk and hosiery they were stable. The ranking of cotton goods remained fairly high, but even here ranking with respect to value of output and value added by manufacture deteriorated. In the leather industry, with the exception of boot and shoe production, employment opportunities steadily declined.

The employment share of automobile production increased throughout the period, although there was some slippage with the onset of the Great Depression. Overall, the data indicate an industry that, precisely when it was hard hit by a profound slump, was becoming more and more important in the creation of jobs for the nation's labor force. In nonferrous metals, building materials (stone, clay, and glass), shipbuilding, locomotives, and textile machinery, shares of national employment secularly declined. Only in rubber products was there im-

7 See the statistical appendix to this chapter.

provement, although the downturn in the thirties jeopardized that progress.

2. The industries that recovered quickly and performed well during the thirties did not simultaneously increase their share of national manufacturing employment. Opportunities for expansion in these sectors were on a secular upswing, but this did not necessarily translate itself into expanded opportunities for workers. The result was an unfortunate combination of tendencies whereby declining industries employed fewer persons, but growing industries failed to absorb the unemployed.

Employment opportunities in the production of food products did not expand during the twenty-eight-year period, despite the overwhelming growth in the industry's share of the value of total manufacturing output. Technical change played a large role both in expanding the sector's output and in the displacement of workers. Despite the development of new product lines, the rank of paper manufacturing in national employment remained fairly steady. In machine tools, employment also was steady, largely as a result of technical change.

For the tobacco, petroleum, and chemical sectors, the contribution to the value of total manufacturing output steadily rose over time. But the employment rankings remained steady or, in the case of tobacco, fell. Rapid technical progress, while contributing to these sectors' impressive output performance in the 1930s, progressively constrained employment. The best economic performance in American manufacturing during the depression occurred in sectors that did not have growing demands for labor.

In electrical and agricultural machinery, aluminum, and rayon, employment shares rose, but the rate of increase was only moderate. In the case of agricultural machinery, the improved position of the worker may have been linked in large part to the farm policies of the New Deal. The sector's employment progressively deteriorated throughout the world agricultural crisis of the 1920s until government action commenced in the early thirties.

3. Certain new industries emerging in the interwar period showed great potential for expansion and for securing a rising share of national employment: radio electronics, home appliances, and aircraft production. These sectors were still too new, however, to be major factors in the economy during the thirties. Although their rankings in employment and value of output rose steadily in the late thirties, they remained quite low. War and several more years of development were necessary

before these sectors could assume the large role in the nation's manufacturing that they came to play in the latter half of the century. Their activity during the Great Depression, however promising, could not lead a broad-based recovery in employment.

Census data from the postwar period show continuation of the long-term shifts in the distribution of employment that began in the interwar years.[8] In textile mills, apparel, lumber products, leather products, and primary metals production, the percentage share of manufacturing employment fell from 1947 to 1972. The employment share for food products, furniture, paper products, building materials, nonelectrical machinery, and transportation equipment remained fairly steady. Rising percentage shares are observed in printing, chemicals, fabricated metals, electrical machinery, and instruments. In rubber products, the employment share rose, but this seems to be linked with the inclusion of the employment share for plastic products in the rubber industry figures. Declining shares in tobacco and petroleum production are found despite the dynamic performance of these sectors in the postwar era. The divergent trends in employment and output are due to the relatively high capital intensity of these industries and, in the case of petroleum, the increasing extent to which plants and drilling sites have been located abroad.

The employment difficulties of the interwar years had long-term characteristics far transcending the cyclical problems after 1929. After achieving its peak just after World War I, manufacturing's share of national employment declined throughout the interwar period. Primary and secondary industries played a dwindling role in employing the nation's labor force, while service industries and government operations expanded. These changes were most prevalent during the 1920s. Their continuation into the 1930s meant that the effective demand failure of the 1930s was both cyclical and secular.

Secular transformation of the industrial distribution of employment in the economy was part of its long-term development. As the theory advanced in Chapter 1 indicated, such secular growth involves the often

8 Percentage shares of total manufacturing employment for each sector in the postwar period are reported in the statistical appendix. Evidence for the early 1940s is not used here because of the distortions created by the war. The reader will note differences in the industrial classifications used for 1909–37 and for 1947–72. The reporting conventions of the U.S. Bureau of the Census changed during World War II.

disruptive propagation of industrial life cycles. The delay in the recovery of the American economy of the 1930s was directly linked with a long-run phenomenon whereby traditional patterns of employment, which might otherwise have provided the demand needed to lead an upturn, were becoming weaker and weaker.

As Chapter 2 showed, some manufacturing industries rebounded quite quickly from the trough of 1932. But such "depression-proof" performance failed to lead the economy as a whole out of the crisis. The secular process whereby manufacturing created fewer and fewer opportunities for employment helps to explain this failure. Despite their relatively robust performance, the dynamic industries of the interwar period were incapable of absorbing the unemployed from the more mature sectors. Demand remained weak, and the economy mired in a stagnant phase.

It is most interesting to note that in the postwar period the secular employment trends of the interwar period reasserted themselves. "The period of the depression, in combination with the employment impact of the war, reversed many of the employment changes of the late 1920s and it was not until the mid-1950s, at least, that these changes began to reappear."[9] This suggests that the secular dynamic of the 1920s represented the initial stages of a major restructuring of the American economy. But the war, by raising the demand for more traditional goods, allowed the economy to delay the day of reckoning. The military buildups of the immediate postwar period and of the Korean conflict further delayed the transformation that began after World War I.

The depression had peculiar cyclical origins, but was very much part of a climacteric that witnessed the start of major new trends in the composition of national output, employment, and technology. Delayed recovery from the downturn of 1929–32 was linked directly with the impact of these secular trends during the interwar years. The outbreak of war in 1939 interrupted these developments, and economic growth on the more traditional basis of earlier decades reasserted itself. But once the artificial stimulus of war subsided, the American economy was again confronted with the difficulties of adjusting to long-term patterns of development. In the postwar period, the adjustment had to take place in the face of complications created by foreign developments and an emerging cold war. These issues will be more thoroughly analyzed in Chapter 8.

9 From Henderson, *Changes in the Industrial Distribution of Employment*, 5.

Statistical appendix to Chapter 5

Time plots of industrial employment, 1927–40

The time plots were generated by monthly employment data (Figures 5-1 through 5-12).

Figure 5-1. Food products employment and total employment.

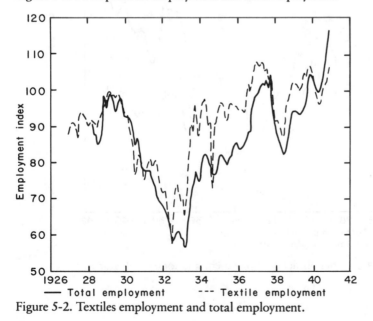

Figure 5-2. Textiles employment and total employment.

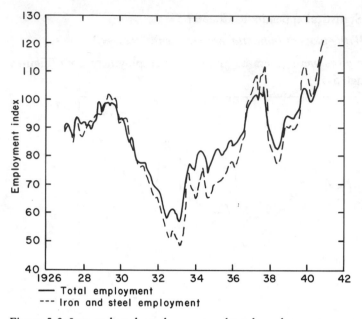

Figure 5-3. Iron and steel employment and total employment.

Figure 5-4. Lumber products employment and total employment.

Figure 5-5. Leather products employment and total employment.

Figure 5-6. Paper and printing employment and total employment.

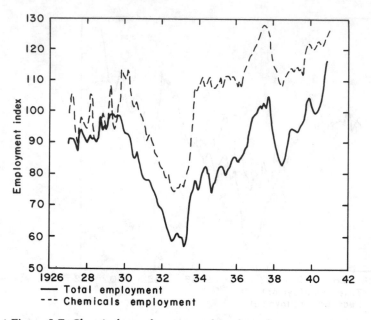

Figure 5-7. Chemicals employment and total employment.

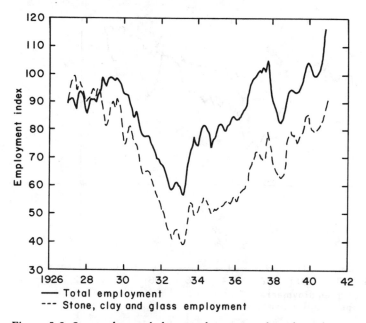

Figure 5-8. Stone, clay, and glass employment and total employment.

Figure 5-9. Nonferrous metals employment and total employment.

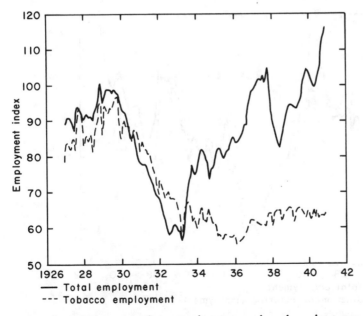

Figure 5-10. Tobacco products employment and total employment.

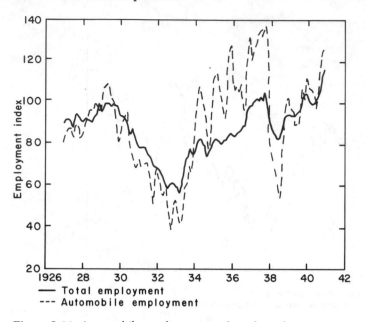

Figure 5-11. Automobile employment and total employment.

Figure 5-12. Other manufacturing employment and total employment.

*Quarterly percentage of the pre-crash peak
in industrial employment, 1927–40*

The tables on the percentage of pre-crash employment achieved in each quarter were computed by finding the average index value for each quarter and dividing it by the pre-crash peak value.

Quarter	1	2	3	4
1. Food products				
1927	83.7	87.5	93.3	90.4
1928	88.5	87.5	90.4	98.1
1929	93.3	95.2	98.2	88.5
1930	91.3	92.3	91.3	88.5
1931		Not available.		
1932	79.9	78	78.7	76.9
1933	75.4	79.1	90.3	97.8
1934	103.7	103.2	106.3	103.8
1935	99	96.2	95.2	96.8
1936	98.3	98.5	100	110.6
1937	112.5	110.6	110.6	119.7
1938	117.7	116.5	117.5	124
1939	122.4	124.4	123.2	126.3
1940	125.3	126.9	122.1	130.4
2. Textiles				
1927	90	86	94	94
1928	94	88	87	98
1929	100	97	97	94
1930	93	84	82	78
1931	79.7	78.6	80	72.2
1932	71	58.5	72.2	70.4
1933	65.4	81.6	88.4	87.3
1934	97.3	92.2	72.9	92.1
1935	96.6	91.7	96.9	96.2
1936	94.6	94.5	100.1	106.8
1937	107	195.4	101	93.4
1938	91.4	87.4	97	102.2
1939	101	101.2	103.6	105.8
1940	99.1	97	102	107.2
3. Iron and steel				
1927	88.2	85.3	90.2	85.3
1928	89.2	91.2	92.2	93.1
1929	97.1	100	99	90.2
1930	91.2	88.2	80.4	76.5
1931	75.1	71.2	66.1	64.1
1932	59.7	53.7	50.3	51.8
1933	47.4	57	73.2	66.3
1934	67.7	74.8	64.1	66.4
1935	69.4	70.3	72.6	76.4

Quarter	1	2	3	4
3. Iron and steel (continued)				
1936	74.6	80.6	85.4	99
1937	104.3	98.7	106.3	95.1
1938	82.2	76.3	79.5	89.1
1939	88.9	88.5	93.8	109.9
1940	101	102	110.8	120
4. Lumber products				
1927	90.2	91.3	96.7	90.2
1928	89.1	91.3	92.4	95.7
1929	93.5	97.8	98.9	89.1
1930	81.5	78.3	70.7	63
1931	60.5	59.1	53.7	49.3
1932	44.8	41.2	39.8	40
1933	35.3	43.5	53.7	54.2
1934	54.1	54.1	52.2	52
1935	56.4	53	60.3	59.2
1936	60.8	62.3	64.2	73.8
1937	77.6	78.6	75.2	72
1938	68.9	65.1	68.8	70.7
1939	68.7	71	73.3	78.7
1940	74	73.3	76.8	81.7
5. Leather products				
1927	93.9	86.7	99	89.8
1928	94.9	87.8	92.9	89.8
1929	93.9	90.8	100	91.8
1930	93.9	86.7	87.8	76.5
1931	83.9	85.6	82.6	76.8
1932	81.8	75.8	76.4	73.5
1933	77.2	85.6	85	84.1
1934	92.3	93.3	84.1	90.7
1935	92.3	88.2	87.1	92.1
1936	88.7	87.7	87.9	100.8
1937	99.4	98.1	91.8	90.8
1938	91.7	86.1	93.2	100.1
1939	101.2	99.1	98.8	98.9
1940	95.7	91.4	91.7	96.2
6. Paper and printing				
1927	97.2	95.3	96.3	98.1
1928	95.3	94.4	95.3	94.4
1929	93.5	93.5	96.3	100
1930	97.2	Not available.		
1931	88.5	87.5	85.1	83.4
1932	80.6	77.4	75.8	75
1933	73.4	76.3	85.2	86.9
1934	87.3	89.3	89.3	89.5
1935	90.4	90.1	91.2	91.6
1936	91.5	92.7	95.4	97.2

Quarter	1	2	3	4
1937	100.4	100.1	100.9	100.4
1938	99.1	96.3	97.2	103.8
1939	104.1	103.8	105.6	108.8
1940	107.5	108.4	108.1	109.6

7. Chemicals

1927	92.1	78.9	86	83.4
1928	92.1	78.9	86	83.4
1929	90.4	82.5	89.5	98.2
1930	99.1	89.5	90.4	86
1931	78.8	78.6	75.2	71.8
1932	68.9	67	64.6	66
1933	66.3	72.2	84.1	93.5
1934	97.4	95.6	94.9	94.8
1935	97.4	97.6	96.8	96.8
1936	96.8	98.2	101.8	104
1937	107.9	111.8	111.8	103.5
1938	99.1	95.1	97.7	99.7
1939	99.5	99.2	101.9	107
1940	105.3	107.9	106.4	109.9

8. Stone, clay, and glass

1927	96	100	98	91.9
1928	89.9	96	96	87.9
1929	84.8	91.9	91.9	82.8
1930	78.8	80.8	75.8	66.7
1931	65.9	65.1	60	55.6
1932	50.6	43.8	42.3	43
1933	39.3	47.3	54.5	50.5
1934	53.6	55.5	51.6	51.7
1935	52.9	54	54.5	57
1936	55.8	58.9	60.6	69.7
1937	73.4	71.2	71.2	74.8
1938	66.4	63.8	66.1	78.6
1939	78.2	78.3	79.8	86.3
1940	80.8	80.6	83.8	91.3

9. Nonferrous metals

1927	92.2	88.3	89.3	86.4
1928	89.3	90.3	92.2	96.1
1929	99	88.3	93.2	87.4
1930	81.6	77.7	70.9	68
1931	64.7	63.5	60.7	59.3
1932	52.7	47.3	45.8	46
1933	39.8	52	66.6	67.2
1934	71.6	74.6	71.5	76.1
1935	79	80.4	84.9	88.7
1936	84.7	88.2	94.3	107.5
1937	109.9	111.7	110.7	94.4
1938	87.8	78.9	84.1	90.4

Quarter	1	2	3	4

9. Nonferrous metals (continued)

1939	90.7	90.1	96.3	108.1
1940	103.5	105	115.1	125.6

10. Tobacco products

1927	83.2	84.2	91.1	88.1
1928	85.1	85.1	88.1	97
1929	93.1	93.1	95	88.1
1930	89.1	88.1	87.1	84.2
1931	82.6	79.6	76.4	69.7
1932	70.1	68.7	67.2	67
1933	57.2	66.2	64.6	61.3
1934	64.3	62.1	62.3	61
1935	57.6	57.5	56.7	57.4
1936	55.8	56.6	57.8	61.4
1937	61.1	59.6	59.6	63.7
1938	64	64.6	63.7	65
1939	61	64.9	63.8	64.1
1940	63.7	64.6	63.1	64.1

11. Automobiles

1927	79.6	78.7	81.5	76.9
1928	84.3	88.9	91.7	88
1929	99.1	95.4	92.6	74.1
1930	84.3	82.4	67.6	63.9
1931	65	65.5	57.4	63.7
1932	56.4	53.7	39.8	47.8
1933	38.8	46.6	56.9	66.5
1934	96	93.6	76	89.5
1935	105.9	94	85.2	118.5
1936	98.4	100.2	89.1	123.1
1937	117.6	124.1	125.9	99.1
1938	68.5	55.6	73.1	94.5
1939	89.8	82.4	92.6	103.7
1940	99.1	94.5	106.5	114.8

12. Other manufacturing

1927	88.8	85.3	84.5	83.6
1928	80.2	81	81.9	84.5
1929	92.2	99.1	99.1	76.7
1930	75	75.9	66.4	62.9
1931	59	65.3	60.2	61.5
1932	57.8	57.8	50.5	54.5
1933	49	58.4	70.9	72.7
1934	76.7	71.7	68.1	69.6
1935	74	67.9	70.4	71.9
1936	63.5	70.4	78.8	88.1
1937	82.8	86.2	85.8	73.4
1938	62.4	61.5	65.5	71.5

Quarter	1	2	3	4
1939	70.9	69.7	74.2	79.7
1940	74.7	72.6	77.3	83.4

Source: U.S. Department of Commerce, Survey of Current Business; computations by the author.

Relative importance of selected U.S. industries for employment, by rank, 1909–37

Sector	'09	'14	'19	'21	'23	'25	'27	'31	'33	'35	'37
Food											
Meat packing	16	19	14	17	16	18	17	18	13	14	15
Flour, grist	37	42	41	40	50	52	55	60	51	65	69
Bakery	14	13	15	10	14	14	14	6	8	5	6
Liquors	28	24	52	66					49	50	49
Dairy	61	87	86	67	55	60	53	80	69	89	96
Canning	26	30	31	38	27	23	23	21	20	15	13
Confectionery	30	28	24	22	31	29	29	27	29	37	40
Soda waters	78		90	84	62	62	61	57	73	98	65
Sugar	136	101	83	81	94	99	101	106	99	116	129
Lumber	1	1	3	3	1	1	2	5	7	3	3
Paper	19	21	23	20	20	17	20	20	19	17	17
Iron and steel	6	5	5	5	5	5	5	4	2	1	1
Foundries	2	3	2	4	4	4	3	2	4	19	16
Blast furnaces	40	50	47	65	46	57	60	95	97	108	85
News printing	5	15	21	18	6	6	6	16	15	13	14
Textiles											
Cotton goods	3	2	4	1	3	2	1	1	1	2	2
Clothing, M.	7	7	10	7	10	13	11	15	12	18	19
Woolens	9	9	12	19	19	27	30	35	31	26	33
Clothing, W.	11	8	13	11	15	16	15	10	9		67
Hosiery	12	11								9	10
Silk	15	17	19	15	18	15	16	17	14		
Leather	25	25	30	32	34	34	35	36	35	38	
Boots, shoes	8	6	8	6	9	9	8	7	5	6	
Tobacco	10	10	16	13	17	19	18	19	54[a]	67[a]	70[a]
Autos	20	22	9	12	7	10	10	12	18	8	8
Petroleum	76	59	32	26	29	28	26	23	22	21	22
Nonferrous metals								31	32	28	23
Copper	70	74	91	130	76	88	102			142	125
Lead	97	137		179	166	164	184				

Sector	'09	'14	'19	'21	'23	'25	'27	'31	'33	'35	'37
Brass	33	41	29	37	30	30	28				
Zinc	101		110			118	120				153
Electrical machinery	17	14	7	9	8	7	7	8	11	7	5
Rubber	50	31	22	28	25	24	24	30	28	32	31
Chemicals	55	46	35	33	24	32	37	32	27	25	25
Stone	24	26	56	49		45	42	49	68	106	92
Brick	18	18	28	25							
Glass	23	23	27	29	26	26	27	29	30	24	24
Cement	49	54	71	52	51	43	47	55	71	78	68
Shipbuilding (steel)			6	21	33	38	33	34	42	43	32
Locomotives	72		69	75	59						
Agricultural machinery	29	33	37	48	58	59	49	72	101	36	26
Machine tools			38		56	44	48	62	93	56	48
Textile machinery			57	46	47	61	64	67	63	86	72
Aluminum				91	101	97	93	82	84	80	
Rayon							63	37	34	39	39
Radio								39	38	44	
Refrigerators									44	51	
Stoves									43	47	20
Aircraft										135	79
Machinery^{NEC}											11
Lighting equipment										100	87

Notes: (1) Where no data are reported, none are available. (2) In cases in which several product lines for one industry are reported in the *Census*, data are for raw materials or intermediate goods. (3) Where classification conventions have changed, between census years, the nearest product categories have been used. (4) NEC, not elsewhere classified. [a]For cigarette production only.

Source: U.S. Department of Commerce, Bureau of the Census, *Biennial Census of Manufactures* (Washington, D.C.: U.S. Government Printing Office, 1909, 1914, 1919, 1921, 1923, 1925, 1927, 1931, 1933, 1935, 1937).

Employment data, 1909–37

Sector	Average annual rank of employment share
Cotton	2
Lumber	2.73

Sector	Average annual rank of employment share
Iron and steel	4
Foundries	5.73
Boots and shoes	7.2
Electrical machinery[a]	9.1
Hosiery	10.5
Bakery[a]	10.8
Clothing, men's	11.73
Automobiles	12.4
Meat packing[a]	16.1
Silk	16.3
Clothing, women's	17.5
Paper	19.4
Brick	22.3
Woolens	22.73
Canning[a]	24.2
Glass	26.2
Tobacco[a]	28.5
Rubber	29.5
Confectionery[a]	29.6
Shipbuilding	31.4
Brass	32.6
Petroleum[a]	33.1
Chemicals[a]	33.7
Leather	33.73
Radio[a]	41.3
Rayon[a]	42.4
Liquors[a]	45.4
Agricultural machinery	49.8
Flour, grist[a]	51.1
Machine tools[a]	55.6
Stone	55.7
Cement	58.1
Textile machinery	62.6
Blast furnaces	68.2
Locomotives	68.8
Dairy[a]	73
Soda waters[a]	73
Aluminum[a]	89.7
Copper	99.8
Sugar[a]	104.1
Zinc	120.4
Lead	154.5

[a]Dynamic sectors during the 1930s.
Source: Census of Manufactures, 1909–1937; computations by the author.

Employment data, 1947–72

Sector	Average annual percentage share of employment
Nonelectrical machinery	9.7
Transportation equipment	9.7
Food[a]	9.6
Apparel	7.9
Electrical machinery[a]	7.9
Primary metals	7.2
Fabricated metals[a]	7.1
Textiles	6.5
Chemicals[a]	4.4
Lumber	3.8
Paper	3.5
Stone, clay, and glass	3.4
Furniture	2.4
Rubber	2.4
Leather	2.2
Instruments	1.9
Petroleum[a]	1.1
Tobacco[a]	0.56

[a]Dynamic sectors during the 1930s.
Source: Census of Manufactures, 1947–1972; computations by the author.

Percentage share of total manufacturing employment, by sector, 1947–72

Sector	1947[a]	1954[a]	1958	1963	1967	1972
Food	NA[b]	9.2	11.1	10.1	8.9	8.7
Tobacco	0.87	0.7	0.55	0.48	0.41	0.37
Textiles	9.6	7.7	5.9	5.3	5	5.3
Apparel	8.2	8.6	7.7	7.9	7.3	7.6
Lumber	NA	4.7	3.8	3.5	3	3.8
Furniture	2.3	2.3	2.3	2.3	2.3	2.6
Paper	3.3	3.5	3.6	3.6	3.5	3.5
Printing	3.7	4	5.6	5.6	5.6	5.9
Chemicals	3.9	4.1	4.5	4.5	4.6	4.6
Petroleum	1.4	1.3	1.2	0.95	0.77	0.77
Rubber[c]	1.8	1.6	2.3	2.6	2.8	3.4
Leather	2.9	2.6	2.3	2	1.8	1.5
Stone, clay, and glass	3.4	3.3	3.6	3.5	3.2	3.5
Primary metals	8.5	7.6	7.1	6.9	6.9	6.3
Fabricated metals	6.9	6.6	6.9	6.7	7.3	8.3

Sector	1947[a]	1954[a]	1958	1963	1967	1972
Nonelectrical machinery	10.5	9.5	8.8	9	10.1	10.1
Electrical machinery	5.3	5.8	7.4	9.3	10.1	9.2
Transportation equipment	8.2	10.7	10.1	9.9	9.9	9.5
Instruments	1.6	1.6	1.9	1.9	2.1	2.5

[a]For production workers only; all other years for total employees.
[b]Data not available.
[c]Includes plastics products.
Sources: Census of Manufactures, 1947, 1954, 1958, 1963, 1967, 1972; computations by the author; not all sectors reported, so total figures do not equal 100.

6. The effective demand problem of the interwar period. II: Cyclical and secular changes in final demand

> Of course the . . . development of cheap luxuries has been a very fortunate thing for our rulers. It is quite likely that fish and chips, art-silk stockings, tinned salmon, cut-price chocolate . . . the movies, the radio, strong tea and the Football Pools have between them averted revolution. Therefore we are sometimes told that the whole thing is an astute manoeuvre by the governing class . . . to hold the unemployed down. What I have seen of our governing class does not convince me that they have that much intelligence. The thing has happened, but by an unconscious process.
>
> – George Orwell

The effective demand problem of the 1930s primarily resulted from persistent unemployment, but cyclical and secular changes in consumer expenditures also played an important role in lengthening the depression. Related changes in the distribution of income also impeded recovery. These changes in consumer expenditures and income distribution provide additional insight as to why the industries that did recover quickly after 1932 nonetheless could not lead a general upturn.

With a massive deficit spending effort, perhaps on the scale of spending undertaken during World War II, consumption could have led the way out of depression.[1] Given the political impossibility of such a strategy, recovery required investment growth. The industries that potentially might have provided such investment leadership were hampered by a low rate of growth in sales, due in part to the cyclical and secular changes in consumer spending discussed in the following sections.

There were two major short-run shocks to consumer spending that enervated the U.S. economy after the panic of 1929: the impact of the downturn on incomes, and the stress placed on consumer credit mar-

---

1 As intimated by Alvin H. Hansen in his *Fiscal Policy and Business Cycles* (New York: Norton, 1941), 84. Indeed, it was in the period 1940–5, not 1935–40, that the federal payroll grew and federal expenditures rose from 13.8% to 39.5% of G.N.P. See U.S. Council of Economic Advisers, *The Midyear Economic Report of the President: July 1951* (Washington, D.C.: U.S. Government Printing Office, 1951), 226; computations from constant-dollar data by the author.

kets that had particularly serious consequences for durable goods industries. From 1929 to 1933, disposable personal income, indexed in constant dollars, fell from $229.5 billion to $169.6 billion – a decline of 26.1%. The level of $229 billion was not reached again until 1939.[2] Moreover, extensive destruction of the value of assets also occurred after 1929. The impact on the demand for goods and services was obviously enormous. But in addition to income shortfalls, deflation followed the crisis, with important implications for the pattern of consumer expenditures.

By 1932 the purchasing power of those still employed had risen greatly because of rapid deflation. Because these income recipients tended to be businessmen and professionals, the demand for luxury items, high-priced durables such as large cars, and nonessential services such as entertainment and tourism rose. Deflation did not, of course, bolster the purchasing power of those who had lost their jobs, except to the extent that they owned assets, borrowed funds, or received relief payments. In essence, there arose a distorted "Pigou effect."[3] The falling trend in the general price level did not strengthen consumption as a whole, but redirected consumer expenditures toward product markets geared mainly to high income recipients. This shift in demand patterns intensified the difficulties of the industries most damaged by the depression. Their markets shrank as the number of inactive workers rose. In more dynamic sectors, the demand emanating from those still employed was not large enough, nor was it sufficiently dispersed among a broad spectrum of commodities, to generate a large advance in revenues and thereby a robust recovery.

The downturn also destroyed the easy conditions in consumer credit markets that had been one of the hallmarks of the prosperity of the twenties. Total consumer credit fell forty-one index points from 1929 to 1933.[4] In addition to the consequences of a restriction in consumer

2   See U.S. Department of Commerce, Bureau of Economic Analysis, *The National Income and Product Accounts of the United States: 1929–1976* (Washington, D.C.: U.S. Government Printing Office, 1981), 73.

3   The Pigou effect occurs when a decline in the overall price level leads to an increase in spending on goods and services because of the rise in real purchasing power resulting from deflation. See A. C. Pigou, "The Classical Stationary State," *Economic Journal*, 53 (April, 1943), 343–51.

4   See Duncan M. Holthausen, *The Volume of Consumer Installment Credit: 1929–38* (New York: National Bureau of Economic Research, 1940), 131; and Rolf Nugent, *Consumer Credit and Economic Stability* (New York: Russell Sage Foundation, 1939).

Table 6-1. *Percentage change in disposable income per capita, 1928–9*

Population category	Change (%)
Total population	13
Nonfarm population	9
Top 1% of nonfarm population	63
Middle 2%–7% of nonfarm population	23
Lower 93% of nonfarm population	−4
Farm population	21

Source: C. F. Holt, "Who Benefited from the Prosperity of the Twenties?" *Explorations in Economic History*, 14 (July, 1977), 283.

credit for new purchases of durable goods, deflation increased the real burden of existing debt.[5] It appears that by the mid-thirties, consumers were so concerned with liquidating the relatively large debt incurred at the start of the decade, and so wary given the experience of the crash, that the aggregate marginal propensity to consume fell. Some have argued that this alone explains the recession of 1937 and the continuation of the depression itself.[6]

Long-run developments also influenced consumption behavior and the recovery mechanisms of the interwar American economy. On the one side these factors were of consequence for the distribution of income. On the other they involved a transition in the composition of consumption expenditures that ultimately favored the sales and profitability of some industries over others.

As to the distribution of national income, the lower 93% of the nonfarm population saw their per capita disposable income fall during the boom of the later twenties. They were the only segment of the population so affected, as Table 6-1 shows. The evidence thus suggests that the interwar years offered relatively limited opportunities for the full-scale development of new mass markets.[7] Not until the war years

5 For another view, cf. F. S. Mishkin, "The Household Balance Sheet and the Great Depression," *Journal of Economic History*, 38 (December, 1978), 918–37.

6 See the work of Alvin Hansen, Ralph Hawtrey, Kenneth D. Roose, and Sumner Slichter cited in the Introduction to this book.

7 Simon Kuznets estimated that the share of income received by the top 5% of recipients rose from 25.76% in 1920 to 32.12% in 1932. Thereafter, the share hovered around 28%, until the 1940s, when it fell below 20%. Raymond Gold-

and after was the distribution of income sufficiently broad to allow for the full emergence of the markets and firms that were beginning to grow during the interwar era. Although the high-income era of the 1920s spawned a new composition of aggregate demand, it also created a demand constraint on the growth of new markets in the form of a highly skewed distribution of income. The severe cyclical reduction in disposable income after 1929 only magnified this obstacle to the transformation of the structures of economic growth.

Perhaps the greatest constraints on the rapid growth of the dynamic industries of the interwar period were those long-term changes in the pattern of consumption behavior that emerged after World War I. The fundamental source of these changes was the secular rise in living standards that began after the turn of the century. These changes in consumption behavior were but another expression of the transformation in the composition of national output theoretically described in the first chapter of this study.

World War I, much like World War II, tended to mask the trends in expenditures that originated in the early part of the century. With the unprecedented prosperity of the 1920s, however, these trends became more evident. Although consumption data for the 1920s suggest a decline in the importance of certain markets that figured prominently in total expenditures in the prewar and wartime periods, they also reveal new demand patterns. For example, between 1923 and 1929 the share of consumer spending devoted to clothing fell from 17% to 15.1%. For housing and utilities the proportion declined from 20.4% to 17.9%. The share of payments going to transportation equipment and services was roughly stable. Increasing percentages of demand ex-

smith estimates the same share to be 30% throughout the first half of the thirties and argues that it fell to 20.9% in 1947 and to just below 20% by 1962. See Jeffrey G. Williamson and Peter H. Lindert, *American Inequality: A Macroeconomic History* (New York: Academic Press, 1980), 315–16. Also see Simon Kuznets, *Shares of Upper Income Groups in Income and Savings* (New York: National Bureau of Economic Research, 1953), 637. And see Robert J. Lampman, *Changes in the Share of the Wealth Held by Top Wealth-Holders, 1922–56.* N.B.E.R. occasional paper 71 (New York: National Bureau of Economic Research, 1960), which discusses increasing income inequality in the United States prior to 1929. In a sample of thirty-three large and middle-sized American cities for the years 1929–33, Horst Mendershausen shows that the absolute dispersion of incomes fell, while the relative dispersion (i.e., inequality) of incomes rose. See his *Changes in Income Distribution during the Great Depression,* vol. 7 of *Studies in Income and Wealth* (New York: National Bureau of Economic Research, 1946).

Table 6-2. *Preferred foods: U.S. consumption trends, 1910–70 (pounds per capita)*

Year	Beef	Poultry	Ice cream	Citrus (processed)
1910	56	17	2	0
1920	47	16	3	0
1930	39	18	10	1
1940	43	18	12	4
1945	47	26	19	8
1950	50	25	19	11
1960	64	34	23	15
1970	84	50	26	19

Source: Lebergott, *The American Economy*, 295. Reprinted by permission of Princeton University Press.

penditures were spent on food products, tobacco, household appliances and operations, medical care and insurance, recreation, and education.[8] It appears, therefore, that the structure of demand in the interwar American economy reflected a long-term transition to what might be called high-income spending behavior. While this conjuncture created severe difficulties for some sectors of the economy, it afforded a new set of opportunities for others.

The percentage of constant-dollar consumption expenditures for food, liquor, and tobacco fell from 1914 to 1927 from 35.3% to 29.5%. From 1929 to 1939 the share for food alone rose steadily from 24.4% to 30.6%. As Table 6-2 shows, the consumption in pounds per capita of preferred foods (beef, poultry, and citrus, for example) increased throughout the thirties.[9] Yet short-term movements in relative prices may have affected the per capita consumption of beef and poultry.

8 For details, see the statistical appendix to this chapter taken from J. Frederic Dewhurst and Associates, *America's Needs and Resources*, 80–2; and William H. Lough, *High-Level Consumption* (New York: McGraw-Hill, 1935), appendix A. Also see *Historical Statistics of the United States*, part 1, series G470–494, p. 320.

9 See Harold Barger, *Outlay and Income in the United States: 1921–1938* (New York: National Bureau of Economic Research, 1942); and J. Weinberger, "Economic Aspects of Recreation," *Harvard Business Review*, 15 (Summer, 1937), 448–63. Also see Stanley Lebergott, *The American Economy* (Princeton, N.J.: Princeton University Press, 1976), 272–88, 355; and F. Stricker, "Affluence for Whom? – Another Look at Prosperity and the Working Class in the 1920's," *Labor History*, 24 (Winter, 1983), 5–33.

Table 6-3. *Percentage of U.S. families with refrigeration, 1910–70*

Year	Total (%)	With ice (%)	With mechanical refrigeration (%)
1910	18.0	18.0	0
1920	48	48	*a*
1930	48	40	8
1940	72.0 *b*	27	44
1950	91	11	80
1960	90		
1970	99	*a*	99

*a*Under 1%.
*b*Includes 1% with refrigeration other than ice or mechanical.
Source: Lebergott, *The American Economy*, 286.
Reprinted by permission of Princeton University Press.

Beef consumption fell from 1910 to 1930, which suggests that rising prices may have reduced beef purchases in a period of rising incomes. Nevertheless, there was an unmistakable change in the pattern of food consumption during the depression decade. This new trend in food consumption was paralleled by changes in the demand for household appliances and equipment.

The share of American incomes expended on appliances, other household equipment, and household operations rose throughout the interwar years. In 1914, 9.3% of real consumption spending was devoted to such items; by the end of the twenties, 11.9%. This trend continued into the thirties, despite the cyclical instability after 1929. Other evidence confirms the impression afforded by the consumption share figures. Eight percent of American families owned washing machines in 1920. By 1930, 24% did. Thirty-five percent of American farms had washing machines by 1941, as did 44% of the rural nonfarm population. The percentage of families with mechanical refrigeration capacity rose steadily from 1910 to 1940. Table 6-3 documents this trend. Despite the depression, the fastest increase in this percentage took place during the thirties. Nine percent of American homes had vacuum cleaners by 1920; the figure rose to 30% by 1930 and 54% by

Table 6-4. *Percentages of homes with electrical appliances, 1912–71*

Category	1912	1932	1953	1971
With major appliances				
Vacuum cleaner	0	30	54	92
Washing machine	0	27	70	92
Refrigerator	0	12	82	100
Range	0	4	22	56
Dishwasher	0	1	3	26
With minor appliances				
Iron	0	65	82	100
Toaster	0	27	65	93
Coffee maker	0	19	47	89
Radio	0	61	94	100
TV	0	0	43	99

Source: Lebergott, *The American Economy*, 288. Reprinted by permission of Princeton University Press.

1953. A quarter of American homes owned radios in 1925. The share rose to 40% in 1930 and 83% by 1940. Table 6-4 summarizes the rise of these new products of the interwar era. Americans enjoyed a new age in household comforts and operation as increasing numbers purchased vacuum cleaners, washing machines, refrigerators, ranges, dishwashers, irons, toasters, coffee makers, radios, and other new products. These changes went hand in hand with the introduction of electricity to American homes. The percentage of households with electricity rose from 35% to 68% during the twenties.

Finally, during the New Era, the share of real expenditures going to clothing fell. But expenditures on personal care, recreation, and amusement rose from 14.3% in 1914 to just over 17% by the mid-twenties. The share held steady during the thirties, despite the downturn after 1929. Moreover, the evidence indicates that the real expenditure shares rose for the following four major groups of nondurable and service goods:

> *Personal and small shop services*: Comprising domestic services, personal appearance services (barbers, hairdressers, and so on), moving expenses and repairs, tailoring and clothes-pressing. . . .
> *Larger-scale commercial services*: laundries, dry-cleaning establishments, theaters, hotels. . . .

Non-professional social-cultural spendings: tuition, contributions, dues and postage. . . .
Public utility services rendered by street railway and other local transportation agencies, electricity and gas companies and telephone companies.[10]

During the interwar years, the fruits of the technological and institutional developments of the late nineteenth and early twentieth centuries were secured – not to mention the consequences of America's rise to world prominence as an economic, financial, political, and military power. Changes in the pattern of consumer demand demonstrate this fact, and they show that despite a recession in the early twenties and the depression of the thirties, the composition of the national product was secularly altered.[11]

10 From Lough, *High-Level Consumption*, 43.
11 The changes during the interwar period in the United States may have been unique in their magnitude, although not their character. Insofar as the United States was one of the wealthiest societies in the world during the New Era, it is understandable that the changing pattern of consumption was more pronounced here than elsewhere. Indeed, as the following table shows, by the late post-World War II period, American and European households continued to differ substantially in the composition of their consumption. In large measure this was an outgrowth of the impact of World War II – in the United States the war stimulated G.N.P., whereas in Europe it systematically destroyed the capital stock and the labor force. But it may also be that just as the United States reached a higher level of consumption during the twenties and thirties than most of Europe, so also the transformation that began at that time in the structure of consumption moved faster in America in the postwar period. See Svennilson, *Growth and Stagnation in the European Economy*. The transformation in the composition of national output in the interwar period is reflected in the change in the commodity composition of trade between industrialized nations between the world wars. See H. Tyszynski, "World Trade in Manufactured Commodities: 1899–1950," *Manchester School of Economic and Social Studies*, 19 (September, 1951), 272–304; and R. E. Baldwin, "The Commodity Composition of Trade: Selected Industrial Countries, 1900–1954," *Review of Economics and Statistics*, 40 (1958), 550–68.

Percent of households with specified item in 1970

	U.S.	Western Europe
Refrigerator	99	72
Washing machine	70	57
Dryer	45	18
Iron	100	93
Vacuum cleaner	92	61

Variations in consumer demand during the interwar years were also brought about by changes in the role of women in the national economy and in family life. The growing scholarship in women's history has shown that the entry of women into the American labor force during the interwar years was not solely due to the economic instability that left households with lower incomes when men were unemployed or underemployed. Evidence suggests that increasing female labor force participation also arose out of a redefinition of an adequate standard of living – to include, for the first time, domestic appliances, automobiles, commercial entertainment, and other services. New expectations regarding appropriate family income levels thus encouraged more women to enter the labor market.[12]

The effective demand problem of the interwar period had both secular and cyclical components affecting employment and final demand. Changes in the pattern of employment opportunities and in final demand expenditures made it extremely difficult for dynamic, recovering industries to lead the way out of economic depression. Although the consequence was a decade of instability, the ultimate outcome was not catastrophe. The economy eventually recovered and thrived; the polity ultimately withstood the immense pressures to which it was subjected. And yet both were forever changed.

Percent of households with specified item in 1970

	U.S.	Western Europe
Dishwasher	26	2
Toaster	93	21
Automobile	80	47
TV	99	75
Running cold water	93	91
Running hot water	87	61
Central heating	66	26
Telephone	91	33

Source: Lebergott, *The American Economy*, 261.

12 See, for example, Winifred D. Wandersee, *Women's Work and Family Values, 1920–1940* (Cambridge, Mass.: Harvard University Press, 1981). As discussed in Chapter 2, the entry of women into the labor force was both a cause and effect in the rising use of home appliances.

Statistical appendix to Chapter 6

Percentage distribution of consumer spending, 1914–27

In the first table, the percentage distribution of consumer spending from 1914 to 1927 is presented. Current-dollar data were gathered from J. Frederic Dewhurst and Associates, *America's Needs and Resources*, 81. The data were deflated to 1967 constant dollars using annual consumer price indices (for all commodities) reported in *Historical Statistics of the United States*, series E135–173, part I, p. 211. The percentage shares of total spending were then computed.

Percentage distribution of consumer spending, 1929–39

In the second table, the percentage distribution of consumer spending from 1929 to 1939 is presented. These data were available in 1972 constant dollars from the U.S. Department of Commerce, *The National Income and Product Accounts of the United States: 1929–65*, 69–101. The percentage shares were computed directly from these data.

Percentage share of real consumer expenditures, major categories, 1946–74

In the third table, the percentage share of real consumer expenditures in major categories from 1946 to 1974 is presented. These shares were computed from 1972 constant-dollar data reported in *The National Income and Product Accounts of the United States, 1929–65*, 92–5.

Over the course of the time periods covered by the tables, some classifications were altered. A fully consistent reporting of consumer expenditure patterns prior to 1929 is not currently available. Evidence for the 1940s is not used here because of the distortions created by World War II.

Percentage distribution of consumer spending, 1914–27

	Food, liquor, tobacco	Clothing, accessories, personal care	Housing and utilities	Household equipment & operation	Consumer transportation	Medical care, insurance, death expenses	Recreation	Private education	Religion, private social welfare
1914	35.3	14.3	23.3	9.3	6.8	3.9	3	1.5	2.4
1919	36.7	16.1	16.8	10.2	8.5	4.6	3.5	1.2	2.5
1921	30.3	16.9	21.8	10	9.3	4.1	3.7	1.2	2.5
1923	29.1	17.1	20.4	11.4	10.5	4.7	3.9	1.2	1.9
1925	29	15.9	20	11.6	11.4	5.1	3.9	1.3	2
1927	29.5	16.1	19.2	11.9	10.3	5.4	4.2	1.3	2

Percentage distribution of consumer spending, 1929–39

	'29	'31	'33	'35	'37	'39
Motor vehicles and parts	4.2	2.6	2.2	3.5	4	3.4
Furniture and household equipment	4.4	3.9	3.3	3.6	4.1	4
Food	24.4	27.1	28	28.4	29.7	30.6
Clothing and shoes	11.9	11.8	10.7	11	10.5	11.1
Gasoline and oil	1.5	1.8	1.9	1.9	2	2.1
Fuel oil and coal	1.8	1.8	2	1.9	1.8	1.8
Other[a]	6	6.1	6.1	6.3	6.4	6.8
Housing	9.5	10.4	11.3	10.8	9.8	9.9
Household operation	6.1	6.2	5.9	6.1	6	5.9
Transportation	4	3.7	3.6	3.5	3.6	3.5
Personal care	2.6	2.5	2.1	2.3	2.4	2.3
Medical care	4.1	4.3	4.3	4.1	3.9	4
Recreation	3.3	3.5	3	3.1	3.3	3.1
Private education	1	1.2	1.1	1.1	1.1	1.1
Religious and welfare activities	1.7	2	1.9	1.7	1.4	1.5

[a] Tobacco, toilet articles, semidurable house furnishings, miscellaneous household supplies, drug preparations, nondurable toys and sports supplies, stationery, net foreign remittances.

Percentage share of real consumer expenditures, major categories, 1946–74

	1946	1947	1948	1949	1950	1951	1952	1953	1954	1955	1956	1957	1958	1959	1960
Total expenditures	301.4	306.2	312.8	320.0	338.1	342.3	350.9	364.2	370.9	395.1	406.3	414.7	419.0	441.5	453.0
Motor vehicles and parts	2.7	3.8	4.3	5.3	6.4	5.5	5.0	5.7	5.6	6.8	5.8	5.7	4.9	5.5	5.6
Furniture and household equipment	4.2	4.7	4.8	4.6	5.0	4.7	4.6	4.6	4.6	4.8	4.8	4.6	4.5	4.5	4.3
Food	31.2	29.5	28.5	28.1	27.0	27.3	27.4	27.2	27.1	26.5	26.6	26.5	26.3	25.9	25.5
Clothing and shoes	10.3	9.6	9.5	9.3	9.1	8.9	9.1	8.8	8.6	8.5	8.5	8.2	8.3	8.2	8.1
Gasoline and oil	2.1	2.2	2.3	2.4	2.4	2.6	2.7	2.9	2.8	2.9	3.0	3.0	3.1	3.1	3.1
Fuel oil and coal	1.7	1.8	1.8	1.5	1.5	1.5	1.4	1.3	1.3	1.3	1.3	1.3	1.3	1.2	1.1
Tobacco products	2.7	2.8	2.8	2.8	2.6	2.7	2.7	2.6	2.5	2.3	2.3	2.4	2.4	2.4	2.4
Toilet articles and preparations	0.6	0.6	0.5	0.5	0.6	0.6	0.7	0.6	0.6	0.6	0.7	0.7	0.7	0.7	0.8
Cleaning and polishing preparations	0.6	0.7	0.7	0.8	0.8	0.8	0.8	0.8	0.8	0.8	0.9	0.9	0.9	1.0	1.0
Housing	9.7	10.4	10.7	11.2	11.3	11.9	12.4	12.5	12.9	12.7	13.0	13.4	13.8	13.8	14.1
Household operation	4.9	5.2	5.2	5.3	5.4	5.6	5.5	5.5	5.5	5.7	5.9	6.0	6.1	6.0	6.1
Telephone and telegraph	0.7	0.7	0.7	0.8	0.8	0.8	0.9	0.9	0.9	1.0	1.0	1.1	1.1	1.1	1.1
Transportation	5.4	5.3	5.2	4.8	4.4	4.5	4.3	4.2	4.0	3.9	3.9	3.9	3.8	3.7	3.7
Medical care services	4.3	4.6	5.0	5.0	5.0	5.2	5.1	5.3	5.4	5.2	5.4	5.5	6.1	5.8	5.9

Percentage share of real consumer expenditures, major categories, 1946–74 (continued)

	1961	1962	1963	1964	1965	1966	1967	1968	1969	1970	1971	1972	1973	1974
Total expenditures	462.2	482.9	501.4	528.7	558.1	586.1	603.2	633.4	655.4	668.9	691.9	733.0	766.3	759.8
Motor vehicles and parts	5.0	5.5	5.9	5.8	6.4	6.1	5.8	6.3	6.3	5.6	6.4	6.9	7.0	5.8
Furniture and household equipment	4.3	4.4	4.5	4.8	5.0	5.3	5.4	5.5	5.6	5.6	5.8	6.1	6.5	6.6
Food	25.4	24.7	24.1	23.7	23.5	23.0	22.7	22.4	22.0	22.0	21.3	20.5	19.6	19.4
Clothing and shoes	8.1	8.1	7.9	8.1	7.9	8.0	7.8	7.7	7.6	7.4	7.5	7.5	7.7	7.8
Gasoline and oil	3.1	3.1	3.1	3.0	3.0	3.0	3.1	3.1	3.2	3.4	3.4	3.4	3.4	3.2
Fuel oil and coal	1.0	1.0	1.0	1.0	1.0	1.0	0.9	0.9	0.9	0.9	0.8	0.9	0.9	0.7
Tobacco products	2.4	2.3	2.3	2.1	2.1	2.0	2.0	1.8	1.7	1.7	1.7	1.7	1.7	1.7
Toilet articles and preparations	0.8	0.9	0.9	0.9	0.9	1.0	1.0	1.1	1.1	1.1	1.1	1.1	1.1	1.1
Cleaning and polishing preparations	1.1	1.1	1.2	1.2	1.2	1.3	1.3	1.3	1.4	1.4	1.3	1.4	1.4	1.3
Housing	14.5	14.6	14.8	14.6	14.6	14.6	14.8	14.8	15.0	15.3	15.4	15.3	15.3	16.2
Household operation	6.1	6.2	6.2	6.1	6.1	6.1	6.3	6.2	6.3	6.4	6.3	6.3	6.3	6.4
Telephone and telegraph	1.2	1.2	1.2	1.2	1.3	1.4	1.4	1.5	1.6	1.7	1.7	1.7	1.8	1.9
Transportation	3.7	3.6	3.6	3.6	3.5	3.5	3.6	3.6	3.6	3.6	3.5	3.5	3.6	3.8
Medical care services	6.0	6.1	5.9	6.6	6.5	6.4	6.2	6.3	6.6	6.9	7.0	7.1	7.2	7.6

7. New Deal economic policy and the problem of recovery

> Industry generally brings together a multitude of men in the same place and creates new and complex relations among them. These men are exposed to sudden great alterations of plenty and want, which threaten public peace. Work of this sort may endanger the health, even the life, of those who make money out of it or who are employed therein. Therefore the industrial classes, more than other classes, need rules, supervision, and restraint, and it naturally follows that the functions of government multiply as they multiply.
>
> – Alexis de Tocqueville

The entire composite of New Deal policies must be considered if one is to assess the political economy of the 1930s. Following common practice, these policies can be divided into the following categories: (1) the measures of relief: the emergency banking bill, the Federal Emergency Relief Administration, the Civilian Conservation Corps, the Farm Credit Act to forestall farm foreclosures, Harry Hopkins's Civil Works Administration, and the first agricultural program for crop and livestock herd curtailment; (2) the measures of recovery: the National Recovery Administration (N.R.A.), Harold Ickes's Public Works Administration, the dollar devaluation and gold and silver purchase programs, the various housing acts, and the lending agencies, including and following the Reconstruction Finance Corporation taken over from the Hoover administration; and (3) the measures of reform: the Tennessee Valley Authority, the Social Security Act, the Securities and Exchange Commission, the Federal Communications Commission, the Rural Electrification Administration, the Banking Act of 1935 reforming the Federal Reserve System, and the Wagner bill setting up the National Labor Relations Board.

It can be argued that the relief measures at least accomplished their immediate objectives – banks reopened, people were fed, and deflation ended and ultimately was reversed. The New Deal reforms had lasting effects that Republican administrations after 1952 have been unwilling or unable to undo. Even in an era of deregulation it is clear that numerous New Deal social programs have become permanent institutions. But New Deal recovery efforts, though they had some "relief" and some "reform" aspects, were not successful.

The questions scholars have posed about the economic recovery policies of the New Deal have generally been molded by the theoretical apparatus used to analyze the depression itself. Monetarists have been predisposed to focus on the actions of the Federal Reserve Board, Keynesians on government spending policies, "new" macroeconomists on labor market behavior and the determinants of the natural rate of unemployment. Analyzing the Great Depression as part of a long-term structural phenomenon – the approach taken here – poses new questions about the political economy of the New Deal and indeed about the general economic history of the postwar era.

A bold generalization would suggest that the New Deal has been viewed in one of three ways: as an aberrant violation of the principles of American democracy, as the triumph of a Whig consensus, or as the manifestation of a corporatist broker-state. Those who viewed the New Deal with a jaundiced eye typically invoked the example of Mussolini's Italy or of National Socialist Germany to underscore their misgivings about a statist approach to the economic crisis of the thirties. Consensus historians understood the unprecedented initiatives of the Roosevelt administrations as responses to an altogether unique "crisis of the Old Order." Their position is best summarized by one of their most eloquent spokesmen, who argued that New Dealers saw "America as off on a tangent but capable of being recalled to the old main road of progress." A later analysis focused on the New Deal as a system "of continued corporate dominance in a political structure where other groups agreed generally on corporate capitalism and squabbled only about the size of the shares."[1]

These interpretations of the New Deal, whatever their relative merits, nonetheless suffer from a common inadequacy. Their focus moves from the top downward; their method of analysis is generally aggregative. Yet a comprehensive examination of New Deal politics and policy making would benefit from a structural approach that allows for the

1 On the "crisis of the Old Order," see Arthur M. Schlesinger, Jr., *The Politics of Upheaval*, vol. 3 of *The Age of Roosevelt* (Boston: Houghton Mifflin, 1959), 393. On the notion of the New Deal as a broker-state system, see B. J. Bernstein, "The New Deal: The Conservative Achievements of Liberal Reform," in B. J. Bernstein, ed., *Towards a New Past: Dissenting Essays in American History* (New York: Pantheon, 1968), 270. Also see N. Sivachev, "The Rise of Statism in 1930's America: A Soviet View of the Social and Political Effects of the New Deal," *Labor History*, 24 (Fall, 1983), 500–25.

interplay of material interest, economic behavior, and political advocacy. Some political scientists and sociologists have employed such an approach in recent years.[2]

Just as the economics of the thirties were driven by the interplay of sectoral dynamics, so the political history of the decade was shaped by similar forces. On the one side, the original architects of the New Deal recognized the structural and sectoral components of the crisis, and I would suggest that the policy initiatives of the early New Deal were in large part informed and motivated by that perspective. On the other side, the response of the business community to the New Deal, and the extent to which their response aided or interfered with New Deal recovery policy, was also determined in large part by the material interests embedded within each sector. These material interests were specified by the particular combination of long-term and cyclical factors that impinged on each industry in the interwar period.

Following its most thorough analysis by Ellis Hawley, New Deal recovery policy has generally been seen as beset by a fundamental contradiction between two strategies. The contradiction was epitomized by the conflict between the advocates of economic planning within Roosevelt's inner circle and the "Brandeisians" committed to trust-busting, who maintained that excessive concentrations of market power in major sectors of the economy caused the economic crisis of the thirties. The result of the contradiction was the strange brew of New Deal policy, the bewildering movement of the president from a planning initiative to a reform initiative, and the generally poor record of Roosevelt's first two terms with respect to economic recovery.[3]

There is a great deal of wisdom in this view. It is hardly my intention here to attempt a general history of New Deal policy or of the transition between the so-called First and Second New Deals.[4] I wish to suggest, however, that the planning initiative of the early New Deal

2 See, for example, T. Skocpol and K. Finegold, "State Capacity and Economic Intervention in the Early New Deal," *Political Science Quarterly*, 97 (Summer, 1982), 255–78; and J. R. Kurth, "The Political Consequences of the Product Cycle: Industrial History and Political Outcomes," *International Organization*, 33 (Winter, 1979), 1–34.

3 See Ellis W. Hawley, *The New Deal and the Problem of Monopoly: A Study in Economic Ambivalence* (Princeton, N.J.: Princeton University Press, 1966), especially ch. 2.

4 The notion of two New Deals was first formulated by Basil Rauch in his *The History of the New Deal: 1933–1938* (New York: Creative Age Press, 1944), vi.

was inspired in part by an awareness of some of the sectoral dynamics I have analyzed. Moreover, I want to argue that the demise of the planning viewpoint within the Roosevelt White House, and the emergence of the Brandeisian and Keynesian views of how to deal with the depression, did not reflect a leftward swing of the president in response to the *Schechter* decision and his anger over the intransigence of his conservative critics. Rather, it was a failure of the planning apparatus to overcome the political opposition – based on material interests molded by both long-term and short-term factors – of firms and industries to a sectoral strategy. The failure of planning had profound consequences for the subsequent ability of the American state to deal with economic problems.

Throughout the first two Roosevelt administrations, recovery policy was derived from several conflicting points of view. This, indeed, may be one of the reasons why New Deal policy seems in retrospect so ad hoc, unsystematic, and at times self-defeating. Rexford Tugwell, the Columbia University economist who came to play a significant role in the First New Deal, suggested in his *The Art of Politics* that there were basically five theories of economic recovery debated within the Roosevelt administration. First, there was what might be called an entrepreneurship theory, which held that deregulation and other strategies to bolster business confidence would end the crisis. Second, there was the monetarist view, which proposed an easy-money strategy. Third, there was the purchasing power idea, which argued that steps had to be taken to raise purchasing power throughout the economy. Fourth, there was the fiscal concept of those whom today we call Keynesian. Finally, there was the notion of "balance" – "the equalizing of income among mutually supporting groups." It was this final policy conception that epitomized the general tenor of the First New Deal.[5]

The man who best exemplified the attitude and position of the planners within the New Deal hierarchy was Tugwell himself. His unorthodox and iconoclastic thinking on economic matters demonstrates

5 See Bernard Sternsher, *Rexford Tugwell and the New Deal* (New Brunswick, N.J.: Rutgers University Press, 1964), 123; and Rexford G. Tugwell, *The Art of Politics, As Practiced by Three Great Americans: Franklin Delano Roosevelt, Luis Munoz Marin and Fiorello LaGuardia* (Garden City, N.Y.: Doubleday, 1958), 184–5. Also see L. L. Lorwin, "The Plan State and the Democratic Ideal," *Annals of the American Academy of Political and Social Science*, 180 (July, 1935), 114–18; and Hugh S. Johnson, *The Blue Eagle From Egg to Earth* (Garden City, N.Y.: Doubleday, Doran, 1935), 162, 222, 235.

the distinctiveness of the First New Deal in its approach to the problem of economic recovery and provides more detailed insight with regard to the understanding of the crisis that prevailed in Washington before *Schechter* and the advent of the Brandeisians.

For Tugwell, the central problem facing advanced capitalist economies was that of the social coordination of investment in order to avoid "disproportionality crises" whereby the various sectors of the economy grew out of balance with one another.[6] Unlike mainstream economists of his day, Tugwell did not believe that the price system alone could ensure that supplies and demands throughout the economic system would balance appropriately. In addition to such difficulties, in times of economic crisis capital tended to go on "strike," avoiding the investment necessary for recovery because of a lack of business confidence and a general fear of political turmoil and government intervention.

Economic imbalance or disproportionality, as Tugwell viewed it, was the result of inappropriate or inadequate dispositions of corporate surpluses. A firm "tended to reinvest its surplus in its own operation without having adequate knowledge of its place within an industry, or of the place of that industry in the total economy." Indeed, it was Tugwell's opinion that Roosevelt himself believed the depression to be the outgrowth of "the antics of the newer rich" that resulted in the "mismanagement of corporate surplus." The task of national policy, therefore, was to ensure that "the capitalists behave."[7]

Whereas the president may have had political notions of what constituted proper behavior by capitalists, Tugwell and others had specific economic arguments for the need to influence the most important activity in which entrepreneurs engaged – investment. In essence, the goal was for capitalists to have a broad vision of the importance and impacts of their decisions, not a short-sighted one. The disposition of surplus funds had to be made on the basis of "a national point of view" if intermittent cyclical instability and secular stagnation were both to be avoided. The basis of economic growth, investment expenditure, had to be coordinated on a national scale; if left to the narrow basis of purely individual decision making, the achievement of economic "balance" would be virtually impossible.[8]

6 The phrase "disproportionality crisis," based on Marx's notion of *unproportionierter Produktion*, is derived from Paul Sweezy, *The Theory of Capitalist Development*, ch. 10.
7 From Sternsher, *Rexford Tugwell*, 113, 316.
8 See Sternsher, *Rexford Tugwell*, 316–17.

In a certain sense, Tugwell (and those of like mind) attempted to find a middle road between the two ideological poles of the early New Deal. With the technocrats of the New Deal he shared a conception of the technological requirements of new production methods and new products – requirements that necessitated large firms and the vertical and horizontal concentration of economic power. With the Progressives of the New Deal, the Brandeisians, the trust-busters, he shared a concern that large firms and economic concentration resulted in lethargy, smugness, and a lack of dynamism. Even so, Tugwell saw the Progressives being "torn between attachment to their traditional attitudes and the demands of a new technological era." And he felt the technocrats tended to overlook the fact that "accumulation of undistributed corporate surpluses [by large firms] was an important cause of overproduction-underconsumption" – that is, of crises.[9]

It was essentially a vision of the technological requirements of modern productive enterprise that informed Tugwell's view of the causes of the Great Depression and its potential policy cures. Large firms, an outgrowth of the large capital commitments required for modern production techniques, accumulated surpluses in order to protect themselves from the vagaries of the market. If firm managers were overly timid, underinvestment resulted; if they were too aggressive, overinvestment was the consequence. What was objectionable to Tugwell was the fact that the tasks of accumulating profits and of allocating surpluses to investment were undertaken by the same individuals – the managers of firms. In order to avoid the instability that resulted from the emergence of large-scale enterprise, state planning and other forms of intervention were necessary.[10]

Industrial planning was an obvious solution to the problems that preoccupied Tugwell. And it was his distinctive economic outlook that

9 See Sternsher, *Rexford Tugwell*, 110; and Daniel R. Fusfeld, *The Economic Thought of Franklin D. Roosevelt and the Origins of the New Deal* (New York: Columbia University Press, 1956), 211.

10 See Allan G. Gruchy, *Modern Economic Thought: The American Contribution* (New York: Prentice-Hall, 1947), 433. It is interesting to note the similarity of Tugwell's thinking to that of John Maynard Keynes. In his massive critique of classical economic theory, Keynes rejected the orthodox notion that "an act of individual saving inevitably leads to a parallel act of investment." He maintained that those who believed in that notion were "fallaciously supposing that there is a nexus which unites decisions to abstain from present consumption with decisions to provide for future consumption; whereas the motives which determine the latter are not linked in any simple way with the motives which determine the former." See Keynes, *The General Theory*, 21.

made him unique among proponents of the planning initiatives of the First New Deal. The core of his policy strategy was the implementation of a taxing scheme to prevent the accumulation of corporate surpluses and to stop the privilege firms had always enjoyed of investing their surpluses at will. Tugwell's novel concern with economic "balance" and with the destabilizing tendencies of modern business enterprise led him to embrace an old idea, the undistributed profits tax.[11]

The undistributed profits tax, embedded in the Revenue Act of 1936, was one of the most unpopular and controversial pieces of legislation to emerge from the New Deal. Indeed, it was repealed in 1938.[12] Most historians of the Roosevelt years have viewed the measure as a punitive device embraced by the president to bolster the left wing of his coalition in the face of conservative thrusts and the aftermath of the *Schechter* decision in 1935. Some have also suggested that the tax was employed as a device to steal the thunder of the followers of the murdered Huey Long and of Father Coughlin.[13]

Yet regardless of the personal motivations of the president, there was an economic motivation for the implementation of the undistributed profits tax that was derived from a particular interpretation of the Great Depression – an interpretation analogous to the one I have advanced in this study. Tugwell and other members of the so-called Brain Trust placed much of the blame for the depression on the tendency of large firms to engage in distorted investment decision making. Moreover, it was Tugwell's and others' conviction that the persistence of the depression was due to the lethargy of capital. Surpluses did not find their way back into productive, high-growth investment outlets. Capital tied up in slowly growing industries did not necessarily move into industries with faster rates of growth, because privately based expenditure decisions were uncoordinated and often chaotic. The solution was to be found in national policies to encourage the kind of expenditure behavior that would generate higher rates of growth and macroeconomic recovery.

The essence of the economic argument in favor of the undistributed

11 See Gruchy, *Modern Economic Thought*, 441–2.
12 See Leuchtenburg, *Franklin D. Roosevelt and the New Deal*, 260. Also see Alfred G. Buehler, *The Undistributed Profits Tax* (New York: McGraw-Hill, 1937).
13 See Leuchtenburg, *Franklin D. Roosevelt and the New Deal*, ch. 11; Raymond Moley, *After Seven Years* (New York: Harper & Bros., 1939), 300–1, 308–9; and Alan Brinkley, *Voices of Protest: Huey Long, Father Coughlin, and the Great Depression* (New York: Knopf, 1982), 247.

profits tax was that the incentive of the tax would lead firms to issue more of their surpluses in the form of productive investment commitments or in the form of dividends. If surpluses went into investment, there might still be disproportionality and instability, but productive expenditure was better than wasteful speculation or no expenditure at all. If surpluses were distributed as dividends, they would then be subject to the discipline of private capital markets. Such discipline would ensure that the allocation of capital was made on the basis of a broader set of information than that available within a single firm. The capital market would be more prone to discriminate between high- and low-growth sectors – more capable of "picking winners and losers." As a result, the mobilization of capital resources would be more efficient and more likely to generate higher rates of growth.[14]

The idea of the macroeconomic benefits of an undistributed profits tax was a relatively old one, tracing its lineage back to the work of a group of economic thinkers in the United States just after World War I.[15] Far from being a punitive measure undertaken on the spur of the moment by Roosevelt, it was the outgrowth of a systematic consideration by several economists of the weaknesses in the interwar American economy.

As early as 1933, in his major work, *The Industrial Discipline and the Governmental Arts*, Tugwell had argued for an undistributed profits tax as a reform measure, not as a means of augmenting the federal revenue. In his acceptance speech to the Democratic National Convention at Chicago in 1932, Roosevelt had held that corporate profits "were eventually invested in unnecessary industrial plants and equipment and in the call-money markets of Wall Street, where they nurtured speculation." For both men the central problem was the establishment of appropriate incentives and safeguards that would ensure that capital funds were mobilized in ways conducive to economic recovery, growth, and development.[16]

14 See Sternsher, *Rexford Tugwell*, 316–17.
15 For a full history of the original proposals regarding an undistributed profits tax, see Buehler, *The Undistributed Profits Tax*, ch. 1. Also see C. William Hazelett, *Incentive Taxation* (New York: Dutton, 1936); and Rexford G. Tugwell, *The Industrial Discipline and the Governmental Arts* (New York: Columbia University Press, 1933).
16 See Buehler, *The Undistributed Profits Tax*, 14, 16–18; Franklin D. Roosevelt, *The Public Papers and Addresses of Franklin D. Roosevelt*, vol. 5 (New York: Macmillan, 1941), 233–4; and Charles F. Roos, *NRA Economic Planning* (Bloomington, Ind.: Principia Press, 1937), 470–1. Also cf. G. N. Nelson,

Such views were also commonly held among Roosevelt's principal aides. Marriner Eccles, governor of the Federal Reserve Board, endorsed the undistributed profits tax on the grounds that it would increase investment and consumption expenditures along with improving the effectiveness of the Federal Reserve System in monitoring capital markets. Henry Morgenthau, Jr., secretary of the treasury, also offered an effective analysis of the usefulness of the tax when he pointed out the weaknesses of the present system. He held that "large corporations by retaining their surpluses could block innovation by their own subsidiaries and withhold profits from stockowners who might otherwise have invested in more venturesome enterprises. Thus the accumulation of surpluses perpetuated business oligarchy and tended to inhibit the whole investment process on which recovery depended." [17]

The major exception among the president's men with regard to support for the tax scheme was Raymond Moley, an original member of the Brain Trust. His views of the measure appear to have been absorbed by most political historians of the New Deal. Moley claimed that "[t]he 'soak-the-rich' and corporate-surplus proposals represented a complete departure from the principles of taxation for revenue and reform in taxation. They signalized the adoption of a policy of reform through taxation [and were] punitive in intent." [18] With the exception of the last thought on the punitive nature of the program, Moley's reflection seems entirely accurate. These proposals did represent a new departure that, though temporary, did suggest that New Deal economic policy had several structuralist components.

"Taxation of Corporate Surplus," in *Proceedings of the 29th Annual Conference of the National Tax Association* (September 28 to October 1, 1936) (Columbia, S.C.: National Tax Association, 1937), 221–52. On August 3, 1934, *Commonweal* ran an article calling for special legislation to move investment funds into the hands of small-scale entrepreneurs. See G. C. McCabe, "Wall Street Recants," *Commonweal* (August 3, 1934), 341–4. Also see Rexford G. Tugwell, *The Democratic Roosevelt: A Biography of Franklin D. Roosevelt* (Garden City, N.Y.: Doubleday, 1957), 467; and E. B. Fricke, "The New Deal and the Modernization of Small Business: The McCreary Tire and Rubber Company, 1930–1940," *Business History Review*, 56 (Winter, 1982), 559–76.

17 See Marriner S. Eccles, *Beckoning Frontiers: Public and Personal Recollections* (New York: Knopf, 1951), 260; John M. Blum, *From the Morgenthau Diaries: Years of Crisis, 1928–1938* (Boston: Houghton Mifflin, 1959), 307; and John M. Blum, *The Progressive Presidents: Roosevelt, Wilson, Roosevelt, Johnson* (New York: Norton, 1980), 128.

18 From Moley, *After Seven Years*, 367. Also see F. R. Macaulay, "Economic Recovery and the New Deal," *Economic Forum*, 3 (Winter, 1936), 245–55.

A sectoral approach to understanding the economic crisis of the 1930s alters our judgment as to the vision and efficacy of New Deal policies. These policies did not, of course, unambiguously assist in the adjustment of the American economy to the new constellation of demand forthcoming during the New Era. But the industries as yet unborn could not lobby for their interests. Only established industries, agriculture, and unionized or unionizing labor could do so. The financial community was alienated and in disgrace. Not until military necessity forced technology and government investment into new lines was it possible to give the future some political clout.

Most evaluations of the effectiveness of New Deal economic policy have rested with second-guessing – arguing that this or that fiscal or monetary policy was good or bad.[19] Depending on the theoretical persuasion of the author, policies are either extolled or condemned. What this literature fails to do is to consider the political economic coalitions within the New Deal created by the Roosevelt administration's strategy of economic intervention. The nature and actions of these coalitions go a long way toward explaining the successes and failures of New Deal recovery policy.

It traditionally has been argued that the New Deal had adverse effects on business confidence. There are two versions of this argument. The first stresses the quantitative distortion of investment decision making created by the intervention of the National Recovery Administration. Costs, particularly labor costs, were forced up by the industry codes, thereby dampening the private sector's potential for economic recovery.[20] The second argument is more qualitative, claiming that the unprecedented scale of the federal government's presence in the nation's markets left the business world intimidated and apprehensive about the future political environment. Confidence in the future, a prerequisite

19 For example, see the work of Milton Friedman and Anna J. Schwartz cited in the Introduction to this book, along with P. B. Trescott, "Federal Reserve Policy in the Great Contraction: A Counterfactual Assessment," *Explorations in Economic History*, 19 (July, 1982), 211–20. Also see L. C. Peppers, "Full Employment Surplus Analysis and Structural Change: The 1930s," *Explorations in Economic History*, 10 (Winter, 1973), 197–210.

20 The most recent and precise statement of this view is provided by Weinstein, *Recovery and Redistribution under the NIRA*, especially ch. 4; and cf. Roose, *The Economics of Recession and Revival: An Interpretation of 1937–38*, chs. 2, 15, 16; and Douglas A. Hayes, *Business Confidence and Business Activity: A Case Study of the Recession of 1937* (Ann Arbor: University of Michigan Press, 1951), ch. 5.

for bold investment strategies, was lost, with economic stagnation the result.

The climate of opinion Roosevelt at times created could easily be construed as a direct attack on the business community and the institution of private property. The president, in his acceptance speech to the Democratic National Convention in 1936, spoke of "[t]he royalists of the economic order [who] complain that we seek to overthrow the institutions of America" and "[who] have maintained that economic slavery was nobody's business." And in his first presidential campaign, Roosevelt declared: "The country needs and, unless I mistake its temper, the country demands bold, persistent experimentation." It is easy to understand the concern of the private sector with the intentions of the New Deal.[21]

But the historical record shows a far more subtle reality than the business confidence argument implies. The available evidence indicates that it was precisely in the industries where economic conditions were worst that the industry codes were most welcome. And it tended to be the older, larger firms that were most eager to secure government regulation. In the textile industry, the older, larger firms in the North embraced the code; the newer, smaller mills in the South did not. The latter had less to lose and more to gain from unrestricted competition.[22]

21 Roosevelt, *The Public Papers and Addresses of Franklin D. Roosevelt*, vol. 5, 233–4; and *New Deal Thought*, H. Zinn, ed. (Indianapolis: Bobbs-Merrill, 1966), 83. Zinn quotes the following, on p. 408, from a letter (of February 1, 1938) to President Roosevelt from John Maynard Keynes warning about the delicate psychology of the entrepreneur: "Business men have a different set of delusions from politicians; and need, therefore, different handling. They are, however, much milder than politicians, at the same time allured and terrified by the glare of publicity, easily persuaded to be 'patriots', perplexed, bemused, indeed terrified, yet only too anxious to take a cheerful view, vain perhaps but very unsure of themselves, pathetically responsive to a kind word. You could do anything you liked with them, if you would treat them (even the big ones), not as wolves and tigers, but as domestic animals by nature, even though they have been badly brought up and not trained as you would wish. It is a mistake to think that they are more *immoral* than politicians. If you work them into the surly, obstinate, terrified mood, of which domestic animals, wrongly handled, are so capable, the nation's burdens will not get carried to market; and in the end public opinion will veer their way." A recent study that finds no adverse effects of the New Deal on business confidence is that of T. Mayer and M. Chatterji, "Political Shocks and Investment: Some Evidence from the 1930s," *Journal of Economic History*, 45 (December, 1985), 913–24.

22 See Galambos, *Competition and Cooperation*, 160.

Steel firms with high overhead and excess capacity welcomed the codes, whereas smaller fabricating companies accepted them only reluctantly.[23]

Although some automobile companies, such as Ford, were involved in bitter labor disputes arising from the New Deal's pro-union policies, most of the industry endorsed the stabilization efforts of the code authorities.[24] In the rubber industry, even the aggressive giant, Firestone Tire and Rubber, pushed for N.R.A. price stabilization, as did almost all the lumber firms – firms that in 1930 had urged President Hoover to regulate the industry through a Timber Conservation Board.[25] It is worth remembering that the most notorious of the N.R.A.'s opponents was not a member of the Fortune 500 but a small food processing firm in Brooklyn, New York, the A. L. A. Schechter Poultry Corporation.

The business confidence argument, at least as formulated in the literature, is too crude and aggregative to withstand close consideration. The issue is not the attitude of the business community as a whole toward the New Deal, but the division of opinion within the business community as to the proper course of antidepression national economic policy. It is telling in this regard that two major evaluations of the N.R.A. and allied policies undertaken during the thrities lamented the tendency of New Deal policy to exacerbate tensions within the business community. And they noted the failure of the Roosevelt administration to establish itself as an impartial and independent arbiter or broker of economic interests.

In 1935, the year of the *Schechter* decision, the Brookings Institution published, under the direction of Leverett Lyon, an appraisal of the National Recovery Administration. The Brookings study found that the primary problem with the code apparatus of the N.R.A. was that it was "not fully representative of all the business interests in a [particular] industry." Moreover, the code administration for each industry was held to be "subordinated to immediate exigencies and interests." It was the control on capacity in each industry, applied by the N.R.A.

23 See Maxwell S. Stewart, *Steel – Problems of a Great Industry* (New York: Public Affairs Committee, 1937), 8; and Daugherty et al., *The Economics of the Iron and Steel Industry*, 447–8.

24 See Kennedy, *The Automobile Industry*, 217; and Rae, *American Automobile Manufacturers*, 201.

25 See Lief, *The Firestone Story*, 199; Pack, *Forestry*, 27; L. M. James, "Restrictive Agreements and Practices in the Lumber Industry, 1880–1939," *Southern Economic Journal*, 13 (October, 1946), 125; and Ralph C. Bryant, *Lumber: Its Manufacture and Distribution* (New York: Wiley, 1938), 394.

codes, that the study found to be most troublesome. It argued that the code authorities were ill-equipped to choose among alternative investments and that the entire structure of capacity restriction "interfere[d] still further with an already too inactive capital market, and thus constitute[d] a distinct hindrance to economic recovery."[26]

The National Recovery Review Board, chaired by Clarence Darrow at the request of President Roosevelt, had been created the year before the Brookings report was issued. Mounting criticism of the N.R.A. appears to have influenced the president to convene this special commission, which reported directly to him rather than to the N.R.A. director, Hugh Johnson. The review board was composed of two attorneys, Darrow and his partner William O. Thompson; a banker, John F. Sinclair; a merchant, Fred P. Mann; and a manufacturer, William R. Neal. It was charged to evaluate the industrial codes.[27]

The review board offered two major criticisms of the N.R.A. code apparatus. One concerned the structure of the code authorities themselves, the other a particular aspect of the code authorities' policy. As to the former, the board found that in "virtually all the codes we have examined, one condition has been persistent . . . the code has offered an opportunity for the more powerful . . . interests to seize control of an industry or to augment and extend a control already obtained." For example, the board found that most of the complaints concerning the code for the petroleum industry focused on the fact that the code authority lacked any representatives of small, independent companies.[28]

In terms of the code authorities' policies, the board singled out for vehement criticism the restrictions in all the industry codes on expansion of existing facilities or erection of new capacity. Board hearings on the steel code produced a uniform complaint from "small enterprises" regarding "a rule that forbids the enlarging of the producing capacity of any unit in the industry." Lumber producers offered similar criticisms of the code in their sector. The conclusions of the board with

---

26 See Leverett S. Lyon et al., *The National Recovery Administration: An Analysis and Appraisal* (Washington, D.C.: Brookings Institution, 1935), 258, 273, 647.

27 See U.S. National Recovery Review Board, *Reports* (n.p.: n.p., n.d.), and Bernard Bellush, *The Failure of the NRA* (New York: Norton, 1975), 142ff. Also see U.S. House of Representatives, Committee on Ways and Means, *Hearings*, "Extension of the National Industrial Recovery Act," 74th Congress, 1st session (Washington, D.C.: U.S. Government Printing Office, 1935), 613, 620, 756, 759.

28 See U.S. National Recovery Review Board, "Third Report," 35, 50–3, in *Reports*.

respect to the steel code well summarize the board's general attitude toward the capacity restriction policy of the N.R.A. In its report on that code, the board argued that "changes in the productive capacity should not be so prohibited as to protect the less economical centers of production and the less efficient mills in favor of the more economical and lower cost sections and mills."[29]

Overall, the Darrow report was a Brandeisian document. It focused on what it held to be the monopolistic bias of the industrial codes and of the entire N.R.A. strategy and apparatus. By not ensuring the representation of smaller firms, and by imposing capacity restrictions at the request of larger companies that hindered the ability of their smaller competitors to enter or get a foothold in an industry, the codes interfered with dynamic and aggressive expenditure strategies that could generate economic recovery at a faster pace. The minimum pricing standards touted by the Roosevelt administration as a device to bolster incomes, spending, and overall economic activity also came in for censure. Such price floors inhibited smaller and more dynamic corporations in their efforts to compete profitably within their particular industries. Whatever its political merits, the N.R.A. apparatus was a decisive obstacle to robust and fast economic recovery. The Darrow commission and the Brookings study both tried to understand some of the nagging problems of the New Deal and the persistence of the depression.

In the attitudes of the business community one finds evidence of the political economic factors that hindered the establishment of a coherent and effective national economic policy. These attitudes suggest differences within the business community that the New Deal failed either to recognize or to resolve differences derived from the particular material interests of each firm and industry. The evidence suggests that the problem with the N.R.A. apparatus was not so much one of favoring large monopolistic firms over smaller enterprises, but rather of failing to pinpoint the new industries that could lead recovery and to implement policies to aid them. Insofar as the N.R.A. code authorities were dominated by older firms within older industries, there was an inherent bias toward aiding slow-growth activities.

Interestingly, in March 1938, the *Wall Street Journal* published a "Review and Outlook" column in which the editors dismissed any suggestion that the difficulty for American industry was a relative

29 See U.S. National Recovery Review Board, "First Report," 11, 58; and see "Second Report," 127.

scarcity of loanable funds or the lack of "an elaborate new industrial credit system." The *Journal* maintained that easier credit would not do small or big firms any good. "What both desperately need," the editors declared, "is better reasons for borrowing and for undertaking the utilization of other people's money. Among such better reasons, now lacking, the first and foremost is assurance that the framework of laws within which they must carry on is not to be suddenly and violently distorted to their unforeseeable injury." In a reference to "men who dare not borrow," the *Journal* made clear its conception of the continuing crisis as a problem of confidence and excessive government intervention.[30]

Yet in January and February of that year the *Journal* ran two articles on the processed foods industry, noting that despite the depressed levels of economic activity and "uncertain prospects," the industry was forging ahead with broad programs of expansion. The introduction of new production techniques, especially for frozen and refrigerated foodstuffs, was the foundation of this industry's expansion in the midst of crisis. Noting that the "oldest industry in the world" was capable of finding sources of growth in new products and processes, the *Journal* wondered what impact such developments might have had earlier in the decade. The *Journal* thus focused on a crisis in confidence as the source of the nation's economic difficulties and clearly recognized the need for new investment projects. Such opinions also emerged in the utterances of industry representatives themselves.[31]

Generally speaking, assessments of the attitudes of the business community toward the New Deal have suffered from a reliance on the records left by cooperative associations such as the U.S. Chamber of Commerce and the National Association of Manufacturers.[32] Such evidence provides no insight into the sectoral issues posed in this study,

30 See "Review and Outlook: The Key to Capital Inertia," *Wall Street Journal*, March 24, 1938, 4. Also see Arthur Dahlberg, *When Capital Goes on Strike: How to Speed Up Spending* (New York: Harper & Bros., 1938), passim.

31 See "Frosted Food Sales Show Sharp Gain for Past Year," *Wall Street Journal*, January 31, 1938, 1ff.

32 See, for example, Arthur M. Schlesinger, *The Coming of the New Deal*, vol. 2 of *The Age of Roosevelt* (Boston: Houghton Mifflin, 1959), and his *The Politics of Upheaval*; also see, for a later example, Albert V. Romasco, *The Politics of Recovery: Roosevelt's New Deal* (Oxford University Press, 1983); and my review of Romasco in the *Journal of Economic History*, 43 (December, 1983), 1048–9. Also see Willard E. Atkins et al., *Economic Problems of the New Deal* (New York: F. S. Crofts, 1934), 96.

and the sampling of opinion that the records of such organizations provide tends to be rather one-sided. Overall, such sources present the image of a fearful and disorganized business community seeking and accepting government intervention at the depth of the depression, but then becoming increasingly hostile as the leftist tendencies of the Roosevelt administration manifested themselves later in the decade. In particular, according to this evidence, the labor provisions of the New Deal, most important Section 7(a) of the National Industrial Recovery Act (N.I.R.A.), received the universal condemnation of the business community and were the basis of a lack of confidence that forestalled recovery.[33]

Review of the *Annual Report* of the U.S. Chamber of Commerce for the decade 1929–39, for example, would suggest that the primary concerns of the American business community during the Great Depression were: (1) relaxation of antitrust laws in order to allow for price and output control by industry members; (2) decrease in federal spending and balancing of the national budget; (3) prohibition of government enterprise in major industries; (4) allowance of industrial "self-government"; (5) elimination of securities and capital markets regulation; and (6) suppression of subversive activities. The chamber's board of directors, in their own *Annual Reports* for the thirties, focused on the impact of excessive government interference on business confidence and the fomenting of labor unrest. Such sentiments were reiterated repeatedly by state chambers of commerce and other spokesmen.[34]

33 See *Resolutions Expressing the Manufacturer's Viewpoint Adopted at the Annual Meeting of the N.A.M.*, December 7–8, 1933 (New York: National Association of Manufacturers, 1933); U.S. Chamber of Commerce, *Outlines of Eleven Talks on Timely Questions Affecting the American Free Enterprise System* (Washington, D.C.: n.p., 1941); and W. H. Wilson, "How the Chamber of Commerce Viewed the NRA: A Reexamination," *Mid-America: An Historical Review*, 44 (April, 1962), 95–108. Also see "Business Agrees to Regulate Itself," *Nation's Business*, 21 (June, 1933), 17ff. *Nation's Business* was the chamber's official magazine. Section 7(a) of the N.I.R.A. required that the codes for each industry specify minimum wages and maximum hours. In addition, it guaranteed the right of labor to bargain collectively.

34 See U.S. Chamber of Commerce, *Annual Reports* (Washington, D.C.: U.S. Chamber of Commerce, 1929–1939); U.S. Chamber of Commerce, *Board of Directors Annual Report* (Washington, D.C.: Chamber of Commerce of the United States, 1933), 6, 24; and U.S. Chamber of Commerce, *Board of Directors Annual Report* (Washington, D.C.: Chamber of Commerce of the United States, 1936), 6. Also see Congress of American Industry and National Association of Manufacturers, *Platform and Resolutions Adopted December 5 and 6, 1934* (New York: National Association of Manufacturers, n.d.), 6, 68; and

Several studies written after World War II found that business attitudes toward the New Deal varied with economic conditions. Early in the thirties, in the worst years of the crisis, support for the interventionist strategies of the Roosevelt presidency was high. As the decade wore on, as some economic indicators improved slightly, as Roosevelt himself seemingly moved left to bolster the labor component of his coalition, businessmen became disaffected with the New Deal. The National Recovery Administration and the other "alphabet agencies" were "no longer a medium of prestige enhancement," and the business community moved into opposition against Roosevelt.[35]

A more detailed consideration of the attitudes of the business community toward the New Deal reveals differences within that community that derived from material interests – interests differentiated by the varied experiences of particular industries in the crisis of the thirties. One authority on business attitudes toward the New Deal has argued that "business was scarcely monolithic in its reaction to the changes of the New Deal years. . . . Perhaps it is time to qualify our simplistic division of the business community into the polar opposites of reactionary small and medium-sized business on the one hand and enlightened big business on the other." Scholars who have attempted to specify the differences of opinion within the business community have focused on the division between small and big firms – the former opposing the N.R.A. and the latter supporting it. But the evidence suggests that "[t]he major line of division within the business community was between the more and the less profitable industries."[36]

Congress of American Industry and National Association of Manufacturers, *The Platform of American Industry* (New York: National Association of Manufacturers, n.d.).

35 See Linda K. Brown, *Challenge and Response: The American Business Community and the New Deal, 1932–1934* (Ph.D. dissertation, University of Pennsylvania, 1972), 204; Wesley C. Clark, *Economic Aspects of a President's Popularity* (Ph.D. dissertation, University of Pennsylvania, 1943); and S. Fine, "The Ford Motor Company and the N.R.A.," *Business History Review*, 32 (Winter, 1958), 353–85. Cf. the opinion of William E. Leuchtenberg, in his *Franklin D. Roosevelt and the New Deal*, 90: "No single act did more to mobilize the business community against Roosevelt than his message of February 9, 1934, asking Congress for legislation to regulate the Stock Exchange." Also see Lee R. Tilman, *The American Business Community and the Death of the New Deal* (Ph.D. dissertation, University of Arizona, 1966).

36 See R. M. Collins, "Positive Business Responses to the New Deal: The Roots of the Committee for Economic Development, 1933–1942," *Business History Review*, 52 (Autumn, 1978), 369–91, especially 390; Robert M. Collins, *The Business Response to Keynes: 1929–1964* (New York: Columbia University

A good example is found in the political conduct of the textile industry during the thirties. With the onset of the crash in 1929, the industry as a whole supported industrial cooperation under the aegis of federal supervision. But as the years passed, a split developed between the textile firms in the North and those in the South. The latter firms were younger, leaner, more mechanized, producing for the faster-growing markets of the interwar period, and served by an unorganized labor force. The attempt by the Cotton Textile Institute (C.T.I.), the industry's trade association, to implement cooperative agreements to fight the depression was thwarted by the split that developed between the northern and southern mills.[37]

The C.T.I. proposal of a "55-50 Plan" (a policy attempting to limit the number of hours worked and thereby the level of output in order to bolster sagging prices) was supported by almost all of the northern firms. But over a third of the southern firms would not join the plan. Indeed, by 1934 the southern mills broke with the rest of the industry over the N.R.A. and sought to pursue their own course. This independence derived on one level from the South's historical opposition to organized labor. Much of the southern firms' opposition to the N.R.A. focused on Section 7(a) of the N.I.R.A. and its labor provisions. But on another level such independence was a logical, indeed a necessary outcome of the southern firms' better economic health in the 1930s.[38]

Within the petroleum industry there was a similar conflict. The large integrated producers favored N.R.A. regulation, especially of output and pricing levels, in order to bolster profits. Smaller independent firms were implacably opposed to such restrictions. In their view, the opportunity to compete offered by depression circumstances could be exploited only by price offensives and marketing practices that were explicitly prohibited by N.R.A. guidelines – guidelines drafted by a code authority dominated by the large integrated companies.[39]

Press, 1981), 32; E. W. Hawley, "The Discovery and Study of a 'Corporate Liberalism'," *Business History Review*, 52 (Autumn, 1978), 309–20; Schlesinger, *The Coming of the New Deal*, 121, 170, 182, 569; and Robert F. Himmelberg, *The Origins of the National Recovery Administration* (New York: Fordham University Press, 1976), 221.

37 See Galambos, *Competition and Cooperation*, 141–2, 176–8, 187, 196.
38 See Galambos, *Competition and Cooperation*, 149, 154, 203; and George B. Galloway et al., *Industrial Planning Under Codes*, chapters on "The Cotton Textile Industry under the NRA" and "The Woolen and Worsted Industry."
39 See Galloway et al., *Industrial Planning Under Codes*, chapter on "The Petroleum Industry." Also see G. Terborgh, "The Roosevelt Government and Ameri-

Relatively new and rapidly recovering industries such as aircraft production and chemicals were also opposed to N.R.A. guidelines that hampered aggressive actions by newcomers. Even within the iron and steel industry, a sector in which the large majority of producers favored N.R.A. controls, smaller firms resisted and protested the efforts of the code authority to restrict capacity expansion, price competition, and marketing offensives. R. E. Flanders, an engineer and spokesman for those opposed to New Deal policies that protected lethargic and inefficient firms, wrote that the primary problem with the code-making practices of the N.R.A. was the tendency to impose limitations "on improvements in management, processes, and equipment; hindrances to the expansion of efficient plants."[40]

The most authoritative study of the opinion of business leaders during the thirties shows that with the exception of bankers and perhaps merchants, businessmen held extremely eclectic views on how to approach the crisis. In part this explains the quick commitment by industrialists to the relaxation (indeed abrogation) of the antitrust laws and their general acceptance of either overproduction or underconsumption theories of the crisis. The same study discovered an intriguing pattern in the attitude of industrialists toward the price maintenance and output restriction policies of the N.R.A. "Businessmen in industries whose nature led them to believe that the demand for their product was inelastic [i.e., inflexible] – textile manufacturers, retailers, steel

ca's Petroleum Problems," *Rotterdamsche Bankvereeniging Monthly Review*, 6 (June, 1933), 147–53; and 7 (July, 1933), 171–7; and "The American Petroleum Code," *Rotterdamsche Bankvereeniging Monthly Review*, 9/10 (September/October, 1933), 225–32; and see S. J. Randall, "Harold Ickes and United States Foreign Petroleum Policy Planning, 1939–1945," *Business History Review*, 57 (Autumn, 1983), 367–87. But cf. D. R. Brand, "Corporatism, the NRA, and the Oil Industry," *Political Science Quarterly*, 98 (Spring, 1983), 99–118.

40 See R. E. Flanders, "Business Looks at the N.R.A.," *Atlantic Monthly*, 152 (November, 1933), 626; *Where Does Steel Stand?* (New York: American Iron and Steel Institute, 1938); and Herman E. Krooss, *Executive Opinion: What Business Leaders Said and Thought on Economic Issues, 1920's–1960's* (Garden City, N.Y.: Doubleday, 1970), 171, 179, 186, 199. Also see "America's Mightiest Industry Discusses Its Economic Problems," *Economic Forum*, 3 (Spring, 1936), 429ff.; Thomas Paul Jenkins, *Reactions of Major Groups to Positive Government in the United States: 1930–1940*. University of California Publications in Political Science, vol. I, no. 3 (Berkeley: University of California Press, 1945), 270, 298; and D. Blanchard, "Should We Try a Partnership of Business and Government? – The Views of Industrial Leaders and the Attitude of the Administration," *Automotive Industries*, 68 (May 13, 1933), 586–7.

men, and so forth – were obsessed by the specter of overproduction. On the contrary, producers who were not overly concerned with price elasticity . . . emphasized productivity and rejected policies that stemmed from overproduction theories."[41]

In the slower-growing industries, those experiencing transformations in the strength of their markets because of long-term changes in the structure of American consumption, the response to the crisis was essentially one of output restriction and price maintenance. Such policies, of course, interfered with the efforts of firms in newer industries, or of newer firms in the older industries, to compete effectively and penetrate the market. On this basis it can be argued that the New Deal apparatus, as exemplified by the N.R.A., obstructed the recovery of the American economy in the crisis of the thirties. But insofar as the code authorities themselves were dominated by the older firms within the older industries, the failure of the New Deal in this regard cannot be ascribed simply to ignorance of economics, or to willful and misguided obstruction of the workings of enterprise. Indeed, such an indictment of the New Deal can be made only if one ignores the peculiar and powerful constellation of material interests thrown up during the crisis of the thirties that made effective government intervention problematic.

As we now know, the interventionist strategy of the First New Deal gave way by mid-decade to an assortment of spending schemes, reform legislation (especially with regard to labor and capital markets), and antitrust enforcement. Whatever the successes and failures of industrial policy in the early thirties under the rubric of the N.I.R.A., such centralized planning was no longer used in response to economic crisis. The spending and monetary solutions of a new learning and a new era came to predominate. As one scholar has argued, "the inter-war decades had, for all their failures, provided corporate managers with a solid base from which to argue for industrial self-regulation under loose federal oversight. So long as the complexities of an emerging techno-industrial order underlined the necessity for managerial expertise supplied mainly by private corporations, articulate businessmen would continue their efforts to mold industrial society closer to their perceptions of a liberalized corporation system."[42]

41 From Krooss, *Executive Opinion*, 376–7.
42 From K. McQuaid, "Corporate Liberalism in the American Business Community, 1920–1946," *Business History Review*, 52 (Autumn, 1978), 342–68,

The opportunity afforded American businessmen "to mold industrial society closer to their perceptions" was provided by World War II, the Korean conflict, and subsequent cold war. The opportunity was seized upon precisely because the business community could control the planning process itself. Moreover, unlike the New Deal years, there was no risk in the undertaking of investment during times of war or rearmament. In their 1936 *Annual Report*, the board of directors of the U.S. Chamber of Commerce focused on this issue in their condemnation of New Deal policy, declaring that "demand must precede supply if economic equilibrium is to be maintained. To revive that demand, to stimulate the confidence which expresses itself in investment, in buying, in building, and in the general expansion of industrial enterprises is the first requirement of recovery." Simply put, the board was calling for a risk-free environment – something secured only later with the start of war.[43]

It seems appropriate, therefore, to regard the American business community of the interwar years (and indeed of subsequent decades) as composed of capitalists against capitalism. They could accept government intervention, but only on their own terms. They wanted centralized cooperation in order to ensure the validation of investments and the resultant generation of high rates of growth. They did not want that cooperation to be so centralized and rigid as to deprive them of the independence and freedom of action characteristic of capitalist ventures. Herein lay the fundamental contradiction in the attitudes of the business community toward government economic intervention.

In their trying to have it both ways, American entrepreneurs were not much different from American workers and American consumers. During the 1930s and in subsequent decades, Americans as a whole expressed their desire for the government to establish policies, programs, and institutions that would guard against shortfalls in income. But they were not willing to endorse fully centralized systems of planning. In

especially 367–8. Also see A. Sweezy, "The Keynesians and Government Policy: 1933–39," *American Economic Review*, 62 (May, 1972), 116–24; Herbert Stein, *The Fiscal Revolution in America* (Chicago: University of Chicago Press, 1969), 86–90, 104; and John M. Blum, *V Was for Victory: Politics and American Culture During World War II* (New York: Harcourt Brace Jovanovich, 1977).

43 From U.S. Chamber of Commerce, *Board of Directors Annual Report* (1936), 6. Also see Blum, *From the Morgenthau Diaries*, 307; and Harold L. Ickes, *The Secret Diary of Harold L. Ickes*, vol. II: *The Inside Struggle, 1936–39* (New York: Simon & Schuster, 1954), 243.

short, Americans wanted the government to eliminate risk to whatever extent possible, but they did not wish to see economic opportunity erased in the rigors of statism. They generally believed in a social and political commitment to protecting incomes from economic instability, but at the same time they remained committed to the principle that the unhindered accumulation of private wealth should be protected.

Roosevelt appears to have been sensitive to this contradiction in American attitudes toward positive government. His pragmatism and seeming lack of consistency derived in part from his awareness of the political realities involved in economic intervention by the federal government. A failure to act would have placed incredible strains on the political coherence of the nation. Yet acting in some ways interfered with the workings and ideology of a system based on the private ownership of capital. Roosevelt himself tried to have it both ways. But the requirements for political stability (not to mention tranquillity) – humane action, aggressive intervention – interfered with the requirements for economic recovery – taking steps to bolster business confidence, meeting the demands of the business community, and the like. Centralized planning might have been a way out, but such an effort was only timidly tried and short-lived, in the First New Deal. The conflict of politics and economics born in the thirties remains.

Throughout the postwar period, in democratic societies, the desire for government action to ensure against macroeconomic instability has been expressed with increasing force. Other alternatives to the "mixed economy" have been unappealing – whether they be fascism, national socialism, communism, or the strategy of a popular front and a social contract. Even in the midst of the Reagan Revolution of the 1980s it is clear that the commitment to economic intervention remains strong. The debate today is over whose economic loss will be compensated by the government and by how much – not over whether or not loss will be ensured against at all.

Political and social historians can praise Roosevelt and his New Deal for protecting American democracy during one of its worst crises. Economic historians can criticize the president and his policies for interfering with recovery. But such exercises tell only one side of the story. The full story is one of contradiction and hard choices. To protect against unemployment and hardship, the freedom to accumulate may be curtailed. Yet to endorse unfettered accumulation of wealth is to leave society open to divisive and potentially catastrophic political turmoil when a slackening of business activity occurs.[44] Recent history has shown that planned systems can eradicate income volatility and unemployment, but they cannot ensure adequate rates of growth in material welfare and income. Capitalist systems, by contrast, have unprecedented records when it comes to the massing of wealth and raising of living standards, but unemployment and income fluctuations cannot be eliminated.[45] Here lies the ultimate paradox and lesson of the thirties, the full implications of which have yet to be understood.

44 See A. S. Baster, *The Twilight of American Capitalism: An Economic Interpretation of the New Deal* (London: P. S. King, 1937), 20, 98, 121–2, 130.

45 See the elegant theoretical consideration of these issues in the work of János Kornai: *Economics of Shortage* (New York: North-Holland, 1980), especially 290–1; and *Anti-Equilibrium: On Economic Systems Theory and the Tasks of Research* (Amsterdam: North-Holland, 1980), especially chs. 19, 23.

8. Contemporary economic problems in historical perspective

> The historical sense involves a perception, not only of the pastness of the past, but of its presence.
>
> – T. S. Eliot

The problem of delayed recovery and the peculiar difficulties created by the incipient reordering of America's industrial structure in the 1930s were quickly overcome by World War II. The war provided a twofold stimulus. The more mature industries of the interwar period were brought out of their doldrums by the particular demands of making war. The new industries were pulled along by government orders, both through their contribution to a general increase in economic activity and through their particular demands on sectors such as petroleum, chemicals, electronics, and aviation. Mature and declining sectors were brought back to life, and new industries were at last provided with the generally high level of sales that the full emergence of new products and processes required. Indeed, the war itself spawned the development of other new industries, products, and processes. Thus, the 1940s helped to lay the foundation of prosperity in the 1950s and 1960s.

By the 1970s, however, the postwar prosperity of the American economy was in jeopardy. Much like the crisis of the interwar period, the persistent instability of the seventies raised fears about the long-term viability of capitalism and made a mockery of the optimism of the "New Frontier" and the "Great Society." Indeed, in the 1970s, the performance of the American economy was somewhat similar to that in the 1930s. In both decades, the growth rate of the gross domestic product (that is, the gross national product net of output produced abroad to which residents have title) fell after several years of robust expansion. Unemployment rates reached disquieting levels, and the attendant downturns were persistent rather than transitory. At the beginning of each of these decades, profound exogenous shocks triggered the difficulties that followed. And in both cases formidable political and intellectual obstacles prevented the adoption of appropriate counter-cyclical policies. Are these similarities merely coincidental? Do they demonstrate a simple isomorphism, or are they expressions of a deeper, homologous connection? Did the manner in which the government attempted to resolve the crisis of the thirties and the ultimate solution provided by war affect the ability of the government to deal with the economic problems of the seventies? Are there insights gained by putting contemporary economic problems within a long-term historical perspective?

Both the thirties and the seventies were fragile and vulnerable periods when financial shocks precipitated economic crises of singular duration. The development and growth of new industries and products were too slow because of a combination of demand-side problems, supply-side shocks, and policy difficulties. The economic difficulties experienced during these two decades did not derive from an absolute inability to shift capital and labor from declining to expanding sectors, but rather arose out of the insufficient magnitude of the new sectors that interfered with the ability to get inputs to flow at a proper and desirable rate.

These two decades were characterized by poor growth rates and high unemployment. In the wake of the financial panic of 1929, industrial production fell by a third; unemployment reached approximately 25% of the labor force. After the dramatic rise in oil prices in 1973, the economy similarly deteriorated. Measured in constant prices, the annual average compound growth rate of the gross domestic product (G.D.P.) fell from 4% (for the period 1960–73) to 1.8% (for the period 1973–82). The percentage change in real G.D.P. went from 5.5% in 1973 to −0.7% the next year. There was a recovery in this rate in mid-decade, but a negative rate prevailed once again by 1980. Annual unemployment rose from 4.8% of the labor force in 1973 to 8.3% two years later. By 1982 that rate rose toward 10%. Overall, the decennial average rate was approximately 6.9%.[1]

1 See Temin, *Did Monetary Forces Cause the Great Depression?* xi; Lebergott, *Manpower in Economic Growth: The American Record Since 1800*; and A. Maddison, "Economic Stagnation Since 1973, Its Nature and Causes: A Six Country Survey," *De Economist*, 131 (1983), 585–608. Maddison reports the following statistics for the decade 1973–82:

Percentage change in real gross domestic product in the United States

1973	5.5%
1974	−0.7
1975	−0.7

To be sure, there was more instability and economic deprivation in the thirties than in the seventies. It would be foolish to suggest that in absolute terms the performances of the American economy in these two decades were similar. Yet in both cases, instability, income losses, and employment shortfalls occurred after several years of outstanding macroeconomic growth. The thirties and the seventies were decades that marked major interruptions in the process of growth in the American economy. The poor performance of these decades appeared to be brought on by exceptional shocks and was relatively long-lived. Policy debates were also quite similar. The resemblances suggest considerable contemporary relevance for our understanding of the Great Depression of the 1930s.[2]

The slumps of both decades were initiated by dramatic shocks, transmitted through the price level, that seriously jeopardized the confidence of firms, households, and investors. In 1929 the collapse of stock prices drastically devalued capital stocks and erased a large segment of the national wealth. The wave of bank failures intensified the deflationary process begun on Wall Street on Black Thursday. Capital markets were deranged, and investment all but disappeared. Business failures and individual bankruptcies and hardship followed. A sustained recovery was not achieved until the outbreak of war.

The poor macroeconomic performance of the 1970s was also initiated by an exogenous shock.[3] In the wake of the Yom Kippur War of

Percentage change in real gross domestic product in the United States *(continued)*

Year	Change
1976	4.9
1977	5.2
1978	4.7
1979	2.4
1980	−0.3
1981	2.3
1982	−1.7

2 Contemporary economists often look on the thirties as an era providing dramatic evidence of the ignorance of policymakers at the time. It is most common to assert that the contemporary relevance of the Great Depression lies in its showing us how much we have learned in subsequent decades. Perhaps the depression's contemporary relevance truly lies in showing us how much we have not learned. A good example of the contemporary view is Friedman and Schwartz, *A Monetary History of the United States*; but also see Brown, "Fiscal Policy in the 'Thirties: A Reappraisal."

3 The term "exogenous" might appear unwarranted to some. Indeed, the U.S. government had anticipated a rise in world oil prices and, as a consequence, had begun preparations to deregulate the domestic price of crude. Some journalists

1973, the Organization of Petroleum Exporting Countries (O.P.E.C.) initiated a series of price increases for crude oil that had disastrous consequences for the United States and other industrialized economies. The price of crude rose 12% in June of 1973 and then took off with the October war in the Middle East. Oil prices rose 66% in October and doubled in January of 1974. From 1952 to 1965 the average inflation rate for the American economy (based on the consumer price index) stood at 1.3%. In the following seven years it rose to 4.1%, and for the decade of the seventies to 8.8%. For the ten years 1972–82, it is estimated that the total change in the American cost of living was some 133%. Poor crop yields in 1971 and 1972 due to drought conditions in the nation's agricultural regions contributed to the inflationary spiral.[4]

The O.P.E.C. shock, while different in form, had many of the same consequences as the 1929 stock debacle. Real incomes fell dramatically. Bank portfolios and the economic position of investors were placed in jeopardy. The confidence of consumers and investors was dealt a serious blow. Investment declined as firms became more and more hesitant and as households postponed major expenditures. Profit margins shrank as costs of production rose. Capacity utilization and employment consequently fell. As the G.D.P. growth rates noted earlier show, the American economy then stumbled through the rest of the decade.

What is particularly arresting about the economic weakness of both the 1930s and the 1970s is its persistence. Indeed, what preoccupies economists in examining these two decades is the absence of recovery for such a long period of time. The length of the crisis during the thirties led to suggestions that the depression was evidence of an ultimate breakdown of the capitalist system. Few have made such a bold suggestion regarding the seventies, but the decade was profoundly disturbing nonetheless for the major industrialized states. In both decades the recovery process was evidently obstructed or slowed. My research suggests that the impediments to recovery in the 1930s and the 1970s in the United States were structurally alike. In fact, they may have been historically linked.

The difficulty experienced by the American economy in both decades

have suggested that the American government implicitly supported a rise in oil prices to further its foreign policy goals, especially in the Middle East. Suffice it to say that the price shock was "exogenous" in the sense that it emanated from outside the American economy.

4 See U.S. Council of Economic Advisers, *Economic Report of the President: 1984* (Washington, D.C.: U.S. Government Printing Office, 1984).

grew out of secular trends in the economy's development. Preceding both crises, the economic system encountered new demand patterns and investment and employment opportunities. These patterns and opportunities were linked with a shift in the composition of national output. But such a reorientation weakened the recovery process in both decades. A sluggish recoupment was the result of the difficulty of altering technology and labor skills to meet the new demands for investment and consumption goods at a time of severe financial restriction occasioned by the stock market and O.P.E.C. shocks.

In the seventies, the factors forestalling recovery were numerous. The fiscal crisis of the Vietnam era and its related international financial development – the demise of the Bretton Woods system – fundamentally altered the relationship of the American economy to world markets. Where trading partners in the past had been content to hold dollar reserves – essentially financing the American trade deficit – the deterioration in the value of the dollar pursuant to the war inflation and the emergence of nationalist elements abroad changed that behavior.

With the collapse of the Bretton Woods system in 1970–1, the United States was freed from the burden of maintaining a fixed exchange rate; the resultant devaluation of the dollar improved America's export position, at least potentially. But the other consequence of the policy change was inflation. Thus, on the very eve of the O.P.E.C. price explosion, the United States had already been placed in an extremely exposed condition. In addition to the monetary changes, technological factors made themselves felt in the early seventies and further weakened the American economy.

By the 1960s the nations devastated by World War II (most significantly Japan and the Federal Republic of Germany) had reestablished their economic presence in world markets. They possessed a most advanced technological base owing to the recent rebuilding of their major industries and their relative insulation, under international treaties and agreements, from the burdens of defense spending.[5] Consequently, their

5 From 1971 to 1980, the United States spent an annual average of 5.8% of real gross national product on defense; the Federal Republic of Germany spent an annual average of 3.4%; and Japan spent an annual average of 0.9%. See U.S. Department of Commerce, *Statistical Abstract of the United States: 1984* (Washington, D.C.: U.S. Government Printing Office, 1983), 348. Also see U.S. Arms Control and Disarmament Agency, *World Military Expenditures: Arms Transfers, Annual Reports: 1971–1980* (Washington, D.C.: U.S. Government Printing Office, 1983), 49, 54. I abstract from the costs – in the case of the

major industries – steel, automobiles, and electronics – became power-ful competitors with their American counterparts. This was the real counterpart to the financial crisis precipitated by the O.P.E.C. and agricultural price increases.

Many scholars have focused on what they see as a managerial failure of American enterprise in the sixties and seventies in meeting foreign competition. Certainly the case of the automobile industry suggests that American producers were locked in a kind of technological rigidity that left them exposed to the full impact of superior Japanese technology – especially when the O.P.E.C. price rise qualitatively altered the demand for cars toward lighter, more fuel-efficient vehicles. The peculiar incen-tives established by American tax codes, and what is often called the present-mindedness of the American corporate elite, may have been factors in this managerial failure.[6]

But there appear to have been other factors involved in the techno-logical stagnation of American industry. The dramatic stimulus afforded by World War II and the Korean conflict brought all of American industry out of the crisis of the thirties. Indeed, it has been suggested that wartime production and the military procurement of the cold war years have been responsible for the prosperity of the American economy in the entire postwar era.[7] It would appear, however, that the fiscal stimulus of the "Arsenal of Democracy," while providing a short-run fillip to national income, may in the long run have enervated major sectors of the economy and curtailed their ability to develop and com-pete on a world scale.

The persistence of the slumps of the 1930s and the 1970s derived from the impact of secular trends in the development process. The crisis of the thirties has been the particular concern here. What about the crisis of the seventies? It, too, exhibited structural changes and distortions

Federal Republic and Japan – of the Allied military occupations and subsequent North Atlantic Treaty Organization and Security Treaty deployments.

6 See, as a good example of this position, Robert B. Reich, *The Next American Frontier* (New York: Penguin, 1983). Also see Barry Bluestone and Bennett Harrison, *The Deindustrialization of America: Plant Closings, Community Abandonment, and the Dismantling of Basic Industries* (New York: Basic, 1982); and Amitai Etzioni, *An Immodest Agenda: Rebuilding America Before the Twenty-First Century* (New York: New Press, 1983).

7 See, for example, the classic study by Baran and Sweezy, *Monopoly Capital: An Essay on the American Economic and Social Order*. But also cf. Robert A. Pollard, *Economic Security and the Origins of the Cold War, 1945–1950* (New York: Columbia University Press, 1985), ch. 10.

Table 8-1. *U.S. trade in manufactured goods, 1965–80 (annual averages; billions of dollars)*

Years	Exports	Imports	Trade ratio[a]
1965–69	20.3	16.6	0.1
1970–73	35.1	34.8	0.004
1974–76	71.7	57	0.11
1977–80	101.4	103.6	−0.01

[a]Trade ratio = (exports − imports)/(exports + imports).
Source: U.S. Department of Commerce, *International Economic Indicators* (September, 1974, and September, 1984).

of a long-term nature. The deterioration in G.D.P. growth rates was merely a coarse example of the economic plight of the decade. Perhaps more significant were the persistently low rates of capacity utilization in manufacturing, the loss of America's share in world manufacturing output, and the structural transformation of the labor market. Taken together, these developments heralded a secular change in the relationship of the American economy to the world market, and therefore of the composition of national output.[8]

U.S. manufacturing operated at 86% of its capacity in 1965, but at less than 70% later in the seventies. Nonfinancial corporate profit rates fell below 10% during the decade. The industries that had been crucial components of America's rise to world economic prominence – steel, automobiles, and textiles – were particularly hard hit.[9] Nowhere is the degeneration in American economic performance during the seventies more vividly stated than in the international trade statistics.

As Table 8-1 shows, U.S. trade in manufactured goods was trans-

8 There was also the added problem in the seventies of the changing distribution of manufacturing profits. The share of manufacturing profits earned by petroleum and coal companies increased from 11% to just over 24% between 1950 and 1979. And yet these large funds were not expended in ways that facilitated the flow of resources out of old into new sectors. They were, on the contrary, often expended in speculative ventures – an action reminiscent of the unproductive investments that characterized the boom market of the late twenties. The redistributive achievements of Lyndon Johnson's Great Society (whereby consumer spending rose as income became more evenly distributed) were vitiated by the maldistribution of corporate profits – the growth of the American economy was thereby further jeopardized. See U.S. Council of Economic Advisers, *Economic Report of the President: 1984*, table B-84, 317; computations by the author.
9 See Reich, *The Next American Frontier*, ch. 7.

Table 8-2. *Percentage market shares of exports of manufactures for selected nations, 1960–77*

Year	U.S.	U.K.	Japan	Italy
1960	25.2	15.3	6.5	4.8
1970	21.3	10.4	8.9	7.1
1977	17.3	9.2	12.6	7.7

Source: U.S. Department of Commerce, *International Economic Indicators* (September, 1974, and September, 1984).

formed during the seventies. By 1977–80 the trade ratio (net exports divided by the sum of exports and imports) was negative for the first time since 1940. America's market share of exports of manufactures, as Table 8-2 demonstrates, was steadily eroded. And, as enumerated in Table 8-3, almost all of the major manufacturing sectors saw their trade performance worsen. Exceptions included particular fields in which the United States held a virtually unassailable technical lead, or where public policy had taken an active role in obstructing the trend.

Accompanying the alteration in the competitiveness of American industry in the world economy was the restructuring of the nation's labor market. The share of the nation's employment accounted for by manufacturing industries fell from 30.3% in 1962 to 23.9% in 1977. Moreover, during the seventies the annual average compound growth rate in employment was zero in manufacturing and agriculture and 2.6% in services. Within the manufacturing sector, employment requirements changed dramatically. As Table 8-4 shows, employment fell from 1966 to 1978 in major "traditional" manufacturing industries (primary metals, textiles, and transportation equipment), while rising in newer "modern" sectors (chemicals, fabricated metals, machinery, and instruments).[10] The structural unemployment created as a result serves to explain the aggregate unemployment over the decade. Of course, it should be noted that the total U.S. working population rose 19.1% between 1960 and 1970 (an increase of just over 13 million

10 See Maddison, "Economic Stagnation Since 1973, Its Nature and Causes," 593. Also see Organization for Economic Cooperation and Development (O.E.C.D.), *Labour Force Statistics: 1960–71* (Paris: O.E.C.D., 1973), 72–3; and O.E.C.D., *Labour Force Statistics: 1966–77* (Paris: O.E.C.D., 1979), 78–9.

Table 8-3. *Trade ratios for selected*
U.S. industries, 1967 and 1977

Industry	1967	1977	Change 1966 to 1977
Textile mill products	−0.36	0.03	0.39
Turbine generators	0.41	0.78	0.37
Leather and leather products	−0.24	−0.02	0.22
Telephone and telegraphic equipment	0.19	0.33	0.14
Wood pulp	−0.22	−0.12	0.10
Paper and paperboard	−0.37	−0.30	0.07
Aerospace	0.80	0.82	0.02
Steel	−0.16	−0.68	−0.52
Rubber tires and tubes	−0.11	−0.51	−0.40
Apparel	−0.54	−0.86	−0.32
Machine tools	0.13	−0.12	−0.25
Photographic equipment	0.38	0.17	−0.21
Automobiles	−0.01	−0.21	−0.20
Chemicals	0.49	0.30	−0.19
House appliances	0.01	−0.14	−0.15
General industrial machinery	0.72	0.57	−0.15
Construction machinery	0.91	0.76	−0.15
Computers	0.78	0.65	−0.13
Farm machinery	0.17	0.15	−0.02

Source: U.S. Department of Commerce, *Survey of Current Business: 1980, U.S. Industrial Outlook for 200 Industries with Projections for 1984.*

persons), compared with a rise of 15.5% during the thirties (an increase of almost 9 million persons). It is clear, therefore, that the "baby boom" of the immediate postwar period was also having an effect in the soft labor market of the 1970s.[11]

Overall, the essence of the historical homology between the 1930s and the 1970s lies in the fact that industrial life cycles served to complicate growth in both decades. In these periods, the American economy underwent a profound recasting of the composition of national output and thereby of employment and capital goods demand. When short-run financial shocks at the beginning of each decade hampered the

11 See *Historical Statistics of the United States*, series D29–41, p. 132; computations by the author.

Table 8-4. *Changes in employment in
selected U.S. manufacturing sectors,
1966 and 1978 (thousands of employees)*

Sector	1966	1978	Change (%)
Instruments and related goods	495	653	31.9
Nonelectrical machinery	1,910	2,326	21.8
Chemicals	961	1,096	14
Fabricated metals	1,489	1,673	12.4
Electrical machinery and equipment	1,856	2,006	8.1
Leather and leather products	364	257	−29.4
Textile mill products	964	899	−6.7
Primary metals	1,297	1,215	−6.3
Apparel	1,402	1,332	−5
Food	1,777	1,724	−3
Transportation equipment	2,052	2,003	−2.4

Source: U.S. Department of Commerce, *Business Statistics: 1982* (Supplement to the *Survey of Current Business*, November, 1983).

conversion, the result was a serious and protracted economic crisis. Moreover, in both crises there emerged profound obstacles to the implementation of appropriate domestic and international policies.

During the interwar period, Keynesianism was virtually unknown. Economists were limited by deep-seated intellectual prejudices in the formulation of countercyclical measures. The lack of a comprehensive theory of macroeconomic behavior was paralleled by the absence of reliable and systematic data on the fiscal and monetary mechanisms of government. The notion of government spending itself was suspect. Budget deficits were equated with national economic ruin, and the plausible yet inaccurate parallel drawn between a family's finances and those of the state reigned supreme in economists' minds. The fallacy of composition was not yet part of the economists' lexicon.[12]

Business cycle theory was in a similarly inchoate and uninformed state. Most economists tended to view the cycle as a therapeutic cure

12 See Sweezy, "The Keynesians and Government Policy, 1933–39," 116–24.

for intermittent yet never well-explained overflows of the economic mechanism. Cycles could not be tamed, much less made obsolete. The notion of potential output and an appreciation of the losses incurred when actual national output fell below that capacity ceiling were yet unexplained. As a result, there was a thoroughly inadequate understanding of the process of inflation. There certainly was no conception that a slack economy would not suffer accelerating inflation under a regime of compensatory fiscal spending. Ignorance contributed to (though it does not fully explain) the virtual impotence and in some cases the unintended perversity of economic policy during the thirties.

The crisis of the seventies found the intellectual foundations of economic policy in similar disarray. With the demise of the Bretton Woods system of fixed exchange rates and the perceived disappearance of the Phillips curve linking lower unemployment rates with higher inflation, confidence in the Keynesian revolution diminished, and the consensus of macroeconomic thinking dissolved.[13] Spending by the government once again was excoriated, although countercyclical action was condemned not so much for its inflationary bias as for its negative impact on incentives for risk taking and productive behavior in the marketplace. In addition, a political reaction against distributive policies and federalism emerged after the Vietnam period.[14]

The seventies also witnessed the revival, in a vigorous and cogent offensive, of old-fashioned policy thinking. The best example of this was the restoration of monetary theory inspired by the work of Milton Friedman. In addition, a resurgence of general equilibrium approaches to cyclical phenomena prompted the formulation of a "new classical macroeconomics" and the rise of a "rational expectations school."[15]

13 See A. W. Phillips, "The Relation Between Unemployment and the Rate of Change of Money Wage Rates in the United Kingdom, 1861–1957," *Economica*, N.S., 25 (November, 1958), 283–99.

14 See J. Steindl, "Reflections on the Present State of Economics," *Banca Nazionale del Lavoro Quarterly Review*, 148 (March, 1984), 3–14; Sweezy, "The Keynesians and Government Policy, 1933–39"; and Maddison, "Economic Stagnation Since 1973, Its Nature and Causes," 598–608. Acceptance of Keynesian fiscal policy in the United States was linked with the emergence of a political consensus in the early sixties regarding increased defense spending and the implementation of redistributive policies derived from the federal government's pursuit of civil rights reform. As that consensus was undermined – for various political and social reasons – the commitment to Keynesianism also waned. In this regard, see R. Griffith, "Dwight D. Eisenhower and the Corporate Commonwealth," *American Historical Review*, 87 (February, 1982), 87–122.

15 It should be pointed out that although inspired by his work, the "new mone-

These intellectual developments, linked with political events having to do with the backlash against the progressive politics of the New Frontier and the Great Society, eliminated Keynesian thinking from the formulation of responses to the crisis. Thus, attempts were made to balance fiscal expenditures and tighten monetary variables in the face of unemployment and G.D.P. shortfalls – the kind of policies once labeled (derisively by some) the "Treasury view." There is, of course, a major difference between the thirties and the seventies in this regard, at least in the United States. Timid countercyclical policy in the interwar period was to some extent the result of ignorance and misplaced confidence in old remedies. In the seventies, slow-growth policies were derived from the politics of reaction and resentment.[16]

The inability of the American government to respond effectively to the crises of the thirties and seventies must also be situated within an international context. Both decades witnessed acute disruptions of international commodities and currency markets. In the interwar period, the difficulties of adjustment throughout the industrialized world, along with the particular problems resulting from the Versailles reparations settlement, led governments to forgo international cooperation and pursue beggar-thy-neighbor and other aggressive and inflammatory trade policies.

After the crash in 1929, the United States implemented the Hawley-Smoot Tariff. That barrier, while crippling America's trading partners, enabled the United States to pursue economic isolationism – a stance epitomized by President Roosevelt's abrogation of the gold standard in 1933. But in the seventies, an isolationist course was no longer open to

tarism" and the "new macroeconomics" have never been endorsed by Milton Friedman and the "old monetarists." Indeed, the most recent reformulations of the classical view are notable for their simplicity. In the work of the "old" monetarists, such as Friedman, one finds a coherent, if controversial, theory of consumer and producer behavior. In the nostrums of the rational expectations and supply-side theorists, one finds a steady drift toward reductionism and sophistry. See Steindl, "Reflections on the Present State of Economics."

16 On the political constraints within which countercyclical policy is often formulated, see the seminal essay of Michal Kalecki, "Political Aspects of Full Employment," in his *The Last Phase in the Transformation of Capitalism* (New York: Monthly Review Press, 1972), 75–83. The "Treasury view," that fiscal spending could not lower unemployment, emerged in Great Britain in 1929 in response to Liberal Party calls for activist policy. See *Memoranda on Certain Proposals Relating to Unemployment*, P.P. 1928–9 (Cmd. 3331), XVI; and K. J. Hancock, "The Reduction of Unemployment as a Problem of Public Policy, 1920–29," *Economic History Review*, 15 (December, 1962), 336.

American politicians. American dependence on export trade rose from an estimated 3.34% of real G.N.P. in the 1930s to almost 10% in the late seventies. The United States was forced to keep its domestic market open in order to maintain export markets abroad. The consequence was a dramatic jolt to older industries once foreign competitors, especially the Federal Republic of Germany and Japan, broke into the North American market. The resemblance to Britain's difficulties is striking.[17]

The growing dependence on exports contributed to the demise of Keynesianism as a policy guide, because fiscal demand management often requires economic independence and the regulation of capital markets.[18] Recent changes in the structure of world markets have further increased the need for economic cooperation and the coordination of national countercyclical policies. But the weakening of the American economy and the demise of the Bretton Woods regime have reduced the ability of international organizations and forums to meet that need.[19] It

17 See *Historical Statistics of the United States*, part 2, series U201–6, p. 887; and U.S. Department of Commerce, *Statistical Abstract of the United States: 1981* (Washington, D.C.: U.S. Government Printing Office, 1981). Also see Bernard Elbaum and William Lazonick, "The Decline of the British Economy: An Institutional Perspective," *Journal of Economic History*, 44 (June, 1984), 567–83. On p. 573, Elbaum and Lazonick write: "Because Britain had already industrialized, its domestic market for such staple commodities as textiles or steel rails had reached a point of at best moderate growth potential. Under these circumstances, British firms could not find at home a market that could match the dramatic rates of expansion of the foreign markets foreclosed to them. Indeed, given its dependence on international markets, British industry was severely constrained to keep its own domestic markets open to the products of foreign firms." Also see John Eatwell, *Whatever Happened to Britain: The Economics of Decline* (London: Duckworth, British Broadcasting Corporation, 1982).

18 See J. R. Crotty, "On Keynes and Capital Flight," *Journal of Economic Literature*, 21 (March, 1983), 59–65. Crotty quotes Keynes, in a letter to Roy Harrod in 1942: "In my view the whole management of the domestic economy depends upon being free to have the appropriate rate of interest without reference to the rates prevailing elsewhere in the world. Capital control is a corollary to this." See John Maynard Keynes, *Activities 1940–1944: Shaping the Post-War World; The Clearing Union*; Donald Moggridge, ed., *The Collected Writings of John Maynard Keynes*, vol. 25 (New York: Macmillan, 1980), 148–9. Also see J. M. Keynes, "National Self-Sufficiency," *Yale Review*, 22 (June, 1933), 755–69; and J. Williamson, "On the System in Bretton Woods," *American Economic Review*, 75 (May, 1985), 74–9.

19 Potential debt crises also emerged on world markets toward the end of the seventies. As difficult and as politically distorted as the lending functions of major international governments and institutions often are, here there seems to be some basis for optimism. Confrontations have been kept to a minimum, and potential disruptions of international credit have been, in large measure, avoided.

is in this regard that the parallels between the thirties and the seventies are perhaps most disturbing.

World War II laid the basis for a new era of government intervention in economic affairs and in the conduct of international transactions. Deficit spending in the forties paved the way for the success of the Keynesian revolution in American policy thinking, and the Bretton Woods conference established a fixed exchange rate system for all currencies and unambiguous lines of authority in the event of a financial crisis in world currency markets. But these developments, apparently progressive and beneficial, ultimately had negative consequences for the postwar American economy – consequences that in part generated the crisis of the seventies.

The technical requirements of making war and confronting the perceived Soviet challenge in the cold war of the fifties and sixties, while providing a fiscal stimulus, interfered with the kinds of innovation and economic dynamism necessary to meet foreign competition later in the postwar period. For example, during the 1930s the Ford Motor Company began experimenting with the development of plastic car bodies. Such research was abandoned with the inflow of war orders in 1939. The American steel industry by 1950 was ready to engage in the full-scale development of new mechanized processes and the scaling-down of capacity in anticipation of the shrinkage of wartime orders. The Korean conflict reversed this trend. It is now well documented that the strategic weapons buildup of the early sixties, along with the escalation of the space program to undertake a manned mission to the moon, slowed the rate of technological innovations in those markets in which the American economy has been challenged in recent years. The "spillover" effects of military research have not been as profound or useful as proponents have suggested.[20]

20 See J. C. Furnas, "Ford's Leftover Idea," letter to the editor, *New York Times*, February 16, 1983, A-30; Henry W. Broude, *Steel Decisions and the National Economy* (New Haven, Conn.: Yale University Press, 1963), ch. 5; and J. E. Ullmann, "The Arms Race and the Decline of U.S. Technology," *Journal of Economic Issues*, 17 (June, 1983), 565–74. Also see Robert W. Degrasse, Jr., *Military Expansion, Economic Decline: The Impact of Military Spending on U.S. Economic Performance* (New York: Council on Economic Priorities, 1983). The technological daring of Henry Ford was not limited to seeking new methods of producing car bodies. In the mid-thirties he became intrigued with the idea of producing plastic from soybeans. "How the soybean could figure in the manufacture of motor vehicles was one of Ford's high-priority concerns. Plastics made from soybeans, he was pleased to learn from his engineers, could be used

A particularly arresting example of a paradoxical outcome of military enterprise is afforded by the impact of the U.S. Air Force on the nation's production of numerically controlled machine tools. Throughout the 1950s, the air force generously funded developments by private manufacturers in the field. Yet by the 1970s, when German and Japanese producers entered the market, domestic producers were at a serious disadvantage. Military design pressures for extremely complicated equipment left American machine toolmakers ill-prepared to compete with the cheaper and more flexible numerically controlled machine tools shipped from overseas. Thus did "defense expenditures 'spill over' into commercial use. . . . While American manufacturers were concentrating on highly sophisticated machinery . . . Japanese and German manufacturers emphasized cheapness, accessibility, and simplicity in their machine designs and software systems [and so by] 1978 the United States became a net importer of machine tools for the first time since the nineteenth century."[21]

These examples suggest that wartime stimuli and defense spending, although providing a general expansion of the national product that can aid the emergence of new industries and techniques and protect the sales of more mature sectors, may also encourage a technological conservatism that has negative long-run consequences. Had the American automobile industry developed plastic car bodies in the 1930s, had the steel industry developed more mechanized processes as early as the mid-fifties, had machine tool producers been more flexible in their designs, would the hardships afforded by foreign competition obtain in the U.S. economy to the same extent today? This speculation suggests that America's contemporary foreign competitors, whose industries were rebuilt in the relative absence of military demands, may be enjoying the consequences of the Arsenal of Democracy of the 1940s, 1950s, and more recent decades.

in gearshift knobs, horn buttons, window frames, accelerator pedals, light-switch assemblies, and ignition-coil casings, and in due course they were. For a while, every Ford car had at least two pounds of soybeans somewhere in it or on it. But Ford dreamed bigger dreams than that . . . he visualized a car upholstered in material made from soybean fibres and with a tough soybean-plastic exterior shell. . . . Then the Second World War came along, and nobody has thought much about soybean auto parts since." From E. J. Kahn, Jr., "The Staffs of Life, V: The Future of the Planet," *The New Yorker*, 61 (March 11, 1985), 68.

21 See D. F. Noble, "Command Performance: A Perspective on Military Enterprise and Technological Change," in M. R. Smith, ed., *Military Enterprise and Technological Change: Perspectives on the American Experience* (Cambridge, Mass.: M.I.T. Press, 1985), 343–4.

There is a final facet of the historical homology examined here. The policy failures of the New Deal had a persistent legacy that expressed itself in the crisis of the seventies. During the First New Deal, an attempt was made to pursue recovery by means of national planning. The National Recovery Administration sought to reallocate capital and labor from declining to expanding industries, regulate inefficient and disruptive competitive practices, and bolster consumer purchasing power through the establishment of minimum pay scales. This planning initiative, unprecedented in the United States in peacetime, was abandoned by the mid-thirties in the face of growing political opposition and bureaucratic confusion. The Second New Deal ushered in an era of fiscal spending (no matter how timidly pursued) and attempted antitrust reform.

The demise of the First New Deal and the emergence of the Second New Deal had long-run effects that impaired the ability of the American government to solve the economic problems of the seventies. The Second New Deal ushered in the fiscal revolution of the Keynesian era, which was further entrenched by the fiscal experience of World War II. But it also eliminated the possibility that the planning techniques and commitments of the First New Deal would become part of established national economic policymaking. This left the federal government ill-equipped to confront the institutional challenges of the seventies, when planning might have again been appropriate. In place of a systematic and comprehensive federal plan to manage the dislocations created by industrial life cycles and international competition, the relatively crude and often expensive solution of deficit spending became the established method for dealing with instability.

There was a further long-run implication of the defeat of the First New Deal. If the planning and regulatory initiatives of the National Recovery Administration had continued, they presumably would have become integrated with the general policy-making apparatus of the federal government. Indeed, the original intention and preoccupation of Roosevelt's Brain Trust was the integration of federal planning with the decentralized democratic institutions of the American republic. The combined opposition of business interests and conservative elements left the government with the rather blunt instrument of compensatory spending – an instrument ill-suited to the peculiar stresses afforded by secular structural changes. Moreover, such fiscal spending was and is particularly vulnerable to short-run political whim and logrolling, with the result that in the stagnation of the seventies, as in the thirties, government action was stifled, misdirected, and certainly not endowed with long-term vision. The weakness of government action in the seventies is more surprising given the intellectual and experiential knowledge won in the thirties and subsequent decades.

Certainly, the introduction of automatic stabilizers in the fiscal mechanisms of government has succeeded in dampening cyclical extremes in the economy's performance since World War II.[22] But deliberations concerning government stabilization policy are embedded in the process of budget making in Congress. The combination of this fact with the legacy of precedents such as the *Schechter* decision outlawing the N.R.A. in the thirties makes it exceedingly difficult for the U.S. government to plan specifically the direct reallocation of investment funds or labor. Note, for example, the similarity between the undistributed profits tax of the thirties and the windfall profits tax of the seventies. Both were partly designed to encourage the movement of funds out of speculative hoards into productive commitments. Both met with extremely limited success. It appears that the political constraints that made the revenue act of 1936 so unpopular were also binding in 1979.[23] However, there was an important difference in perceptions during the two decades. What was politically tolerable in the thirties – an average unemployment rate over the decade of 18% – was out of the question in the seventies.

There is another important difference between the thirties and the seventies concerning government policy. During the thirties, labor unions (aided by favorable legislation) expanded their membership, while management sought government support for the stabilization of profits. By contrast, the seventies brought a period of union retreat during which

22 See Baily, "Stabilization Policy and Private Economic Behavior," *Brookings Papers on Economic Activity*, 11–59. This proposition, however, has recently been challenged by C. D. Romer, "Is the Stabilization of the Postwar Economy a Figment of the Data?" *American Economic Review*, 76 (June, 1986), 314–34. In turn, Romer has been criticized elsewhere by D. R. Weir, "The Reliability of Historical Macroeconomic Data for Comparing Cyclical Stability," *Journal of Economic History*, 46 (June, 1986), 353–65.

23 In April of 1979, President Carter proposed a 50% tax on windfall profits by oil companies after the deregulation of domestic oil prices. After a bitter congressional struggle and the passage of many amendments, the tax was signed into law in April of 1980. In 1981, President Reagan ruled out any possibility of a similar tax being levied on windfall profits gained from the deregulation of domestic natural gas prices.

labor sought to stabilize workers' incomes through governmental measures such as import restrictions, domestic content bills, or requirements for the advance announcement of plant closings. But in neither case did management or labor seek explicit government planning to facilitate industrial transformation. On the contrary, each sought to forestall economic change insofar as it threatened their income position. What was perhaps required in both decades was a strong government program to hasten structural transformation while simultaneously softening, through subsidies or tax benefits, the impact of long-term economic change on particular segments of the population or industry.

The thirties and the seventies, therefore, are homologous decades. Both endured an economic crisis with profound secular and cyclical components. The length of the crisis in each case was related to the conjunction of cyclical events and a particular point in the process of structural transformation. Moreover, problems in formulating effective policies were transmitted from the thirties to the seventies through the institutional effects described earlier. Finally, the wars and military confrontations separating the two decades contributed to the enervation of American industry and sapped its ability to confront a reconstructed world economy.

What of the consequences? The economic and political turmoil of the interwar years, coupled with the policy failures, ineptitude, and paralysis of the American and other governments, contributed in some degree to the disaster of war in the forties. Indeed, one could argue that the legacy was longer than six years of war and involved the division of the world into two, perhaps three, worlds separated by distrust, deceit, and the perpetual escalation of arms production. The price has been obvious in lives, dreams, principles, and ideals lost. As the end of the century looms before us, we feel perhaps less secure, less confident, less hopeful of the future.

Apocalyptic visions notwithstanding, the legacy of the seventies is yet to be known. Exercises in historical homology may provide some useful insight. But as one examines the crisis of the 1930s, it becomes clear that its relevance does not lie in offering obvious or direct solutions to current problems. The thirties afford a perspective on the contemporary world that shows not how far we have come, but how far we have yet to go.

Bibliography

I   Books, monographs, and documents

Arthur B. Adams, *Trend of Business: 1922–1932* (New York: Harper & Bros., 1932).

Derek H. Aldcroft, *From Versailles to Wall Street: 1919–1929* (London: Allen Lane, 1977).

Carl E. Allen, *The Financing of American Automobile Manufacturing Companies* (Urbana, Ill.: n.p., 1930).

Hugh Allen, *The House of Goodyear* (Akron, Ohio: n.p., 1936).

Alling and Cory Company, *One Hundred and Twenty-Five Years in the Paper Business, 1819–1944* (Rochester, N.Y.: Alling and Cory Company, 1944).

American Economic Association, *Readings in Business Cycle Theory* (Homewood, Ill.: Richard D. Irwin, 1951).

Readings in Business Cycles (Homewood, Ill.: Richard D. Irwin, 1965).

American Iron and Steel Institute, *Where Does Steel Stand?* (New York: n.p., 1938).

American Journal of Agricultural Economics, vol. 65 (December, 1983).

American Petroleum Institute, *Petroleum Facts and Figures* (New York: American Petroleum Institute, annual).

Petroleum-Industry Hearings before the Temporary National Economic Committee (Baltimore: Lord Baltimore Press, 1942).

Rudolph E. Anderson, *The Story of the American Automobile: Highlights and Sidelights* (Washington, D.C.: Public Affairs Press, 1950).

H. W. Arndt, *The Economic Lessons of the Nineteen-Thirties* (New York: Augustus M. Kelley, 1965).

Willard E. Atkins et al., *Economic Problems of the New Deal* (New York: F. S. Crofts and Company, 1934).

Automobile Manufacturers Association, *Automobile Facts and Figures* (New York: Automobile Manufacturers Association, 1937).

Robert T. Averitt, *The Dual Economy: The Dynamics of American Industry Structure* (New York: Norton, 1968).

Jules Backman, M. R. Gainsbrugh, *Economics of the Cotton Textile Industry* (New York: National Industrial Conference Board, 1946).

Willis N. Baer, *The Economic Development of the Cigar Industry in the United States* (Lancaster, Pa.: Art Printing Company, 1933).

Harold A. Baker, *Marketing and Consumption Trends in the Automobile Industry, 1929–1933* (Chicago: n.p., 1938).

225

Paul A. Baran, Paul M. Sweezy, *Monopoly Capital: An Essay on the American Economic and Social Order* (New York: Monthly Review Press, 1966).

Harold Barger, *Outlay and Income in the United States, 1921–1938* (New York: National Bureau of Economic Research, 1942).

P. W. Barker, *Rubber Industry of the United States, 1839–1939* (Washington, D.C.: U.S. Government Printing Office, 1939).

A. S. Baster, *The Twilight of American Capitalism: An Economic Interpretation of the New Deal* (London: P. S. King, 1937).

P. T. Bauer, *The Rubber Industry: A Study in Competition and Monopoly* (Cambridge, Mass.: Harvard University Press, 1948).

William J. Baumol, *Business Behavior, Value and Growth* (New York: Harcourt, Brace & World, 1967).

William J. Baumol, Alan S. Blinder, *Economics: Principles and Policy* (New York: Harcourt Brace Jovanovich, 1982).

David M. Beights, *Financing American Rubber Manufacturing Companies* (Urbana, Ill.: n.p., 1932).

Bernard Bellush, *The Failure of the NRA* (New York: Norton, 1975).

Margarete A. Beney, *Wages, Hours and Employment in the United States, 1914–1936* (New York: National Industrial Conference Board, 1936).

Quincy Bent, *75 Years of Steel* (n.p.: The Newcomen Society, 1939).

John M. Blair, *The Control of Oil* (New York: Pantheon, 1976).

Barry Bluestone, Bennett Harrison, *The Deindustrialization of America: Plant Closings, Community Abandonment, and the Dismantling of Basic Industries* (New York: Basic, 1982).

John M. Blum, *From the Morgenthau Diaries: Years of Crisis, 1928–1938* (Boston: Houghton Mifflin, 1959).

  V Was for Victory: Politics and American Culture During World War II (New York: Harcourt Brace Jovanovich, 1977).

  The Progressive Presidents: Roosevelt, Wilson, Roosevelt, Johnson (New York: Norton, 1980).

Harry Braverman, *Labor and Monopoly Capital: The Degradation of Work in the Twentieth Century* (New York: Monthly Review Press, 1974).

Alan Brinkley, *Voices of Protest: Huey Long, Father Coughlin, and the Great Depression* (New York: Knopf, 1982).

British Rubber Growers' Association, *Statistics Relating to the Rubber Industry, 1928* (London: n.p., 1928).

Brookings Institution, *The Recovery Problem in the United States* (Washington, D.C.: Brookings Institution, 1936).

Henry W. Broude, *Steel Decisions and the National Economy* (New Haven, Conn.: Yale University Press, 1963).

Nelson C. Brown, *The American Lumber Industry: Embracing the Principal Features of the Resources, Production, Distribution, and Utilization of Lumber in the United States* (New York: Wiley, 1923).

Timber Products and Industries: The Harvesting, Conversion, and Marketing of Materials other than Lumber, including the Principal Derivatives and Extractives (New York: Wiley, 1937).

Lumber: Manufacture, Conditioning, Grading, Distribution, and Use (New York: Wiley, 1947).

William H. Brown Collection, Sterling Memorial Library, Yale University.

Ralph C. Bryant, *Lumber: Its Manufacture and Distribution* (New York: Wiley, 1938).

Alfred G. Buehler, *The Undistributed Profits Tax* (New York: McGraw-Hill, 1937).

J. Herbert Burgy, *The New England Cotton Textile Industry: A Study in Industrial Geography* (Baltimore: Waverly Press, 1932).

Ralph Cassady, Jr., *Price Making and Price Behavior in the Petroleum Industry* (New Haven, Conn.: Yale University Press, 1954).

Gustav Cassel, *The Crisis in the World's Monetary System* (Oxford: Clarendon Press, 1932).

Alfred D. Chandler, Jr., *The Visible Hand: The Managerial Revolution in American Business* (Cambridge, Mass.: Harvard University Press, 1977).

Lester V. Chandler, *America's Greatest Depression: 1929–41* (New York: Harper & Row, 1970).

Walter A. Chudson, *The Pattern of Corporate Financial Structure: A Cross-Section View of Manufacturing, Mining, Trade, and Construction, 1937* (New York: National Bureau of Economic Research, 1945).

J. Stanley Clark, *The Oil Century: From the Drake Well to the Conservation Era* (Norman: University of Oklahoma Press, 1958).

Robert M. Coen, Bert G. Hickman, *An Annual Growth Model of the U.S. Economy* (New York: North-Holland, 1976).

Robert M. Collins, *The Business Response to Keynes: 1929–1964* (New York: Columbia University Press, 1981).

Congress of American Industry and National Association of Manufacturers, *Platform and Resolutions Adopted December 5 and 6, 1934* (New York: National Association of Manufacturers, n.d.).

The Platform of American Industry (New York: National Association of Manufacturers, n.d.).

Reavis Cox, *Competition in the American Tobacco Industry, 1911–1932: A Study of the Effects of the Partition of the American Tobacco Company by the United States Supreme Court* (New York: Columbia University Press, 1933).

Daniel Creamer, *Capital and Output Trends in Manufacturing Industries: 1880–1948*, N.B.E.R. occasional paper 41 (New York: National Bureau of Economic Research, 1954).

Daniel Creamer et al., *Capital in Manufacturing and Mining: Its Formation and Financing* (Princeton, N.J.: Princeton University Press, 1960).

Arthur Dahlberg, *When Capital Goes on Strike: How to Speed Up Spending* (New York: Harper & Bros., 1938).

Erik Dahmén, *Entrepreneurial Activity and the Development of Swedish Industry: 1919–1939*, trans. A. Leijonhufvud (Homewood, Ill.: Richard D. Irwin, 1970).

Carroll R. Daugherty, Melvin G. de Chazeau, Samuel S. Stratton, *The Economics of the Iron and Steel Industry* (New York: McGraw-Hill, 1937).

Lance E. Davis et al., *American Economic Growth: An Economist's History of the United States* (New York: Harper & Row, 1972).

Pearce Davis, *The Development of the American Glass Industry* (Cambridge, Mass.: Harvard University Press, 1949).

Robert W. Degrasse, Jr., *Military Expansion, Economic Decline: The Impact of Military Spending on U.S. Economic Performance* (New York: Council on Economic Priorities, 1983).

J. Frederic Dewhurst and Associates, *America's Needs and Resources* (New York: The Twentieth Century Fund, 1947), appendix 21.

David Dietz, *The Goodyear Research Laboratory* (Akron, Ohio: Goodyear Tire and Rubber Company, 1943).

Benjamin Disraeli, *Endymion* (New York: Longmans, Green, 1919).

Sergei P. Dobrovolsky, *Corporate Income Retention: 1915–43* (New York: National Bureau of Economic Research, 1951).

James S. Duesenberry, *Business Cycles and Economic Growth* (New York: McGraw-Hill, 1958).

Richard A. Easterlin, *Population, Labor Force, and Long Swings in Economic Growth: The American Experience* (New York: National Bureau of Economic Research, 1968).

John Eatwell, *Whatever Happened to Britain: The Economics of Decline* (London: Duckworth; British Broadcasting Corporation, 1982).

Marriner S. Eccles, *Beckoning Frontiers: Public and Personal Recollections* (New York: Knopf, 1951).

Electrical Merchandising Magazine (New York: McGraw-Hill, 1946).

T. S. Eliot, *The Wasteland* (New York: Harcourt Brace Jovanovich, 1971).

Ralph C. Epstein, *The Automobile Industry: Its Economic and Commercial Development* (New York: A. W. Shaw Company, 1928).

Amitai Etzioni, *An Immodest Agenda: Rebuilding America Before the Twenty-First Century* (New York: New Press, 1983).

Michael K. Evans, *Macroeconomic Activity: Theory, Forecasting, and Control* (New York: Harper & Row, 1969).

Solomon Fabricant, *The Output of Manufacturing Industries, 1899–1937* (New York: National Bureau of Economic Research, 1940).

John C. H. Fei, Gustav Ranis, *Development of the Labor Surplus Economy: Theory and Policy* (Homewood, Ill.: Richard D. Irwin, 1964).

Harvey S. Firestone, *Men and Rubber: The Story of Business* (New York: Doubleday, Page, 1926).

Irving Fisher, *The Stock Market Crash – and After* (New York: Macmillan, 1930).

   Booms and Depressions: Some First Principles (New York: Adelphi Company, 1932).

Milton Friedman, Anna J. Schwartz, *A Monetary History of the United States, 1867–1960* (Princeton, N.J.: Princeton University Press, 1963).

Monetary Statistics of the United States: Estimates, Sources, Methods (New York: National Bureau of Economic Research, 1970).

Daniel R. Fusfeld, *The Economic Thought of Franklin D. Roosevelt and the Origins of the New Deal* (New York: Columbia University Press, 1956).

John D. Gaffey, *The Productivity of Labor in the Rubber Tire Manufacturing Industry* (New York: Columbia University Press, 1940).

Louis Galambos, *Competition and Cooperation: The Emergence of a National Trade Association* (Baltimore: Johns Hopkins University Press, 1966).

John K. Galbraith, *The Great Crash, 1929* (Boston: Houghton Mifflin, 1972).

George B. Galloway et al., *Industrial Planning Under Codes* (New York: Harper & Bros., 1935).

William C. Geer, *The Reign of Rubber* (New York: Century Company, 1922).

General Motors Corporation, *The Dynamics of Automobile Demand* (New York: General Motors Corporation, 1939).

George S. Gibb, *The Saco-Lowell Shops: Textile Machinery Building in New England, 1818–1949* (Cambridge, Mass.: Harvard University Press, 1950).

C. B. Glasscock, *The Gasoline Age: The Story of the Men Who Made It* (New York: Bobbs-Merrill, 1937).

Raymond W. Goldsmith, *A Study of Saving in the United States*, 3 vols. (Princeton, N.J.: Princeton University Press, 1955).

Robert A. Gordon, *Business Fluctuations* (New York: Harper & Row, 1961).

Michael Gort, *Diversification and Integration in American Industry* (Princeton, N.J.: Princeton University Press, 1962).

Groundwood Paper Manufacturers Association, *Ten Year Trends in the Groundwood Paper Industry, 1935–1944* (New York: n.p., 1945).

Allan G. Gruchy, *Modern Economic Thought: The American Contribution* (New York: Prentice-Hall, 1947).

John A. Guthrie, *The Newsprint Paper Industry: An Economic Analysis* (Cambridge, Mass.: Harvard University Press, 1941).

Gottfried Haberler, *The World Economy, Money, and the Great Depression: 1919–1939* (Washington, D.C.: American Enterprise Institute for Public Policy Research, 1976).

Walton Hamilton et al., *Price and Price Policies* (New York: McGraw-Hill, 1938).

E. C. Hampe, M. Wittenberg, *The Lifeline of America: Development of the Food Industry* (New York: McGraw-Hill, 1964).

Alvin H. Hansen, *Fiscal Policy and Business Cycles* (New York: Norton, 1941).

Full Recovery or Stagnation? (New York: Norton, 1941).

Business Cycles and National Income (New York: Norton, 1951).

C. O. Hardy, Jacob Viner, *Report on the Availability of Bank Credit in the*

Seventh Federal Reserve District (Washington, D.C.: U.S. Government Printing Office, 1935).

Seymour Harris, *Saving American Capitalism: A Liberal Economic Program* (New York: Knopf, 1948).

Ellis W. Hawley, *The New Deal and the Problem of Monopoly: A Study in Economic Ambivalence* (Princeton, N.J.: Princeton University Press, 1966).

Ralph G. Hawtrey, *Economic Destiny* (New York: Longmans, Green, 1944).

Douglas A. Hayes, *Business Confidence and Business Activity: A Case Study of the Recession of 1937* (Ann Arbor: University of Michigan Press, 1951).

William Haynes, *American Chemical Industry: The Merger Era, 1923–1929* (New York: Van Nostrand, 1948).

American Chemical Industry: Decade of New Products, 1930–1939 (New York: Van Nostrand, 1954).

C. William Hazelett, *Incentive Taxation* (New York: Dutton, 1936).

John P. Henderson, *Changes in the Industrial Distribution of Employment: 1919–59.* Bulletin 87 (University of Illinois, Bureau of Economic and Business Research, 1959).

Bert G. Hickman, *Growth and Stability of the Postwar Economy* (Washington, D.C.: Brookings Institution, 1960).

Investment Demand and U.S. Economic Growth (Washington, D.C.: Brookings Institution, 1965).

Robert F. Himmelberg, *The Origins of the National Recovery Administration* (New York: Fordham University Press, 1976).

History of the Rubber Industry, P. Schidrowitz, T. R. Dawson (eds.) (Cambridge, Mass.: W. Heffer and Sons, 1952).

Henry V. Hodson, *Slump and Recovery, 1929–1937* (Oxford University Press, 1930).

William T. Hogan, *Productivity in the Blast-Furnace and Open-Hearth Segments of the Steel Industry: 1920–1946* (New York: Fordham University Press, 1950).

Economic History of the Iron and Steel Industry in the United States (Lexington, Mass.: D. C. Heath, 1971).

Stewart H. Holbrook, *Iron Brew: A Century of American Ore and Steel* (New York: Macmillan, 1939).

Duncan M. Holthausen, *The Volume of Consumer Installment Credit: 1929–38* (New York: National Bureau of Economic Research, 1940).

Donald S. Howard, *The W.P.A. and Federal Relief Policy* (New York: Russell Sage Foundation, 1943).

Thomas P. Hughes, *Networks of Power: Electrification in Western Society, 1880–1930* (Baltimore: Johns Hopkins University Press, 1983).

Harold L. Ickes, *The Secret Diary of Harold L. Ickes*, vol. II: *The Inside Struggle, 1936–39* (New York: Simon & Schuster, 1954).

Iron Age, vol. 117 (January–June, 1927).

Neil H. Jacoby, Raymond J. Saulnier, *Term Lending to Business* (New York: National Bureau of Economic Research, 1941).

Thomas Paul Jenkins, *Reactions of Major Groups to Positive Government in the United States: 1930–1940*. University of California Publications in Political Science, vol. I, no. 3 (Berkeley: University of California Press, 1945).

Hugh S. Johnson, *The Blue Eagle From Egg to Earth* (Garden City, N.Y.: Doubleday, Doran, 1935).

Michal Kalecki, *Studies in Economic Dynamics* (London: George Allen & Unwin, 1943).

Theory of Economic Dynamics: An Essay on Cyclical and Long-Run Changes in Capitalist Economy (New York: Monthly Review Press, 1968).

Studies in the Theory of Business Cycles, 1933–39 (New York: Augustus M. Kelley, 1969).

Selected Essays on the Dynamics of the Capitalist Economy, 1933–1970 (Cambridge University Press, 1971).

The Last Phase in the Transformation of Capitalism (New York: Monthly Review Press, 1972).

William J. Kemnitzer, *Rebirth of Monopoly: A Critical Analysis of Economic Conduct in the Petroleum Industry of the United States* (New York: Harper & Bros., 1938).

John W. Kendrick, *Productivity Trends in the United States* (Princeton, N.J.: Princeton University Press, 1961).

E. D. Kennedy, *The Automobile Industry: The Coming of Age of Capitalism's Favorite Child* (New York: Reynal & Hitchcock, 1941).

Stephen J. Kennedy, *Profits and Losses in Textiles: Cotton Textile Financing Since the War* (New York: Harper & Bros., 1936).

John Maynard Keynes, *The General Theory of Employment, Interest, and Money* (London: Macmillan, 1936).

Activities 1940–1944: Shaping the Post-War World; The Clearing Union; The Collected Writings of John Maynard Keynes, vol. 25, Donald Moggridge (ed.) (New York: Macmillan, 1980).

Lewis H. Kimmel, *The Availability of Bank Credit: 1933–1938* (New York: National Industrial Conference Board, 1939).

Charles P. Kindleberger, *The World in Depression: 1929–1939* (Berkeley: University of California Press, 1973).

Lawrence R. Klein, *Economic Fluctuations in the United States, 1921–1941* (New York: Wiley, 1950).

Jan Kmenta, *Elements of Econometrics* (New York: Macmillan, 1971).

Albert R. Koch, *The Financing of Large Corporations: 1920–1939* (New York: National Bureau of Economic Research, 1943).

Jürgen Kocka, *White Collar Workers in America, 1890–1940: A Social-Political History in International Perspective* (London: Sage Publications, 1980).

János Kornai, *Anti-Equilibrium: On Economic Systems Theory and the Tasks of Research* (Amsterdam: North-Holland, 1980).

Economics of Shortage (New York: North-Holland, 1980).

Herman E. Krooss, *Executive Opinion: What Business Leaders Said and*

    Thought on Economic Issues, 1920's–1960's (Garden City, N.Y.: Doubleday, 1970).

Simon Kuznets, *Shares of Upper Income Groups in Income and Savings* (New York: National Bureau of Economic Research, 1953).

    Capital in the American Economy: Its Formation and Financing (Princeton, N.J.: Princeton University Press, 1961).

    Modern Economic Growth: Rate, Structure, and Spread (New Haven, Conn.: Yale University Press, 1966).

Robert J. Lampman, *Changes in Income Distribution During the Great Depression*, vol. 7 of *Studies in Income and Wealth* (New York: National Bureau of Economic Research, 1946).

    Changes in the Share of the Wealth Held by Top Wealth-Holders: 1922–56. N.B.E.R. occasional paper 71 (New York: National Bureau of Economic Research, 1960).

James C. Lawrence, *The World's Struggle with Rubber, 1905–1931* (New York: Harper & Bros., 1931).

League of Nations, *World Economic Survey: 1938–39* (Geneva).

Stanley Lebergott, *Manpower in Economic Growth: The American Record Since 1800* (New York: McGraw-Hill, 1964).

    The American Economy (Princeton, N.J.: Princeton University Press, 1976).

William E. Leuchtenburg, *Franklin D. Roosevelt and the New Deal, 1932–1940* (New York: Harper & Row, 1963).

David P. Levine, *Economic Theory: The System of Economic Relations as a Whole* (London: Routledge & Kegan Paul, 1981).

W. Arthur Lewis, *Economic Survey, 1919–1939* (Philadelphia: Blakiston, 1950).

Licensed Beverage Industries, Incorporated, *Beverage Distilling Industry: Facts and Figures, 1934–1945* (New York: Licensed Beverage Industries, Incorporated, 1946).

Alfred Lief, *Harvey Firestone: Free Man of Enterprise* (New York: McGraw-Hill, 1951).

    The Firestone Story: A History of the Firestone Tire and Rubber Company (New York: Whittlesey House, 1951).

Lockwood Trade Journal Company, *250 Years of Papermaking in America* (New York: Lockwood Trade Journal Company, 1940).

William H. Lough, *High-Level Consumption* (New York: McGraw-Hill, 1935).

Erik Lundberg, *Instability and Economic Growth* (New Haven, Conn.: Yale University Press, 1968).

David Lynch, *The Concentration of Economic Power* (New York: Columbia University Press, 1946).

Leverett S. Lyon et al., *The National Recovery Administration: An Analysis and Appraisal* (Washington, D.C.: Brookings Institution, 1935).

E. D. McCallum, *The Iron and Steel Industry in the United States: A Study in Industrial Organization* (London: P. S. King & Son, 1931).

James W. McKie, *Tin Cans and Tin Plate: A Study of Competition in Two*

Related Markets (Cambridge, Mass.: Harvard University Press, 1959).

John McLean, Robert Haigh, *The Growth of Integrated Oil Companies* (Norwood, Mass.: Plimpton Press, 1954).

Russell H. Mack, *The Cigar Manufacturing Industry: Factors of Instability Affecting Production and Employment* (Philadelphia: University of Pennsylvania Press, 1933).

Jesse W. Markham, *Competition in the Rayon Industry* (Cambridge, Mass.: Harvard University Press, 1952).

Robin Marris, *The Economic Theory of 'Managerial' Capitalism* (London: Macmillan, 1967).

Karl Marx, *Capital*, trans. S. Moore, E. Aveling (New York: International Publishers, 1967).

Robert C. O. Matthews, *A Study in Trade-Cycle History* (Cambridge University Press, 1954).

Gardiner C. Means, Adolf A. Berle, *The Modern Corporation and Private Property* (New York: Harcourt, Brace & World, 1968).

Memoranda on Certain Proposals Relating to Unemployment, P.P. 1928-9 (Cmd. 3331), XVI.

Horst Mendershausen, *Changes in Income Distribution during the Great Depression*, vol. 7 of *Studies in Income and Wealth* (New York: National Bureau of Economic Research, 1946).

Gerhard Mensch, *Stalemate in Technology: Innovations Overcome the Depression* (Cambridge, Mass.: Ballinger, 1979).

H. E. Michl, *The Textile Industries: An Economic Analysis* (Washington, D.C.: The Textile Foundation, 1938).

Broadus Mitchell, *Depression Decade: From New Era through New Deal, 1929-1941* (New York: Rinehart & Company, 1955).

Wesley C. Mitchell, *Business Cycles* (Berkeley: University of California Press, 1913).

Business Cycles: The Problem and Its Setting (New York: National Bureau of Economic Research, 1927).

Raymond Moley, *After Seven Years* (New York: Harper & Bros., 1939).

G. H. Moore, *Statistical Indications of Cyclical Revivals and Recessions.* N.B.E.R. occasional paper 31 (New York: National Bureau of Economic Research, 1950).

National Bureau of Economic Research, *Recent Economic Changes in the United States* (New York: McGraw-Hill, 1929).

National Industrial Conference Board, *The Petroleum Almanac* (New York: National Industrial Conference Board, annual).

National Resources Committee, *Technological Trends and National Policy, Including the Social Implications of New Inventions* (Washington, D.C.: U.S. Government Printing Office, 1937).

New Deal Thought, H. Zinn (ed.) (Indianapolis: Bobbs-Merrill, 1966).

News Print Service Bureau, *The Story of News Print Paper* (New York: News Print Service Bureau, 1936).

William H. Nicholls, *Price Policies in the Cigarette Industry: A Study of*

234   Bibliography

"*Concerted Action" and Its Social Control, 1911–1950* (Nashville: Vanderbilt University Press, 1951).

Stephen Nickell, *The Investment Decisions of Firms* (Welwyn, England: J. Nisbet, 1978).

Rolf Nugent, *Consumer Credit and Economic Stability* (New York: Russell Sage Foundation, 1939).

G. Warren Nutter, Henry A. Einhorn, *Enterprise Monopoly in the United States: 1899–1958* (New York: Columbia University Press, 1969).

Organization for Economic Cooperation and Development, *Labour Force Statistics: 1960–71* (Paris: O.E.C.D., 1973).

Labour Force Statistics: 1966–77 (Paris: O.E.C.D., 1979).

Economic Outlook: July, 1983 (Paris: O.E.C.D., 1983).

George Orwell, *The Road to Wigan Pier* (London: V. Gollancz Ltd., 1937).

R. J. Overy, *The Nazi Economic Recovery: 1932–1938* (London: Macmillan, 1982).

Arthur N. Pack, *Forestry: An Economic Challenge* (New York: Macmillan, 1933).

William N. Parker, *Europe, America and the Wider World*, vol. I (Cambridge University Press, 1984).

Don Patinkin, *Money, Interest, and Prices* (New York: Harper & Row, 1965).

Leonard Peckitt, *Iron in Industry: Progress of 100 Years* (n.p.: The Newcomen Society, 1940).

Edith T. Penrose, *The Theory of the Growth of the Firm* (New York: Wiley, 1959).

George Perazich, Philip M. Field, *Industrial Research and Changing Technology*. National Research Project report M4 (Philadelphia: Works Progress Administration, 1940).

Frances Perkins, *The Roosevelt I Knew* (New York: Viking, 1946).

Josephine Perry, *The Rubber Industry* (New York: Longmans, Green, 1946).

Robert A. Pollard, *Economic Security and the Origins of the Cold War, 1945–1950* (New York: Columbia University Press, 1985).

Alexander Pope, *An Essay on Criticism*, Raymond Southall (ed.) (Glasgow: Collins Publishers, 1973).

Arthur Pound, *The Turning Wheel: The Story of General Motors through Twenty-Five Years, 1908–1933* (Garden City, N.Y.: Doubleday, Doran, 1934).

Clifford F. Pratten, *Economies of Scale in Manufacturing Industry* (Cambridge University Press, 1971).

John B. Rae, *American Automobile Manufacturers: The First Forty Years* (New York: Chilton, 1959).

The American Automobile: A Brief History (Chicago: University of Chicago Press, 1965).

Climb to Greatness: The American Aircraft Industry, 1920–1960 (Cambridge, Mass.: M.I.T. Press, 1968).

Basil Rauch, *The History of the New Deal: 1933–1938* (New York: Creative Age Press, 1944).

Robert B. Reich, *The Next American Frontier* (New York: Penguin Books, 1983).

Reports of the New York Rubber Exchange, 1929-31.

Resolutions Expressing the Manufacturer's Viewpoint Adopted at the Annual Meeting of the N.A.M. (December 7-8, 1933) (New York: National Association of Manufacturers, 1933).

David Ricardo, *The Principles of Political Economy and Taxation* (New York: J. M. Dent & Sons, 1929).

George B. Richardson, *Information and Investment: A Study in the Working of the Competitive Economy* (Oxford University Press, 1960).

J. J. Riley, *Organization in the Soft Drink Industry: A History of the American Bottlers of Carbonated Beverages* (Washington, D.C.: American Bottlers of Carbonated Beverages, 1946).

A History of the American Soft Drink Industry: Bottled Carbonated Beverages, 1807-1957 (Washington, D.C.: American Bottlers of Carbonated Beverages, 1958).

Lionel Robbins, *The Great Depression* (New York: Macmillan, 1934).

Joseph C. Robert, *The Story of Tobacco in America* (New York: Knopf, 1949).

Dennis H. Robertson, *A Study of Industrial Fluctuation* (London: P. S. King & Son, 1915).

Joan Robinson, *An Essay on Marxian Economics* (London: Macmillan, 1972).

Economic Heresies (New York: Basic, 1971).

Wilhelm Roepke, *Crises and Cycles* (London: William Hodge & Company, 1936).

L. T. C. Rolt, *A Short History of Machine Tools* (Cambridge, Mass.: M.I.T. Press, 1965).

Albert V. Romasco, *The Politics of Recovery: Roosevelt's New Deal* (Oxford University Press, 1983).

Charles F. Roos, *NRA Economic Planning* (Bloomington, Ind.: Principia Press, 1937).

Kenneth D. Roose, *The Economics of Recession and Revival: An Interpretation of 1937-38* (New Haven, Conn.: Yale University Press, 1954).

Franklin D. Roosevelt, *The Public Papers and Addresses of Franklin D. Roosevelt* (New York: Macmillan, 1941).

Nathan Rosenberg, *Perspectives on Technology* (Cambridge University Press, 1976).

Walt W. Rostow, *The Stages of Economic Growth: A Non-Communist Manifesto* (Cambridge University Press, 1971).

A. E. Safarian, *The Canadian Economy in the Great Depression* (Toronto: University of Toronto Press, 1959).

J. A. Salter, *Recovery: The Second Effort* (New York: Century Company, 1932).

Arthur Schlesinger, *The Crisis of the Old Order, 1919-1933* (Boston: Houghton Mifflin, 1957).

Arthur M. Schlesinger, *The Coming of the New Deal*, vol. 2 of *The Age of Roosevelt* (Boston: Houghton Mifflin, 1959).

The Politics of Upheaval, vol. 3 of *The Age of Roosevelt* (Boston: Houghton Mifflin, 1959).

Jacob Schmookler, *Invention and Economic Growth* (Cambridge, Mass.: Harvard University Press, 1966).

Gertrude G. Schroeder, *The Growth of Major Steel Companies, 1900–1950* (Baltimore: Johns Hopkins University Press, 1953).

Joseph A. Schumpeter, *Business Cycles: A Theoretical, Historical, and Statistical Analysis of the Capitalist Process* (New York: McGraw-Hill, 1939).

Capitalism, Socialism and Democracy (New York: Harper & Bros., 1947).

John W. Scoville, *Behavior of the Automobile Industry in Depression* (n.p.: n.p., 1935).

Reasons for the Fluctuations in Automobile Production (Columbus: Ohio State University Publications, 1938).

Warren C. Scoville, *Revolution in Glass-making: Entrepreneurship and Technological Change in the American Industry, 1880–1920* (Cambridge, Mass.: Harvard University Press, 1948).

Lawrence H. Seltzer, *A Financial History of the American Automobile Industry: A Study of the Ways in which the Leading American Producers of Automobiles Have Met Their Capital Requirements* (Boston: Houghton Mifflin, 1928).

Norman J. Silberling, *The Dynamics of Business* (New York: McGraw-Hill, 1943).

J. Russell Smith, *The Story of Iron and Steel* (New York: D. Appleton & Company, 1927).

Philip H. Smith, *Wheels Within Wheels: A Short History of American Motor Car Manufacturing* (New York: Funk & Wagnalls, 1968).

Standard and Poor's, *Industry Surveys* (June 27, 1947), section 2, 53–6.

Herbert Stein, *The Fiscal Revolution in America* (Chicago: University of Chicago Press, 1969).

Josef Steindl, *Small and Big Business: Economic Problems of the Size of Firms* (Oxford: Basil Blackwell, 1945).

Maturity and Stagnation in American Capitalism (New York: Monthly Review Press, 1979).

Bernard Sternsher, *Rexford Tugwell and the New Deal* (New Brunswick, N.J.: Rutgers University Press, 1964).

Louis T. Stevenson, *The Background and Economics of American Papermaking* (New York: Harper & Bros., 1940).

Maxwell S. Stewart, *Steel–Problems of a Great Industry* (New York: Public Affairs Committee, 1937).

George W. Stocking, *Basing Point Pricing and Regional Development: A Case Study of the Iron and Steel Industry* (Chapel Hill: University of North Carolina Press, 1954).

Peter A. Stone et al., *Economic Problems of the Lumber and Timber Products*

Industry. N.R.A. work materials no. 79 (Washington, D.C.: National Recovery Administration, 1936).

William Stoneman, *A History of the Economic Analysis of the Great Depression in America* (New York: Garland, 1979).

Folke W. Sundblad, *The American Steel Industry: At the Cross-Roads of Progress and Reaction* (Philadelphia: Dorrance & Company, 1938).

Ingvar Svennilson, *Growth and Stagnation in the European Economy* (Geneva: United Nations Economic Commission for Europe, 1954).

Paul M. Sweezy, *The Theory of Capitalist Development* (New York: Monthly Review Press, 1968).

Paolo Sylos-Labini, *Oligopoly and Technical Progress*, trans. E. Henderson (Cambridge, Mass.: Harvard University Press, 1969).

Peter Temin, *Did Monetary Forces Cause the Great Depression?* (New York: Norton, 1976).

George Terborgh, *The Bogey of Economic Maturity* (Chicago: Machinery and Allied Products Institute, 1945).

The Development of American Industries: Their Economic Significance, J. G. Glover, W. B. Cornell (eds.) (Englewood Cliffs, N.J.: Prentice-Hall, 1932).

The National Advertising Records (New York: Denney Publishing Company, 1929–34).

The Structure of American Industry: Some Case Studies, W. Adams (ed.) (New York: Macmillan, 1961).

Willard Thorp, *The Integration of Industrial Operation* (Washington, D.C.: U.S. Government Printing Office, 1924).

Business Annals (New York: National Bureau of Economic Research, 1926).

Vladimir P. Timoshenko, *World Agriculture and the Depression*, Michigan Business Studies, vol. 5 (Ann Arbor: University of Michigan Press, 1933).

James Tobin, *Essays in Economics* (London: North-Holland, 1971).

Rexford G. Tugwell, *The Industrial Discipline and the Governmental Arts* (New York: Columbia University Press, 1933).

The Democratic Roosevelt: A Biography of Franklin D. Roosevelt (Garden City, N.Y.: Doubleday, 1957).

The Art of Politics, As Practiced by Three Great Americans: Franklin Delano Roosevelt, Luis Munoz Marin and Fiorello LaGuardia (Garden City, N.Y.: Doubleday, 1958).

United States Arms Control and Disarmament Agency, *World Military Expenditures: Arms Transfers, Annual Reports: 1971–1980* (Washington, D.C.: U.S. Government Printing Office, 1983).

United States Board of Governors of the Federal Reserve System, *Banking and Monetary Statistics* (Washington, D.C.: National Capital Press, 1943).

United States Bureau of the Census, *Annual Survey of Manufactures* (Washington, D.C.: U.S. Government Printing Office).

Census of the United States: 1910 (Washington, D.C.: U.S. Government Printing Office, 1913).

Census of Manufactures, 1947, 1954, 1958, 1963, 1967, 1972 (Washington, D.C.: U.S. Government Printing Office).

United States Bureau of Foreign and Domestic Commerce, Rubber Division, *Circular 2865* (Washington, D.C.: U.S. Government Printing Office, 1929).

United States Renewal Tire Market Analysis (Washington, D.C.: U.S. Government Printing Office, 1937).

United States Bureau of Labor Statistics, *Employment and Earnings* (Washington, D.C.: U.S. Government Printing Office, 1923–38).

Capital Stock Estimates for Input–Output Industries: Methods and Data. Bulletin 2034 (Washington, D.C.: U.S. Government Printing Office, 1979).

United States Chamber of Commerce, *Annual Reports* (Washington, D.C.: Chamber of Commerce of the United States, 1929–39).

Board of Directors Annual Report (Washington, D.C.: Chamber of Commerce of the United States, 1933).

Board of Directors Annual Report (Washington, D.C.: Chamber of Commerce of the United States, 1936).

Outlines of Eleven Talks on Timely Questions Affecting the American Free Enterprise System (Washington, D.C.: n.p., 1941).

United States Council of Economic Advisers, *The Midyear Economic Report of the President: July 1951* (Washington, D.C.: U.S. Government Printing Office, 1951).

Economic Report of the President: 1972 (Washington, D.C.: U.S. Government Printing Office, 1972).

Economic Report of the President: 1984 (Washington, D.C.: U.S. Government Printing Office, 1984).

United States Department of Agriculture, *Consumption of Food in the United States, 1909–1948* (Washington, D.C.: U.S. Government Printing Office, 1949).

Technology in Food Marketing: A Survey of Developments and Trends in the Processing and Distribution of Farm-Produced Foods, 1930–1950 (Washington, D.C.: U.S. Government Printing Office, 1952).

Agricultural Statistics, 1957 (Washington, D.C.: U.S. Government Printing Office, 1958).

United States Department of Commerce, Bureau of the Census, *Biennial Census of Manufactures* (Washington, D.C.: U.S. Government Printing Office, 1901–37).

Biennial Census of Manufactures, 1921–37 (Washington, D.C.: U.S. Government Printing Office, 1924–39).

Historical Statistics of the United States, 1789–1945 (Washington, D.C.: U.S. Government Printing Office, 1949).

The National Income and Product Accounts of the United States, 1929–1965: Statistical Tables (Washington, D.C.: U.S. Government Printing Office, 1965).

Survey of Current Business (Washington, D.C.: U.S. Government Printing Office, August, 1965).

Historical Statistics of the United States: Colonial Times to 1970 (Washington, D.C.: U.S. Government Printing Office, 1975).

Survey of Current Business: 1980, U.S. Industrial Outlook for 200 Industries with Projections for 1984 (Washington, D.C.: U.S. Government Printing Office, 1980).

Bureau of Economic Analysis, *The National Income and Product Accounts of the United States: 1929–1976* (Washington, D.C.: U.S. Government Printing Office, 1981).

Statistical Abstract of the United States: 1981 (Washington, D.C.: U.S. Government Printing Office, 1981).

Statistical Abstract of the United States: 1984 (Washington, D.C.: U.S. Government Printing Office, 1983).

Business Statistics: 1982 (supplement to the *Survey of Current Business*, November, 1983).

International Economic Indicators (September, 1974, and September, 1984).

United States Department of the Interior, Bureau of Mines, *Minerals Yearbook* (Washington, D.C.: U.S. Government Printing Office).

United States Department of Labor, United States Department of Commerce, *Construction Volume and Costs, 1915–1956* (Washington, D.C.: U.S. Government Printing Office, 1956).

United States Federal Trade Commission, *Report on Motor Vehicle Industry* (Washington, D.C.: U.S. Government Printing Office, 1939).

Distribution Methods and Costs: Part IV, Petroleum Products (Washington, D.C.: U.S. Government Printing Office, 1944).

United States House of Representatives, Committee on Ways and Means, *Hearings*, "Extension of the National Industrial Recovery Act," 74th Congress, 1st session (Washington, D.C.: U.S. Government Printing Office, 1935).

United States Internal Revenue Service, *Statistics of Income* (Washington, D.C.: U.S. Government Printing Office).

United States National Recovery Administration, *Work Materials.*

United States National Recovery Review Board, *Reports.*

United States National Resources Planning Board, *Security, Work, and Relief Policies* (Washington, D.C.: U.S. Government Printing Office, 1942).

United States Patent Office, *Index of Patents* (Washington, D.C.: U.S. Government Printing Office).

United States Securities and Exchange Commission, Research and Statistics Section of the Trading and Exchange Division, *Cost of Flotation for Small Issues: 1925–29 and 1935–38* (Washington, D.C.: n.p., 1940).

Research and Statistics Section of the Trading and Exchange Division, *Cost of Flotation for Registered Securities: 1938–39* (Washington, D.C., n.p., 1941).

United States Temporary National Economic Committee, *Investigation of Concentration of Economic Power* (Washington, D.C.: U.S. Government Printing Office, 1941).

Petroleum Industry Hearings (New York: American Petroleum Institute, 1942).

Homer B. Vanderblue, William L. Crum, *The Iron Industry in Prosperity and Depression* (New York: A. W. Shaw Company, 1927).

Harless D. Wagoner, *The United States Machine Tool Industry from 1900 to 1950* (Cambridge, Mass.: M.I.T. Press, 1966).

Henry A. Wallace, *Technology, Corporations, and the General Welfare* (Chapel Hill: University of North Carolina Press, 1937).

Winifred D. Wandersee, *Women's Work and Family Values, 1920–1940* (Cambridge, Mass.: Harvard University Press, 1981).

Michael M. Weinstein, *Recovery and Redistribution under the NIRA* (New York: North-Holland, 1980).

John P. Wernette, *The Control of Business Cycles* (New York: Farrar & Rinehart, 1940).

Charles R. Whittlesey, *Banking and the New Deal* (Chicago: University of Chicago Press, 1935).

Harold F. Williamson et al., *The American Petroleum Industry: The Age of Energy, 1899–1959* (Evanston, Ill.: Northwestern University Press, 1963).

Jeffrey G. Williamson, Peter H. Lindert, *American Inequality: A Macroeconomic History* (New York: Academic Press, 1980).

Howard Wolf, Ralph Wolf, *Rubber: A Story of Glory and Greed* (New York: Covici, Friede, 1936).

Seymour L. Wolfbein, *The Decline of a Cotton Textile City: A Study of New Bedford* (New York: Columbia University Press, 1944).

Robert S. Woodbury, *Studies in the History of Machine Tools* (Cambridge, Mass.: M.I.T. Press, 1972).

II   Articles and chapters in anthologies

M. Abramovitz, "The Nature and Significance of Kuznets Cycles," *Economic Development and Cultural Change*, vol. 9 (April, 1961), 225–48.

"The Passing of the Kuznets Cycle," *Economica*, N.S., vol. 35 (November, 1968), 349–67.

"Welfare Quandaries and Productivity Concerns," *American Economic Review*, vol. 71 (March, 1981), 1–17.

M. Abramovitz, R. A. David, "Reinterpreting Economic Growth: Parables and Realities," *American Economic Review*, vol. 63 (May, 1973), 428–39.

"America's Mightiest Industry Discusses Its Economic Problems," *Economic Forum*, vol. 3 (Spring, 1936), 429ff.

C. E. Ayres, "The Impact of the Great Depression on Economic Thinking," *American Economic Review*, vol. 35 (May, 1946), 112–25.

J. Backman, "Price Inflexibility and Changes in Production," *American Economic Review*, vol. 29 (September, 1939), 480–6.

M. N. Baily, "Stabilization Policy and Private Economic Behavior," *Brookings Papers on Economic Activity*, vol. 1 (1978), 11–59.

R. E. Baldwin, "The Commodity Composition of Trade: Selected Industrial Countries, 1900–1954," *Review of Economics and Statistics*, vol. 40 (1958), 550–68.

C. L. Barber, "On the Origins of the Great Depression," *Southern Economic Journal*, vol. 44 (January, 1978), 432.

J. P. Barry, "The Marginal Utility of Lumber and Lumber Substitutes," *The Timberman*, vol. 37 (February, 1936), 18–31.

B. S. Bernanke, "Nonmonetary Effects of the Financial Crisis in the Propagation of the Great Depression," *American Economic Review*, vol. 73 (June, 1983), 257–76.

   "Employment, Hours, and Earnings in the Depression: An Analysis of Eight Manufacturing Industries," *American Economic Review*, vol. 76 (March, 1986), 82–109.

B. J. Bernstein, "The New Deal: The Conservative Achievements of Liberal Reform," in *Towards a New Past: Dissenting Essays in American History*, B. J. Bernstein (ed.) (New York: Pantheon, 1968).

M. A. Bernstein, Review of Romasco's *The Politics of Recovery, Journal of Economic History*, vol. 43 (December, 1983), 1048–9.

M. A. Bernstein, "A Reassessment of Investment Failure in the Interwar American Economy," *Journal of Economic History*, vol. 44 (June, 1984), 479–88.

C. D. Blachly, "Some Technological Changes for the Consideration of Planners," *Plan Age*, vol. 1 (May, 1935), 13.

D. Blanchard, "Should We Try a Partnership of Business and Government? – The Views of Industrial Leaders and the Attitude of the Administration," *Automotive Industries*, vol. 68 (May 13, 1933), 586–7.

B. Bolch, R. Fels, M. McMahon, "Housing Surplus in the 1920's?" *Explorations in Economic History*, vol. 8 (Spring, 1971), 259.

B. Bolch, J. D. Pilgrim, "A Reappraisal of Some Factors Associated with Fluctuations in the United States in the Interwar Period," *Southern Economic Journal*, vol. 39 (January, 1973), 327–44.

W. Bowden, "Labor in Depression and Recovery, 1929 to 1937," *Monthly Labor Review*, vol. 45 (November, 1937), 1045–81.

D. R. Brand, "Corporatism, the NRA, and the Oil Industry," *Political Science Quarterly*, vol. 98 (Spring, 1983), 99–118.

M. D. Brockie, "Theories of the 1937–38 Crisis and Depression," *Economic Journal*, vol. 60 (June, 1950), 292–310.

E. C. Brown, "Fiscal Policy in the 'Thirties: A Reappraisal," *American Economic Review*, vol. 46 (December, 1956), 857–79.

W. H. Brown, "Innovation in the Machine Tool Industry," *Quarterly Journal of Economics*, vol. 71 (1957), 407.

G. Burck, C. Silberman, "What Caused the Great Depression?" *Fortune*, vol. 51 (February, 1955), 94.

242   Bibliography

A. E. Burns, P. Kerr, "Recent Changes in Work-Relief Wage Policy," *American Economic Review*, vol. 31 (March, 1941), 56–66.

"Business Agrees to Regulate Itself," *Nation's Business*, vol. 21 (June, 1933), 17ff.

E. H. Chamberlin, "The Product as an Economic Variable," *Quarterly Journal of Economics*, vol. 67 (1953), 13.

A. D. Chandler, "The Structure of American Industry in the Twentieth Century: A Historical Overview," *Business History Review*, vol. 43 (Autumn, 1969), 255.

L. Chawner, "Capital Expenditures for Manufacturing Plant and Equipment – 1915 to 1940," *Survey of Current Business* (March, 1941), 9–14.

"Capital Expenditures in Selected Manufacturing Industries," *Survey of Current Business* (May, 1941), 17–56.

"Capital Expenditures in Selected Manufacturing Industries – Part II," *Survey of Current Business* (December, 1941), 14–23.

C. Clark, "A System of Equations Explaining the United States Trade Cycle, 1921 to 1941," *Econometrica*, vol. 17 (April, 1949), 93.

D. Cochrane, G. H. Orcutt, "Application of Least-Squares Regressions to Relationships Containing Auto-correlated Error Terms," *Journal of the American Statistical Association*, vol. 44 (1949), 32–61.

A. J. Cohen, "Technological Change as Historical Process: The Case of the U.S. Pulp and Paper Industry, 1915–1940," *Journal of Economic History*, vol. 44 (September, 1984), 775–99.

R. M. Collins, "Positive Business Responses to the New Deal: The Roots of the Committee for Economic Development, 1933–1942," *Business History Review*, vol. 52 (Autumn, 1978), 369–91.

W. L. Compton, "The Lumber Industry Is Not Defeated," *American Lumberman* (June 11, 1932), 1, 38.

J. R. Crotty, "On Keynes and Capital Flight," *Journal of Economic Literature*, vol. 21 (March, 1983), 59–65.

W. Crounse, "The New Status of Shipbuilding," *Iron Age*, vol. 99 (January, 1917), 27.

L. Currie, "The Decline of the Commercial Loan," *Quarterly Journal of Economics*, vol. 45 (August, 1931), 698–709.

M. R. Darby, "Three-and-a-Half Million Employees Have Been Mislaid: Or, an Explanation of Unemployment, 1934–1941," *Journal of Political Economy*, vol. 84 (February, 1976), 1–16.

P. Darling, M. Lovell, "Factors Influencing Inventory Investment," in *The Brookings Quarterly Econometric Model of the United States*, J. Duesenberry (ed.) (Chicago: Rand McNally & Company, 1965).

L. Davis, "The Capital Markets and Industrial Concentration: The U.S. and U.K., a Comparative Study," *Economic History Review*, second series, vol. 19 (August, 1966), 255–72.

M. DeVroey, "A Regulation Approach Interpretation of Contemporary Crisis," *Capital and Class*, vol. 23 (Summer, 1984), 45–66.

E. F. DuBrul, "Economics of the Machine Tool Industry," *Machinery*, vol. 29 (1923), 564.

J. Durbin, G. S. Watson, "Testing for Serial Correlation in Least-Squares Regression," *Biometrika*, vol. 37 (June, 1950), 409–28; vol. 38 (June, 1951), 159–78.

Richard Easterlin, "American Population Since 1940," in *The American Economy in Transition*, M. Feldstein (ed.) (Chicago: University of Chicago Press, 1980), 275–321.

G. A. Eddy, "Security Issues and Real Investment in 1929," *Review of Economics and Statistics*, vol. 19 (May, 1937), 79.

"The Present Status of New Security Issues," *Review of Economics and Statistics*, vol. 21 (August, 1939), 116–21.

C. C. Edmonds, "Tendencies in the Automobile Industry," *American Economic Review*, vol. 13 (March, 1923), 422.

Bernard Elbaum, William Lazonick, "The Decline of the British Economy: An Institutional Perspective," *Journal of Economic History*, vol. 44 (June, 1984), 567–83.

P. T. Ellsworth, "The Output of New Corporation Issues," *Review of Economic Statistics*, vol. 14 (November 15, 1932), 195–200.

E. Engel, "Die Productions- und Consumtionsverhältnisse des Königreichs Sachsen," reprinted in *International Statistical Institute Bulletin*, vol. 9, no. 1, supplement 1.

R. C. Epstein, "The Rise and Fall of Firms in the Automobile Industry," *Harvard Business Review*, vol. 5 (1926–7), 157.

E. A. Erickson, "The Great Crash of October, 1929," in *The Great Depression Revisited: Essays on the Economics of the Thirties*, H. van der Wee (ed.) (The Hague: Martinus Nijhoff, 1972), 3–12.

S. Fabricant, "Profits, Losses and Business Assets, 1929–1934," N.B.E.R. bulletin 55 (n.p.: National Bureau of Economic Research, n.d.).

W. Fellner, "The Technological Argument of the Stagnation Thesis," *Quarterly Journal of Economics*, vol. 55 (August, 1941), 638–51.

"Full Use or Underutilization: Appraisal of Long-Run Factors Other than Defense," *American Economic Review*, vol. 44 (May, 1954), 423–33.

S. Fine, "The Ford Motor Company and the N.R.A.," *Business History Review*, vol. 32 (Winter, 1958), 353–85.

R. E. Flanders, "The Economics of Machine Production," *Mechanical Engineering*, vol. 54 (1932), 605.

"Business Looks at the N.R.A.," *Atlantic Monthly*, vol. 152 (November, 1933), 626.

E. B. Fricke, "The New Deal and the Modernization of Small Business: The McCreary Tire and Rubber Company, 1930–1940," *Business History Review*, vol. 56 (Winter, 1982), 559–76.

Milton Friedman, Anna J. Schwartz, "The Quantity Theory of Money – A Restatement," in *Studies in the Quantity Theory of Money*, M. Friedman (ed.) (Chicago: University of Chicago Press, 1956).

"Frosted Food Sales Show Sharp Gain for Past Year," *Wall Street Journal*, January 31, 1938, 1ff.

J. C. Furnas, "Ford's Leftover Idea." Letter to the editor. *New York Times*, February 16, 1983, A-30.

W. A. Gibbons, "The Rubber Industry, 1839–1939," in *Annual Report of the Smithsonian Institution, 1940* (Washington, D.C.: U.S. Government Printing Office, 1941), 196.

R. A. Gordon, "Business Cycles in the Interwar Period: The 'Quantitative-Historical' Approach," *American Economic Review*, vol. 39 (May, 1949), 47–63.

"Cyclical Experience in the Interwar Period: The Investment Boom of the 'Twenties," in *Conference on Business Cycles* (New York: National Bureau of Economic Research, 1951).

"The Stability of the U.S. Economy," in *Is the Business Cycle Obsolete?* M. Bronfenbrenner (ed.) (New York: Wiley, 1969), 3.

R. Griffith, "Dwight D. Eisenhower and the Corporate Commonwealth," *American Historical Review*, vol. 87 (February, 1982), 87–122.

F. H. Hahn, R. C. O. Matthews, "The Theory of Economic Growth: A Survey," *Economic Journal*, vol. 74 (December, 1964), 779–902.

R. L. Hall, C. J. Hitch, "Price Theory and Business Behavior," *Oxford Economic Papers*, vol. 2 (May, 1939), 12.

K. J. Hancock, "The Reduction of Unemployment as a Problem of Public Policy, 1920–29," *Economic History Review*, vol. 15 (December, 1962), 328–43.

A. H. Hansen, "Economic Progress and Declining Population Growth," *American Economic Review*, vol. 29 (March, 1939), 1–15.

"Was Fiscal Policy in the Thirties a Failure?" *Review of Economics and Statistics*, vol. 45 (August, 1963), 320–3.

C. O. Hardy, "An Appraisal of the Factors ('Natural' and 'Artificial') Which Stopped Short the Recovery Development in the United States," *American Economic Review*, vol. 29 (March, 1939, supplement), 170–82.

E. W. Hawley, "The Discovery and Study of a 'Corporate Liberalism'," *Business History Review*, vol. 52 (Autumn, 1978), 309–20.

C. Heim, "Structural Transformation and the Demand for New Labor in Advanced Economies: Interwar Britain," *Journal of Economic History*, vol. 44 (June, 1984), 585–95.

"Industrial Organization and Regional Development in Interwar Britain," *Journal of Economic History*, vol. 43 (December, 1983), 931–52.

J. S. Hekman, "The Product Cycle and New England Textiles," *Quarterly Journal of Economics*, vol. 94 (June, 1980), 697.

D. F. Hendry, "Econometrics – Alchemy or Science?" *Economica*, vol. 47 (November, 1980), 387.

C. H. Hession, "The Metal Container Industry," in *The Structure of American Industry*, W. Adams (ed.) (New York: Macmillan, 1961).

B. G. Hickman, "What Became of the Housing Cycle?" in *Nations and Households in Economic Growth: Essays in Honor of Moses Abramovitz*, P. A. David, M. W. Reder (eds.) (New York: Academic Press, 1974).

J. R. Hicks, "Mr. Keynes and the 'Classics': A Suggested Interpretation," *Econometrica*, vol. 5 (April, 1937), 147–59.

G. W. Hill, "The Newer Competition," *World's Work*, vol. 58 (June, 1929), 72–4, 130–44.

C. F. Holt, "Who Benefited from the Prosperity of the Twenties?" *Explorations in Economic History*, vol. 14 (July, 1977), 277–89.

H. M. Hunter, "The Role of Business Liquidity during the Great Depression and Afterwards: Differences between Large and Small Firms," *Journal of Economic History*, vol. 42 (December, 1982), 883–902.

H. Jaeger, "Business in the Great Depression," in *The Great Depression Revisited: Essays on the Economics of the Thirties*, H. van der Wee (ed.) (The Hague: Martinus Nijhoff, 1972), 137.

L. M. James, "Restrictive Agreements and Practices in the Lumber Industry, 1880–1939," *Southern Economic Journal*, vol. 13 (October, 1946), 115.

D. W. Jorgenson, "Econometric Studies of Investment Behavior: A Survey," *Journal of Economic Literature*, vol. 9 (December, 1971), 1111.

E. J. Kahn, Jr., "The Staffs of Life, V: The Future of the Planet," *The New Yorker*, vol. 61 (March 11, 1985), 68.

N. Kaldor, "The Relation of Economic Growth and Cyclical Fluctuations," *Economic Journal*, vol. 64 (March, 1954), 53.

"Capitalist Evolution in the Light of Keynesian Economics," in *Essays on Economic Stability and Growth* (Glencoe, Ill.: Free Press, 1960).

M. Kalecki, "Observations on the Theory of Growth," *Economic Journal*, vol. 72 (March, 1962), 134–53.

R. R. Keller, "Factor Income Distribution in the United States During the 1920's: A Reexamination of Fact and Theory," *Journal of Economic History*, vol. 33 (March, 1973), 252–73.

J. M. Keynes, "National Self-Sufficiency," *Yale Review*, vol. 22 (June, 1933), 755–69.

"Some Economic Consequences of a Declining Population," *Eugenics Review*, vol. 29 (April, 1937), 13–17.

T. C. Koopmans, "Measurement without Theory," in *Readings in Business Cycles*, R. A. Gordon, L. R. Klein (eds.) (Homewood, Ill.: Richard D. Irwin, 1965), 186.

J. R. Kurth, "The Political Consequences of the Product Cycle: Industrial History and Political Outcomes," *International Organization*, vol. 33 (Winter, 1979), 1–34.

S. Kuznets, "Long Swings in the Growth of Population and in Related Economic Variables," *Proceedings of the American Philosophical Society*, vol. 102 (February, 1958), 25–52.

"Quantitative Aspects of the Economic Growth of Nations, VI: Long Term Trends in Capital Formation Proportions," *Economic Development and Cultural Change*, vol. 9 (July, 1961), part 2, 34–5.

J. E. La Tourette, "Potential Output and the Capital-Output Ratio in the United States Private Business Sector: 1909–1959," *Kyklos*, vol. 18 (1965), 316–32.

"Sources of Variation in the Capital-Output Ratio in the United States Private Business Sector: 1909–1959," *Kyklos*, vol. 18 (1965), 635–57.

J. C. Lawrence, "Pioneers in the Commercial Development of Rubber," *Journal of Chemical Education*, vol. 7 (August, 1930), 1788.

W. H. Lazonick, "Industrial Relations and Technical Change: The Case of the Self-Acting Mule," *Cambridge Journal of Economics*, vol. 3 (September, 1979), 236.

"Production Relations, Labor Productivity, and Choice of Technique: British and U.S. Cotton Spinning," *Journal of Economic History*, vol. 41 (September, 1981), 491.

E. Lederer, "The Problem of Development and Growth in the Economic System," *Social Research*, vol. 2 (February, 1935), 20–38.

D. P. Levine, "The Theory of the Growth of the Capitalist Economy," *Economic Development and Cultural Change*, vol. 24 (October, 1975), 47–74.

"Determinants of Capitalist Expansion," *Economic Development and Cultural Change*, vol. 30 (January, 1982), 314–20.

W. A. Lewis, "Economic Development with Unlimited Supplies of Labour," *Manchester School of Economic and Social Studies*, vol. 22 (May, 1954), 139–91.

L. L. Lorwin, "The Plan State and the Democratic Ideal," *Annuals of the American Academy of Political and Social Science*, vol. 180 (July, 1935), 114–18.

R. E. Lucas, "An Equilibrium Model of the Business Cycle," *Journal of Political Economy*, vol. 83 (December, 1975), 1113–44.

"Understanding Business Cycles," in *Stabilization of the Domestic and International Economy*, K. Brunner, A. H. Meltzer (eds.) (New York: North-Holland, 1977), 7–29.

H. Lydall, "A Theory of Distribution and Growth with Economies of Scale," *Economic Journal*, vol. 81 (March, 1971), 91.

F. R. Macaulay, "Economic Recovery and the New Deal," *Economic Forum*, vol. 3 (Winter, 1936), 245–55.

George C. McCabe, "Wall Street Recants," *Commonweal* (August 3, 1934), 341–4.

G. E. McLaughlin, R. J. Watkins, "The Problem of Industrial Growth in a Mature Economy," *American Economic Review*, vol. 29 (March, 1939, supplement), 1–14.

K. McQuaid, "Corporate Liberalism in the American Business Community, 1920–1946," *Business History Review*, vol. 52 (Autumn, 1978), 342–68.

F. Machlup, "Theories of the Firm: Marginalist, Behavioral, Managerial," *American Economic Review*, vol. 57 (March, 1967), 1–33.

A. Maddison, "Economic Stagnation Since 1973, Its Nature and Causes: A Six Country Survey," *De Economist*, no. 131 (1983), 585–608.

T. G. Marx, "The Development of the Franchise Distribution System in the U.S. Automobile Industry," *Business History Review*, vol. 59 (Autumn, 1985), 465–74.

E. Maschke, "Outline of the History of German Cartels from 1873 to 1914," in *Essays in European Economic History: 1789–1914*, F. Crouzet, W. H. Chaloner, W. M. Stern (eds.) (London: Edward Arnold, 1969), 226–58.

T. Mayer, M. Chatterji, "Political Shocks and Investment: Some Evidence from the 1930s," *Journal of Economic History*, 45 (December, 1985), 913–24.

G. C. Means, "Price Inflexibility and the Requirements of a Stabilizing Monetary Policy," *Journal of the American Statistical Association*, vol. 30 (June, 1935), 401–13.

L. J. Mercer, W. D. Morgan, "Alternative Interpretations of Market Saturation: Evaluation for the Automobile Market in the Late Twenties," *Explorations in Economic History*, vol. 9 (Spring, 1972), 269.

"The American Automobile Industry: Investment Demand, Capacity, and Capacity Utilization, 1921–1940," *Journal of Political Economy*, vol. 80 (December, 1972), 1214–31.

J. P. Miller, "Measures of Monopoly Power and Concentration: Their Economic Significance," in *Business Concentration and Price Policy* (Princeton, N.J.: Princeton University Press, 1955), 119–39.

F. S. Mishkin, "The Household Balance Sheet and the Great Depression," *Journal of Economic History*, vol. 38 (December, 1978), 918–37.

G. H. Moore, "Some Secular Changes in Business Cycles," *American Economic Review*, vol. 64 (May, 1974), 133.

J. J. B. Morgan, "Manic-Depressive Psychoses of Business," *Psychological Review*, vol. 42 (January, 1935), 91–3, 98–107.

C. T. Murchison, "Requisites of Stabilization in the Cotton Textile Industry," *American Economic Review*, vol. 23 (March, 1933), 72.

R. F. Muth, "The Demand for Non-Farm Housing," in *The Demand for Durable Goods*, A. C. Harberger (ed.) (Chicago: University of Chicago Press, 1960), 29–96.

G. N. Nelson, "Taxation of Corporate Surplus," in *Proceedings of the 29th Annual Conference of the National Tax Association* (September 28 to October 1, 1936) (Columbia, S.C.: National Tax Association, 1937).

D. F. Noble, "Command Performance: A Perspective on Military Enterprise and Technological Change," in *Military Enterprise and Technological Change: Perspectives on the American Experience*, M. R. Smith (ed.) (Cambridge, Mass.: M.I.T. Press, 1985), 329–46.

W. Nordhaus, "The New Brand of Economics," *New York Times*, February 22, 1981, section 3, p. 2.

R. D. Norton, "Industrial Policy and American Renewal," *Journal of Economic Literature*, vol. 24 (March, 1986), 1–40.

C. R. Noyes, "The Gold Inflation in the United States, 1921–1929," *American Economic Review*, vol. 20 (June, 1930), 181–98.

G. Osborne, "The Development of the Cotton Textile Industry of the United States from 1920 to 1930," *Journal of the Textile Institute*, vol. 27 (1936), 4.

H. T. Oshima, "The Growth of U.S. Factory Productivity: The Significance of New Technologies in the Early Decades of the Twentieth Century," *Journal of Economic History*, vol. 44 (March, 1984), 161–70.

R. J. Overy, "Cars, Roads, and Economic Recovery in Germany, 1932–38," *Economic History Review*, 2nd series, vol. 28 (August, 1975), 466–83.

P. Patnaik, "A Note on External Markets and Capitalist Development," *Economic Journal*, vol. 82 (December, 1972), 1316–23.

L. C. Peppers, "Full Employment Surplus Analysis and Structural Change: The 1930's," *Explorations in Economic History*, vol. 10 (Winter, 1973), 197–210.

C. E. Persons, "Credit Expansion, 1920 to 1929, and Its Lessons," *Quarterly Journal of Economics*, vol. 45 (November, 1930), 94–130.

L. L. Peters, "Cooperative Competition in German Coal and Steel: 1893–1914," *Journal of Economic History*, vol. 42 (March, 1982), 227–30.

J. S. Peterson, "Auto Workers and their Work, 1900–1933," *Labor History*, vol. 22 (Spring, 1981), 213–36.

R. W. Pfouts, C. E. Ferguson, "Market Classification Systems in Theory and Policy," *Southern Economic Journal*, vol. 26 (October, 1959), 111–18.

A. W. Phillips, "The Relation Between Unemployment and the Rate of Change of Money Wage Rates in the United Kingdom, 1861–1957," *Economica*, N.S., vol. 25 (November, 1958), 283–99.

A. C. Pigou, "The Classical Stationary State," *Economic Journal*, vol. 53 (April, 1943), 343–51.

S. J. Randall, "Harold Ickes and United States Foreign Petroleum Policy Planning, 1939–1945," *Business History Review*, vol. 57 (Autumn, 1983), 367–87.

"Review and Outlook: The Key to Capital Inertia," *Wall Street Journal*, March 24, 1938.

L. G. Reynolds, "Competition in the Rubber Tire Industry," *American Economic Review*, vol. 28 (September, 1938), 463–5.

"Producers' Goods Prices in Expansion and Decline," *Journal of the American Statistical Association*, vol. 34 (March, 1939), 32–40.

G. B. Richardson, "Equilibrium, Expectations and Information," *Economic Journal*, vol. 69 (June, 1959), 223.

R. Robinson, "The Economics of Disequilibrium Price," *Quarterly Journal of Economics*, vol. 75 (May, 1961), 199.

C. D. Romer, "Is the Stabilization of the Postwar Economy a Figment of the Data?" *American Economic Review*, vol. 76 (June, 1986), 314–34.

K. D. Roose, "The Recession of 1937–38," *Journal of Political Economy*, vol. 56 (June, 1948), 239–48.

E. Rothschild, "Reagan and the Real American," *New York Review of Books*, vol. 28 (February 5, 1981), 12.

R. Ruggles, "The Nature of Price Flexibility and the Determinants of Relative Price Changes in the Economy," in Universities–National Bureau Committee for Economic Research, *Business Concentration and Price Policy* (Princeton, N.J.: Princeton University Press, 1955).

A. Sachs, "Summary of a Comprehensive Financial Analysis of the Causes of the Slump," *The Annalist*, vol. 51 (January 14, 1938), 35–6.

"The Financial Dynamics of the Recovery since 1933 and Latest Constriction Phase in Capital Flow," in American Management Association, *Corporate Finance and Taxation*. Financial management series number 53 (New York: American Management Association, 1938), 13, 17, 23–4, 27–9.

P. A. Samuelson, "Interactions between the Multiplier Analysis and the Principle of Acceleration," *Review of Economics and Statistics*, vol. 21 (May, 1939), 75–8.

T. J. Sargent, "A Classical Macroeconometric Model for the United States," *Journal of Political Economy*, vol. 84 (April, 1976), 207–37.

J. A. Schumpeter, "The Decade of the Twenties," *American Economic Review*, vol. 36 (May, 1946), 1–10.

G. Sirkin, "The Stock Market of 1929 Revisited: A Note," *Business History Review*, vol. 49 (Summer, 1975), 223–31.

N. Sivachev, "The Rise of Statism in 1930's America: A Soviet View of the Social and Political Effects of the New Deal," *Labor History*, vol. 24 (Fall, 1983), 500–25.

T. Skocpol, K. Finegold, "State Capacity and Economic Intervention in the Early New Deal," *Political Science Quarterly*, vol. 97 (Summer, 1982), 255–78.

S. H. Slichter, "The Downturn of 1937," *Review of Economics and Statistics*, vol. 20 (August, 1938), 97–110.

"Corporate Price Policies as a Factor in the Recent Business Recession," *Proceedings of the Academy of Political Science*, vol. 18 (January, 1939), 20–33.

E. E. Slutsky, "On the Theory of the Budget of the Consumer," in American Economic Association, *Readings in Price Theory* (Chicago: Richard D. Irwin, 1952).

G. Smiley, "Recent Unemployment Rate Estimates for the 1920's and 1930's," *Journal of Economic History*, vol. 43 (June, 1983), 490.

A. Smithies, "The American Economy in the Thirties," *American Economic Review*, vol. 36 (May, 1946), 11.

"Economic Fluctuations and Growth," *Econometrica*, vol. 20 (January, 1952), 52.

C. S. Solo, "Innovation in the Capitalist Process: A Critique of the Schumpeterian Theory," *Quarterly Journal of Economics*, vol. 65 (August, 1951), 417.

L. Spaventa, "Dualism in Economic Growth," *Banca Nazionale del Lavoro*

Quarterly Review, vol. 12 (December, 1959), 386–434, especially 418–19.

A. M. Spence, "The Learning Curve and Competition," *Bell Journal of Economics*, vol. 12 (Spring, 1981), 49–70.

J. Steindl, "On Maturity in Capitalist Economies," in *Problems of Economic Dynamics and Planning: Essays in Honour of Michal Kalecki* (New York: Pergamon Press, 1966), 423–32.

"Stagnation Theory and Stagnation Policy," *Cambridge Journal of Economics*, vol. 3 (January, 1979), 1.

"Reflections on the Present State of Economics," *Banca Nazionale del Lavoro Quarterly Review*, no. 148 (March, 1984), 3–14.

G. J. Stigler, "The Early History of Empirical Studies of Consumer Behavior," *Journal of Political Economy*, vol. 62 (April, 1954), 95–113.

W. L. Stoddard, "Small Business Wants Capital," *Harvard Business Review*, vol. 18 (Spring, 1940), 265–74.

F. Stricker, "Affluence for Whom? – Another Look at Prosperity and the Working Class in the 1920's," *Labor History*, vol. 24 (Winter, 1983), 5–33.

E. W. Swanson, "The Economic Stagnation Thesis, Once More," *Southern Economic Journal*, vol. 22 (January, 1956), 287.

J. A. Swanson, S. H. Williamson, "Estimates of National Product and Income for the United States Economy, 1919–1941," *Explorations in Economic History*, vol. 10 (Fall, 1972), 53.

A. R. Sweezy, "Population Growth and Investment Opportunity," *Quarterly Journal of Economics*, vol. 55 (November, 1940), 64–79.

"The Keynesians and Government Policy: 1933–39," *American Economic Review*, vol. 62 (May, 1972), 116–24.

P. M. Sweezy, "Demand Under Conditions of Oligopoly," *Journal of Political Economy*, vol. 47 (August, 1939), 568.

"Karl Marx and the Industrial Revolution," in *Events, Ideology, and Economic Theory*, R. Eagly (ed.) (Detroit: Wayne State University Press, 1968).

G. Terborgh, "The Roosevelt Government and America's Petroleum Problems," *Rotterdamsche Bankvereeniging Monthly Review*, no. 6 (June, 1933), 147–53; no. 7 (July, 1933), 171–7.

"Estimated Expenditures for New Durable Goods: 1919–1938," *Federal Reserve Bulletin*, vol. 25 (September, 1939), 731.

"The American Petroleum Code," *Rotterdamsche Bankvereeniging Monthly Review*, no. 9/10 (September/October, 1933), 225–32.

"The Immediate Impact of War on the American Economy," by the editors, *Plan Age*, vol. 5 (December, 1939), 313–26.

"The Textile Industry in the United States of America," *Plan Age*, vol. 3 (May-June, 1937).

G. V. Thompson, "Intercompany Technical Standardization in the Early American Automobile Industry," *Journal of Economic History*, vol. 14 (Winter, 1954), 1–20.

W. L. Thorp, W. F. Crowder, "Concentration and Product Characteristics as Factors in Price-Quantity Behavior," *American Economic Review*, vol. 30 (February, 1941), 390–408.

J. Tobin, "Liquidity Preference and Monetary Policy," *Review of Economics and Statistics*, vol. 29 (February, 1947), 124–31.

"The Wage-Price Mechanism," in *Essays in Economics*, vol. 2: *Consumption and Econometrics* (New York: North-Holland, 1975).

P. B. Trescott, "Federal Reserve Policy in the Great Contraction: A Counterfactual Assessment," *Explorations in Economic History*, vol. 19 (July, 1982), 211–20.

G. N. von Tunzelmann, "Structural Change and Leading Sectors in British Manufacturing, 1907–68," in *Economics in the Long View: Essays in Honour of W. W. Rostow*, C. P. Kindleberger, G. di Tella (eds.) (New York: New York University Press, 1982), vol. 3, 1–49.

H. Tyszynski, "World Trade in Manufactured Commodities: 1899–1950," *Manchester School of Economics and Social Studies*, vol. 19 (September, 1951), 272–304.

J. E. Ullmann, "The Arms Race and the Decline of U.S. Technology," *Journal of Economic Issues*, vol. 17 (June, 1983), 565–74.

United States Department of Labor, "Productivity of Labor in Eleven Manufacturing Industries," *Monthly Labor Review*, vol. 30 (March, 1930), 501–17.

United States Federal Reserve Board, "New Index of Industrial Production," *Federal Reserve Bulletin*, vol. 13 (January, 1927), 100; vol. 13 (March, 1927), 170–7.

"Index of Industrial Production," *Federal Reserve Bulletin*, vol. 29 (October, 1943), 953.

"Used Car Sales in 1980 at Record," *New York Times*, July 21, 1981, D2.

H. B. Vanderblue, "Pricing Policies in the Automobile Industry," *Harvard Business Review*, vol. 17 (Summer, 1939), 385–401.

H. G. Vatter, "The Closure of Entry in the American Automobile Industry," *Oxford Academic Papers*, N.S., vol. 4 (October, 1952), 215.

"The Atrophy of New Investment and Some Consequences for the U.S. Mixed Economy," *Journal of Economic Issues*, vol. 16 (March, 1982), 237–53.

R. Vernon, "International Investment and International Trade in the Product Cycle," *Quarterly Journal of Economics*, vol. 80 (May, 1966), 190–207.

J. Viner, "Recent Legislation and the Banking Situation," *American Economic Review*, vol. 26 (March, 1936), 106–7.

Clark Warburton, "Monetary Expansion and the Inflationary Gap," *American Economic Review*, vol. 34 (June, 1944), 303–27.

"Monetary Theory, Full Production, and the Great Depression," *Econometrica*, vol. 13 (April, 1945), 114–28.

"The Volume of Money and the Price Level Between the World Wars," *Journal of Political Economy*, vol. 53 (June, 1945), 150–63.

"Quantity and Frequency of Use of Money in the United States, 1919–1945," *Journal of Political Economy*, vol. 54 (October, 1946), 436–50.

S. Webb, "Tariffs, Cartels, Technology, and Growth in the German Steel Industry, 1879 to 1914," *Journal of Economic History*, vol. 40 (June, 1980), 309–29.

J. Weinberger, "Economic Aspects of Cooperation," *Harvard Business Review*, vol. 15 (Summer, 1937), 448–63.

D. Weintraub, "Effects of Current and Prospective Technological Developments upon Capital Formation," *American Economic Review*, vol. 29 (March, 1939, supplement), 32.

D. R. Weir, "The Reliability of Historical Macroeconomic Data for Comparing Cyclical Stability," *Journal of Economic History*, vol. 46 (June, 1986), 353–65.

J. Williamson, "On the System in Bretton Woods," *American Economic Review*, vol. 75 (May, 1985), 74–9.

W. H. Wilson, "How the Chamber of Commerce Viewed the NRA: A Reexamination," *Mid-America: An Historical Review*, vol. 44 (April, 1962), 95–108.

L. Wolman, "Consumption and the Standard of Living," in Committee on Recent Economic Changes of the President's Conference on Unemployment, *Recent Economic Changes in the United States* (New York: McGraw-Hill, 1929).

R. B. Zevin, "The Economics of Normalcy," *Journal of Economic History*, vol. 42 (March, 1982), 43–52.

III   Unpublished papers, dissertations, and manuscripts

Michael A. Bernstein, *Long-Term Economic Growth and the Problem of Recovery in American Manufacturing: A Study of the Great Depression in the United States, 1929–1939* (unpublished Ph.D. dissertation, Yale University, 1982).

Linda K. Brown, *Challenge and Response: The American Business Community and the New Deal, 1932–1934* (unpublished Ph.D. dissertation, University of Pennsylvania, 1972).

A. D. Chandler, Jr., "Global Enterprise: Economic and National Characteristics – A Comparative Analysis" (unpublished paper, Harvard University, 1980).

Wesley C. Clark, *Economic Aspects of a President's Popularity* (unpublished Ph.D. dissertation, University of Pennsylvania, 1943).

Avi J. Cohen, *Technological Change in the North American Pulp and Paper Industry: A Case Study, 1920–1940* (unpublished paper, Stanford University, 1981).

Gordon Donald, *The Depression in Cotton Textiles, 1924 to 1940* (unpublished Ph.D. dissertation, University of Chicago, 1951).

E. Fano, "Instability, Increasing Productivity and Unemployment in the Great

Depression" (unpublished paper, May, 1985, Dipartimento di Economia Politica, University of Rome I, "La Sapienza").

Carol Heim, *Uneven Regional Development in Interwar Britain* (unpublished Ph.D. dissertation, Yale University, 1982).

Israel I. Holland, *Some Factors Affecting the Consumption of Lumber in the United States with Emphasis on Demand* (unpublished Ph.D. dissertation, University of California, Berkeley, 1955).

D. P. Levine, Nai Pew Ong, "Competition and Economic Fluctuations" (unpublished paper, Yale University and University of California, Riverside, 1979).

Martha L. Olney, *Advertising, Consumer Credit, and the 'Consumer Durables Revolution' of the 1920's* (unpublished Ph.D. dissertation, University of California, Berkeley, 1985).

Elyce J. Rotella, *From Home to Office: U.S. Women at Work 1870–1930.* University Microfilms (1982).

"Statement by Surgeon General Thomas Parran, Public Health Service, before the Special Senate Committee to Investigate Unemployment and Relief" (March 16, 1938), processed (Sterling Memorial Library, Yale University).

Robert Paul Thomas, *An Analysis of the Pattern of Growth of the Automobile Industry: 1895–1929* (unpublished Ph.D. dissertation, Northwestern University, 1965).

Lee R. Tilman, *The American Business Community and the Death of the New Deal* (unpublished Ph.D. dissertation, University of Arizona, 1966).

Ronald C. Tobey, Charles Wetherell, "Electrical Modernization of American Households, 1920–1940" (unpublished paper, University of California, Riverside, 1986).

John Joseph Wallis, "Employment in the Great Depression" (unpublished paper, University of Maryland, College Park, 1986).

Index